AEMILIUS PAULLUS
CONQUEROR OF GREECE

William Reiter

CROOM HELM
London • New York • Sydney

© 1988 William Reiter
Croom Helm Ltd, Provident House, Burrell Row,
Beckenham, Kent, BR3 1AT
Croom Helm Australia, 44-50 Waterloo Road,
North Ryde, 2113, New South Wales

Published in the USA by
Croom Helm
in association with Methuen, Inc.
29 West 35th Street,
New York, NY 10001

British Library Cataloguing in Publication Data

Reiter, William
   Aemilius Paullus, conquerer of Greece.
   1. Paullus, Lucius Aemilius, *Macedonicus*
   2. Generals — Rome — Biography
   3. Consuls, Roman — Biography
   I. Title
   937'.04'0924   DG253.P38
   ISBN 0-7099-4285-0

Library of Congress Cataloging-in-Publication Data

ISBN 0-7099-4285-0

Printed and bound in Great Britain by
Biddles Ltd, Guildford and King's Lynn

CONTENTS

I.	INTRODUCTION	1
II.	POLYBIUS AND THE IMAGE	20
	A. Background	20
	B. Polybius and Paullus	32
	C. Polybius, the House of Macedon, and Paullus	40
III.	LIVY AND THE IMAGE	69
	A. Livy, Paullus and the Third Macedonian War	69
	B. Livy and Roman Foreign Policies	80
IV.	PLUTARCH AND THE IMAGE	97
V.	ANOTHER LOOK	109
	A. Early Years	109
	B. Policies of Imperium	118
BIBLIOGRAPHY		163
INDEX		169

To my wife, Phyllis

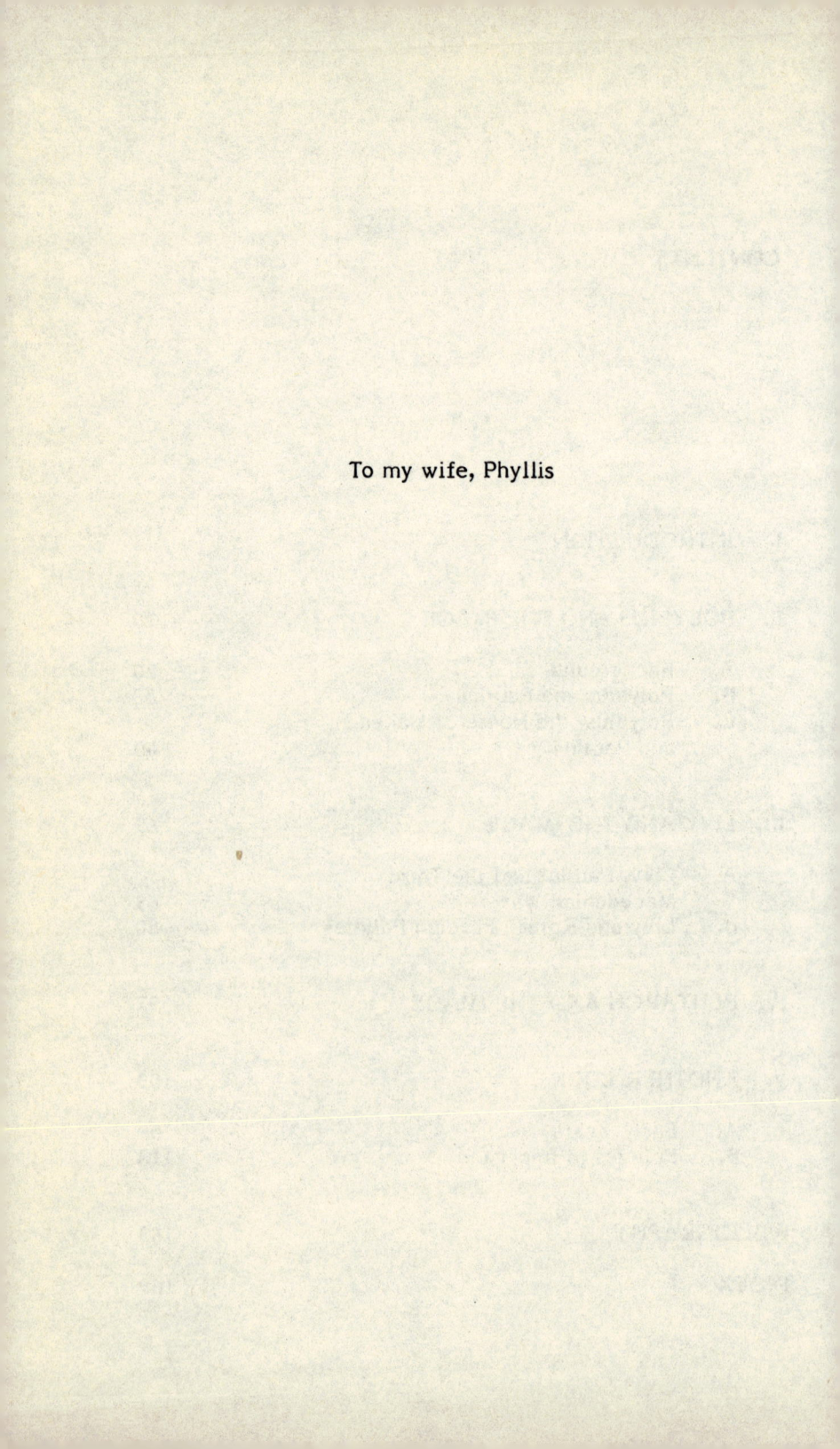

Chapter One

INTRODUCTION

Fortunate is the man whose life and deeds are held as exempla by his fellows. Within the communal memory of his people he is remembered as having possessed all those virtues and traits which characterize, indeed crystalize, the essence of what they imagined to be perfection in a man. He was noble in bearing, aloof to the whims of the masses, but humble in victory and forbearing in the face of personal tragedy; discipline was his, for he conducted his life disdaining the vainglory which other men craved; on the battlefield, stern and crafty, but in the home, a loving father who educated his children in the ways of culture and in the truths of the ancestors; a man who more than any one else coveted the ancient mores of his people and in doing so inherited the quality of gravitas. For the Romans such a man was Lucius Aemilius Paullus, twice consul and the conqueror of King Perseus of Macedon. It was to him that Romans of later ages looked in order to discover those attributes which made a man of the Republic. Paullus epitomized the greatness of a golden age, an age when men still revered Rome itself, and not some petty creature who proclaimed himself dictator or emperor. Paullus' life served as an image, an ideal of antique morality upon which people could model themselves and find escape from troubled times; Paullus the individual was forgotten amidst the image. (1)

An understanding of the genesis and growth of this image is crucial in any attempt to come to grips with Paullus the man. Yet the tradition of portraying Paullus as a virtuous and just person is exceedingly strong and not easily criticized. It extends from the time of Polybius in the

Introduction

second century B.C. down to modern times and shows little sign of abating. To the ancients Paullus was a man of Republican virtues, and to modern scholars he most often represents a unification of the best elements of Greco-Roman culture, a philhellene in every sense of the word. Even the prosopographers, who claim to be more 'scientific' in their approach and analysis of Roman history, tend to condition their ideas on the belief that Paullus and his faction rested foreign policy decisions upon philhellenic convictions. (2) When the facade slips somewhat in the sources to expose a less than noble act which Paullus inflicted on the Greeks, even these notices are often dismissed or explained away - rarely is the image brought into question. The ancients - chiefly Polybius, Livy, and Plutarch - did their work well. Among modern scholarship, no single nationality can lay claim to the dubious honor of according the most praise to the consul of 168; Germans, French, Italians, British, and Americans all, at one time or another, have found it in their hearts to accept blindly the vision offered up by the ancient authors. To be sure, there have been protestations by those less susceptible to ancient eloquence and modern sentimentality, but they have been few and relatively unheard by the majority of historians. Thus, the image of Paullus still stands, and it is not without profit to trace the variety of opinions which men of learning have held concerning the man who figured so highly in Rome's conquest of the Mediterranean world. (3)

Of the more important commentators on Roman history and men, Machiavelli has surprisingly little to say regarding Paullus, although there is no question that he read of Paullus in both Livy and Plutarch. He knows Paullus as a man of virtue, military ability, and commendable poverty. (4) Yet Paullus deserved no extended discussion; rather, Machiavelli prefers to use him as one of many examples of Roman virtue within the larger context on the reasons for Rome's greatness which is found in the Discourses. Rome's astounding success was seen, at least in part, by Machiavelli as being based on strict military discipline, outstanding valor, and the beneficial poverty of its leading citizens; (5) and, again, Paullus is but one example of this type of behavior.

Nor is one able to see any advancement over the space of two centuries. Indeed, Charles Rollin's Ancient History, which appeared in 1729/30 to the acclaim of his countrymen, the French, and others, is less impressive on an

Introduction

intellectual level than Machiavelli's Discourses, since Rollin's driving force was to show, through the study of 'profane history,' the workings and power of God in history. (6) Rollin's History is, nonetheless, a work of immense learning and labor, his purpose being, as he states, 'to extract from the Greek and Latin authors all that I shall judge most useful and entertaining with respect to the transactions, and most instructive with regard to the reflections.' (7) His effort is as unsatisfying as it is uncritical. Nowhere is there any attempt at a 'scientific' analysis of the sources, and everywhere the hand of God intrudes, along with an overabundance of Rollin's pious moralizing. For Paullus himself and for the Third Macedonian War, Rollin does no more than provide a rather free paraphrase of Livy with an occasional note referring to Plutarch and Polybius. (8) Only once does Rollin stray from his Livian narrative to voice brief indignation over the manner in which Paullus handled the sack of Epirus, saying that 'so disgraceful a stratagem was called prudence.' (9) Of course, there is no further notice of the darker side of Paullus, and, in any case, this barbaric deed was 'contrary to his natural disposition, which was gentle and humane.' (10) To read Rollin is to read Livy flavored by a dash of Plutarch.

The other side of the English Channel provided nothing better during the 1700s with which to evaluate Paullus. The first edition of the Encyclopaedia Britannica in 1771 had no room for Paullus. Seven years later the editors of the second edition thought otherwise and included a very matter-of-fact entry on Paullus - unfortunately, their chronology was quite wrong and they assumed that he conquered Perseus, triumphed, and died all in the same year, 168. Equally unfortunate, the entry survived through the seventh edition (1842) with the same error and only the most minor of changes to the article itself. By any standard of measurement, the result is exceedingly poor.

If the popular wisdom of the 1700s and early 1800s was deficient, one receives quite a different picture from more sober scholarship. From Barthold Niebuhr's great History of Rome comes a critical evaluation of Paullus and his actions during the Third Macedonian War. Niebuhr had no illusions about the nobility of this man or of Roman intentions after Perseus' defeat, and he plainly stated so in a passage which puts many moderns to shame - it is worth quoting in full:

Introduction

> L. Aemilius Paullus made a cruel use of his victory, if we may judge from our own feelings of humanity: one hundred and ten years after the war with Pyrrhus the Romans took vengence on Epirus. ... a massacre took place in the midst of a population which believed itself to be in perfect safety. (There follows a description of the attack). After such a cruelty which was perpetrated at the command of L. Aemilius Paullus, he cannot possibly be reckoned among the number of great and virtuous Romans. This mode of acting would have been cruel enough even in the course of a war; and I cannot see the reason why many persons (unnamed) call Aemilius Paullus a mild and humane man. It was a similar manner that he acted in Boeotia, and throughout Greece those places in which a party favored the cause of the Romans received Roman soldiers to crush their opponents. In Aetolia they broke into the senate house, and the senators were put to death instantaneously, at the request of the leading men of the Roman party. It was by the same kind of policy that ten commissioners were sent to settle the affairs of Macedonia, and others to Achaia, who compelled the Achaeans to pass a decree, that all those who had been supporters of Perseus should be put to death. (11)

For perhaps the first time, the interpretations and excuses which Polybius, Livy, and Plutarch laid over the facts are completely rejected, exposing the ruthless character of Paullus. There is no special pleading on the basis of philhellenism or of tears which Aemilius shed on behalf of the captive Perseus. Niebuhr, who was quite capable of eulogizing Roman generals, in particular, Flamininus, (12) found nothing to admire or absolve in the vicious retribution carried out against Epirus and other enemies of Rome. Yet, beyond his scholarly acumen, his opinion of Paullus' cruelty was conditioned by the love and affinity he felt toward the Greeks of his own day who were fighting for their independence. Again and again, Niebuhr's letters reveal a deep hatred for those who were suppressing the Greeks, and it is not difficult to see how these same passions were aroused when he gazed on a Greece humbled and dominated by Paullus and Rome. (13) While Flamininus could be excused by the apology that he set Greece 'free', Paullus certainly could not.

Writing in order to show that France could and should

Introduction

claim a portion of a Rome which was once theirs, and to prove that the French sword of history was keener than the German, J. Michelet composed his History of the Roman Republic as an answer to Niebuhr. (14) Michelet's commentary on Paullus is not nearly so harsh as Niebuhr's, and there are times when he even appears to praise Aemilius. (15) Yet, he is, perhaps, more subtle in his criticism of Paullus than Niebuhr. Niebuhr saw the realities of power politics, while Michelet cared correspondingly little for politics and policies, and painted a picture of Greece as a ravished victim of a rude conqueror:

> ... Paulus Aemilius celebrated games, at which weeping Greece was obliged to appear. Then by order of the senate, he passed into Epirus, declared to the inhabitants that they should enjoy the same liberty as the Macedonians, made them bring their gold and silver to the treasury, and then sold them as slaves, to the number of one hundred and fifty thousand. (16)

Thus far, nineteenth century scholarship had found little praiseworthy in the figure of Paullus.

This was to change, however, with the article on Paullus in the Allgemeine Encyclopädie which appeared in 1840. (17) Written by F.A. Eckstein, the article bristles with erudition and was, without question, the most comprehensive piece of work on Paullus up to that time. It is still worth reading, and it may be stated that the later Realencyclopädie article on Paullus barely, if at all, surpasses what Eckstein had to say. But Eckstein, for all his learning, fails to turn a perspicacious eye on Paullus, and, as he himself freely admits, (18) for most of the article Livy's narrative and, consequently, his interpretation, was adopted. Eckstein surely could have provided a balanced account, yet he deliberately chose to follow Livy - his reasoning is evident, since he makes no secret that he saw Paullus as a prime example of a Roman noble schooled in antique ways. All Paullus' classic attributes are praised to the skies; he was the loving father who was careful to educate his children correctly, he was a military genius who felled Macedon and restored ancient discipline, and, what seems to catch Eckstein's fancy, 'als staatsman gehörte er zu der patrischen Partei.' (19) Most interesting of all is how Paullus' conduct during the Third Macedonian War and the sack of Epirus is characterized and exculpated:

5

Introduction

> Gegen die Überwundenen war er mild und leutselig, er suchte sie aufzurichten in ihrem Schmerz und ihre Lage, so weit es möglich war, zu erleichtern; die grausame Execution gegen die epirotischen Städte darf man nicht ihm Schuld geben ... (20)

One could hardly ask for a more laudatory estimation of Paullus.

But all this fades into obscurity and is nearly forgotten when compared with the next major commentary on Paullus, Theodor Mommsen's History of Rome. The Allgemeine Encyclopädie is little more than a curiosity today, but Mommsen's influence still pervades. Nothing concerning Perseus' conqueror was inherited from Niebuhr; Mommsen's Paullus is the complete opposite of what Niebuhr had seen. Not only was Mommsen convinced that philhellenism motivated both Roman foreign policy and the chief directors of that policy, but his personal ideal of German unification also appears to have affected his judgement of Paullus; the establishment of a Roman hegemony lorded over by benevolent men of culture was hardly something to be condemned by Mommsen, especially when a similar goal was desired for Germany. Mommsen could never have accepted Niebuhr's severe verdict on the Roman hero in the war with Perseus. His summation of Paullus' career and life was to entrance many:

> At length the Romans resolved to send the right man to Greece. This was Lucius Aemilius Paullus, the son of the consul of the same name that fell at Cannae; a man of the old nobility but of humble means, and therefore not so successful in the comitia as on the battlefield, where he had remarkably distinguished himself in Spain and still more so in Liguria. The people elected him for the second time consul in the year 586 on account of his merits - a course which was at that time rare and exceptional. He was in all respects the fitting man: an excellent general of the old school, strict as respected himself and his troops, and, notwithstanding his sixty years, still hale and vigorous - 'one of the few Romans of that age to whom one could not offer money,' as a contemporary (Polybius) says of him - and a man of Hellenic culture, who, when commander-in-chief, embraced the opportunity of travelling through Greece to inspect its works of art. (21)

Introduction

Still, Mommsen may have harbored some unspoken doubts over his beloved philhellene. He notes with obvious disapproval the path the Senate took after the defeat of Perseus, a path 'unworthy of a great power, (which) showed that the epoch of the Fabii and the Scipios was at an end.' (22) The catalog of misdeeds which follows this statement is enough to shake even the true believer, and it very well may have disturbed Mommsen when it came to answering for Paullus' actions. The sack of Epirus is excused, but in every other instance where Paullus was involved, his name is absent from Mommsen's narrative. (23) Better to overlook several indiscretions than to ruin an image.

Nevertheless, the image of Paullus the philhellene does not seem to have been seriously questioned. Victor Duruy's narrative of Paullus and the Third Macedonian War is hardly any better than what Rollin had written a century before; indeed, when the sources are not merely being copied and commentary intrudes, it is either borrowed from Mommsen or is patently out of touch with the facts. Duruy's description of Paullus is a compression of what Mommsen had to say:

> The new consul was a man of antique valor, a man of letters moreover, as were many of the nobles of Rome, a friend of the civilization and arts of Greece, although a devout observer of ancient custom; strict with the soldiers and the people, indifferent to popularity gained in the Forum, and a merit becoming every day more rare, a man of principle. 'No one,' says an old writer, who by this very utterance makes a grave charge against his contemporaries, 'no one would have dared offer him money.' (24)

Later, when the sack of Epirus is mentioned, it is not the Senate or Paullus which receive the blame; Duruy make the astounding assertion (found nowhere in the sources) that the assemblies had ordered this frightful deed. (25) Duruy's work lent more credence to the now-shining image of Paullus, but on a level beneath that of German investigators.

In the English speaking world of 1885, the ninth edition of the Britannica also presented its public with a noble, philhellenic Paullus. He 'was a fine specimen of a Roman noble ... an aristocrat to the backbone ... (whose) sympathy with Greek learning and art is (well) attested ...' This is but a sampling; the unnamed author of the Briannnica's article is

Introduction

boundless in his praise of Paullus. It is unclear if the author drew directly off one source, but there is no doubt that his inspiration came from Mommsen's vision.

The Realencyclopädie on Paullus, appearing eight years after the Britannica, also furthers the same view. The praises remain unchanged over a half century, and the author, Klebs, seems to have combined both Eckstein and Mommsen:

> Paullus war ein Mann, in dem altrömische Tüchtigkeit durch hellenische Bildung geadelt war. Ein echter Aristokrat, verschmähte er es, um die Gunst die Masse zu buhlen ... Streng, wo es das Amt erforderte, war er persönlich mild gegen die Besiegten und Unterworfenen. Hellenisch ist sein masshaltender Sinn ... (26)

Klebs had neither the desire nor the motivation to challenge what he had inherited, and his views now stand enshrined in the Realencyclopädie; they represent the collective verdict of a large portion of the nineteenth century.

The twentieth century opened with a momentous work, the still unsurpassed Geschichte der Griechischen und Makedonischen Staaten of Benedictus Niese. Its level of scholarship leaves nothing wanting, and it remains both indispensible and important. Niese was certainly influenced by the predominant voice of preceding scholars concerning the role and behavior of the consul of 168, and his estimation of the man and his influence reflects much of the earlier sentiment. The first notice of Paullus is very favorable - there is the all too familiar picture of the stern general and disciplinarian faithfully serving the fatherland. (27) One is led to believe that Niese will do no more than parrot previous writings. And this impression is furthered by the statement that Paullus 'war ein Mann von guter hellenischer Bildung ...' (28) Niese cannot, however, have been entirely at ease with his own acceptance of the pristine Paullus. As the historian approaches the narrative detailing the raiding parties authorized by Paullus just before the Roman returned to Italy, doubts must have entered Niese's mind. While commenting on the attack launched against a number of Illyrian cities by Scipio Nasica and Fabius Maximus, under, of course, Paullus' aegis, Niese goes to extremes to excuse the deed: 'Was für Illyrier gemeint sind, wissen wir nicht; es müssen solche sein, die

Introduction

sich noch nicht unterworfen hatten.' (29) Yet, almost immediately after mention of this, Niese abandons all pretence of standing up for Paullus. A note concerning the sack of Epirus is a complete turn-about from earlier praises:

> Das Verfahren gegen die Molosser ist, wie Plut. Aem. 30 berichtet, nicht nach dem Sinne des Aemilius Paullus gewesen, der nach Polyb. XXX.13.11 auch an den Verleumdungen des Kallikrates und Lykiskos keinen Gefallen fand. Dies wollen wir gerne glauben, aber es ist schwer zu erweisen und macht mehr den Eindruck einer nachträgliche Entschuldigung. Wenigstens hat Aemilius Paullus nichts getan, um die Schicksal der Hellenen zu verbessern, was er besonders zu Anfang wohl gekonnt hätte. Er muss doch die Politik des Senata durchaus gebilligt haben. (30)

No touch of the idealistic Paullus remains. Although Paullus, in Niese's mind, may have deserved the earlier compliments, Aemilius' actions following the end of the Third Macedonian War were a different matter.

Nor were the French to be outdone. G. Colin, in his work, Rome et la Grece, finds absolutely nothing to commend in the figure of Paullus. His commentary is devastating and harkens back to Niebuhr in its fervor. Moreover, Colin seems to be the first to question the motives of the sources which mention Paullus. (31) But the most damning statement of all takes to task all those who had earlier closed their eyes to the realities of Paullus' career, and saw only what they wanted to see:

> Tout en goutant leur (the Greeks') civilisation, il n'eprouve guere pour de sympathie, et, par exemple, sur un ordre du Senat, sans aucune protestation, il va organiser et executer methodiquement le pillage de l'Epire. Cependant il peut avoir juge bon d'epargner aux Macedoniens les dernieres rigueurs, mais pour des raisons etrangeres a leur propre interet. (32)

There is no whitewash of the treachery at Epirus, no applause that Macedon was set 'free'. Colin had enough sense to distrust sources openly favorable to Paullus and Rome, nor was he awed by the concensus of recent historical opinion which had excused the maneuvers of a Roman general.

Introduction

One would have hoped that America's premier historian of Rome during the early twentieth century, Tenny Frank, would have paid more attention to what his European counterparts were saying. Frank's thesis, revolving around the application of 'sentimental politics', is hard, if not impossible, to apply to a man such as Paullus; but Frank insists on trying. Many of the usual niceties are repeated, (33) with the most extensive digression affirming what Mommsen and those like him had said:

> Paullus may well be considered the spokesman of what remained of the Scipionic circle. His love for things Greek was fully as genuine as that of the former leaders, though perhaps it expressed itself in a less sentimental form. In his employment of practical political methods he justifies the inference that he did not subscribe to all the enthusiastic sentiment that Flamininius had uttered in his after-dinner speech in 196. (34)

Apparently, the last sentence is a veiled criticism of the sack of Epirus, but Paullus had fit too well into Frank's scheme for the historian to see the reality that Niese had forced himself to see and that Colin had observed with no difficulty.

The first half of the twentieth century was also to introduce onto the historical scene some of the more important scholarly British opinion concerning Paullus. The respected Oxford Classical Dictionary was published in 1949, bringing with it what may be characterized as the epitome of current British thought. The article on Paullus was written by A.H. McDonald, and remains unchanged in the second edition of the O.C.D. which appeared in 1970. The choice of McDonald as the author was well-founded, as he is noted for both his work on the text of Livy's last extant books and for his in-depth studies of second century Roman history. Unfortunately, McDonald's estimation of Paullus offers no advance from what Mommsen had written, and one is tempted to imagine that McDonald saw Aemilius as an Oxford don:

> Aemilius symbolizes the union of Roman tradition with Hellenism. Cultured yet conservative, a fine soldier and just administrator, strict in religious observance, he played an honorable and authoritative part in public

and private life at Rome. (35)

The description might fit an English gentleman, yet one may well question whether it can be applied to Paullus.

In any case, McDonald was in good company. In 1951 there appeared a major study, H.H. Scullard's Roman Politics, and this agreed completely with, and, indeed, went beyond the O.C.D. in its judgement of Paullus. Scullard's work was prosopographical in nature and sought to explain the machinations of the political factions during the period of the Third Macedonian War by determining the attitudes of each coalition toward the East. Following this line of attack, Scullard came to see the members of the older patrician houses as philhellenes who only wanted the best for the Greeks, while opposite them were the new plebeian nobles who are seen as unprincipled and vainglorious, desirous of advancing their reputations and power. In effect, what Scullard has done, although he does not recognize it, is to take over as his thesis the very same dramatic pattern of plebeian vs patrician conflict around which Livy himself constructed much of the last extant pentad. Thus, for Scullard (and Livy) it was the 'violent plebeian clique' which thirsted for war and which pursued the conflict against Perseus in so ignoble a fashion. (36) On the other hand, the patricians, finally regaining power in 169/8, found a natural leader in Aemilius Paullus, 'an upright and capable general who did not lack sympathy for Greek life.' (37) Paullus is the man of old ways whose beliefs and convictions were conditioned by his philhellenism. (38) Furthermore, the action in Epirus was hardly Paullus' fault; Scullard imagines that Charops, the pro-Roman quisling in Epirus, had conspired with 'extreme plebeian leaders' who, in turn, had forced Paullus, through the use of a senatorial order, to execute their ambitious and frightful plans. (39) It is unfortunate that a scholar of Scullard's caliber chose to base his analysis of Paullus and the Third Macedonian War on such a shaky thesis as a plebeian-patrician confrontation. Livy would have applauded this approach, although one can hardly trust the Augustan historian's motivations or interpretations. Scullard's choice of theses has boxed him in; he must, of necessity, see a noble, philhellenic Paullus, or damage would be done to his entire analysis, prosopographical and otherwise.

But the author of a massive study dealing with Perseus, Piero Meloni, was not impressed with Scullard's Paullus. As

Introduction

one might expect from a scholar who wrote Perseo e la fine della Monarchia Macedone and who was sympathetic toward the last king of Macedon, Meloni had no praise for Paullus. He found Paullus to be a rather distasteful man; and Meloni hardly needed to be reminded of the fact that the sources were all biased in favor of Aemilius. Concerning Paullus' various speeches and the character of the man who delivered them, Meloni had some harsh words:

> I discorsi pronunciati a Roma ed in Grecia che la tradizione pervenutaci gli attribuisce - indipendentemente dalla loro scarsa credibilita - ci mostrano proprio un uomo siffatto, esigente ed intransigente verso i suoi subordinati, di grande ascendente sulle truppe, pronto ad addossarsi tutte le responsabilita di una decisione. (40)

And, in the same vein, the destruction dealt Epirus is laid at Paullus' feet, and there is no attempt to excuse the deed. (41) Meloni's level of criticism never reaches the ferocity of Niebuhr or Colin, but it does provide a well needed balance to the O.C.D. and to Scullard.

The remainder of the 1950s found opinion on Paullus somewhat divided. The dissertation by Alice Stanley on the life and career of Paullus is disappointing since it repeats the usual eulogies and adds little, if anything, new. (42) S.I. Oost, in his 1954 work on Roman policies in Epirus and Acarnania, systematically demolished the argument that Paullus disapproved of the order to pillage Epirus. (43) In 1958, Ernst Badian, in his Foreign Clientelae, noted the utter ruthlessness of Paullus, but, as it was not to the purpose of the book, failed to carry his discussion to any length. (44) In the English speaking world, two realistic historians had forsaken idealism and had seen Paullus without the facade of nobility with which so many others had hidden him. Unfortunately, the complete reverse was occuring in Germany. H.E. Stier's study of Roms Aufstieg zur Weltmacht retreated to an acceptance of Mommsen's philhellenism and thesis in Roman politics. (45) Here, as in so many past instances, Paullus is the good philhellene whose love of Greece affects his conduct. (46) And, if German scholarship of the early 1960s may be included at this point, the image of Paullus received another authoritative boost with the article in the Kleine Pauly. (47) H.G. Gundel, who wrote the article, cites Steir, and

Introduction

concludes on a highly laudatory note: 'Streng und Gewissenhaftigkeit, Gerechtigkeit und Milde zeichneten ihn aus. Er war ein Philhellene, verstand die griech. Sprache und führte trotzdem als Vertreter der röm.' (48) For whatever the reason, recent German opinion has preferred to dismiss all which does not agree with the vision of Mommsen, and to cling to the belief that an ability to speak Greek, appreciate Greek art, and the like is indicative not only of a person's character but also of his politics.

Aside from the unheard admonitions of Meloni, Oost, and Badian, contemporary wisdom seems bent on perpetuating the ancients' interpretation of Paullus. E. Will, whose Histoire Politique du Monde Hellenistique appeared in 1966/67, followed much of this. (49) His is the only study to challenge Niese on scope, depth, and erudition, and although he has not surpassed Niese, Will's succinct narrative and modern bibilography are always useful. To be sure, Will's treatment of Paullus nowhere approaches the adoration of Stier and Gundel; nevertheless, there is no critical estimation of Aemilius, who is accorded most of the standard traits. (50) On the destruction of Epirus, perhaps the most reliable barometer for measuring an author's judgement of Paullus, Will chooses a poor guide and follows the explanation of Scullard: 'l'ordre (to sack Epirus), que Paul-Emile parait avoir desapprouve, venait de Rome, où il semble que le Senat ait accepte de se faire l'instrument de luttes obscures entre clans et factions epirotes.' (51) It is difficult to see why Will would accept Scullard, especially in light of the fact that he was familiar with Oost's work. Still, the damage has been done; the French, continuing in the path of their European counterparts, have lent their authority to the Paullus cult.

The Italians, too, soon joined in. In a 1972 article by Rosanna Vianoli devoted entirely to an analysis of Paullus' character and the nature of the sources which speak about him, little new light is shed on the subject. Although Vianoli does recognize the biases which the ancients had for Paullus, she never seems to doubt their claims of the humanity, justice, and rectitude of this Roman condottiere. (52) She sees, however, a basic dichotomy in Paullus' personality, a dichotomy which allowed this noble Roman to destroy Epirus. (53) Her result leads to a schizophrenic Paullus who can only be explained by imagining that he represents a man caught in a process of transition from the ideals of philhellenic aristocracy (to which he belongs by

Introduction

birth) to the political methods advocated by 'democrats' such as Cato. (54) Vianoli promises further work.

But, for an finale, one must turn to a recent and rather silly little book by Nels Forde, Cato the Censor. (55) The book itself is dedicated to a curious collection of people, and in the words of the author,

> ... etched deeply upon these pages is my inner turmoil, raging derision, and shocked contempt for the events of the past year in America (1973/74). It is precisely because we have experienced so much, but learned so little, that I cynically dedicate Cato the Censor: To the Watergate Generation. (56)

The book, as the author openly claims, both moralizes and is didactic:

> One must objectivize relevantly, explaining such as Cato in current venacular and contemporary ratiocination. If Cato sounds like a late twentieth century American statesman, it is all too deliberate; but as I have allowed him to speak only from his Latin setting it must be-a 'Romanesque' statecraft. (57)

After all, are not the young taught by example? In magical fashion, Cato is transformed into a type of Senator Sam Ervin; and, to turn to Paullus, the resemblance between Aemilius and Lt. William Calley is amazing. For, it should be noted, Forde has vivid memories of American activity in Vietnam (although he will not admit to it), and he writes of Roman foreign policy with this in mind. For example, 'Cato seems genuinely to have believed that Rome could not afford to garrison or police the world because of the moral involvement and the energy drain from domestic affairs ...' (58) And when Paullus is criticized, it is only because he symbolized the harshness of the Vietnam years and was, in Forde's mind, the Roman twin to America's Calley. (59) As it stands, the book is florid rhetoric and little more; the few worthwhile points that are made fall by the side amidst the purple prose. Nor should it be forgotten when appraising the value of the work that, besides righteous moral indignation, the author wrote the book in order to secure tenure in, as he puts it, 'our grim 'publish or perish' scholastic environment.' (60)

When all is considered, Aemilius Paullus has emerged

Introduction

from the hands of modern historians with far more acclaim than do most figures of antiquity. Much of continental scholarship, from the second edition of the O.C.D. and Scullard's Roman Politics, to the Kleine Pauly, to the French and Italian works of consequence, has left no doubt as to what verdict it passes on Paullus - a collective 'not guilty', accompanied by a shower of approbation. Vigorous protests which, beginning with Niebuhr, still manage to surface even in the face of almost universal acceptance of the opposite view have been largely ignored. But, far worse, those scholars who accept the validity of politics governed by cultural tastes, and announce that Paullus was the epitome of such behavior, leave themselves open to the charge that they have thereby distorted not only the man, but also the era. They have believed sources where there was every reason for doubt; they have imposed patterns on politics where none belong; and they have chosen to excuse rather than explain. Polybius, Livy, and Plutarch would be pleased if they could but note the applause heaped upon their hero, since it is from their pens that the image of Paullus first emanated. And it is to these same ancients that one must look if there is to be any hope of piercing the. myths surrounding the life and career of Aemilius Paullus. For there remains the certainty that Polybius, Livy, and Plutarch were not infallible and that their motives, prejudices, and purposes can be discovered.

NOTES

1. There is surprisingly little secondary material concerning Paullus. He is usually discussed only in relation to his part in the Third Macedonian War, and even then the reader is given little more than a recitation of events. In any case, one can consult several works which deal with Paullus. Rosanna Vianoli, 'Caraterre e tendenza della tradizione su L. Emilio Paolo,' Contributi dell' Instituto di storia antica 1 (1972), 78-90. Alice D. Stanley, 'Lucius Aemilius Paullus' (Unpublished Ph.D. dissertation, Bryn Mawr College, 1954). A.H. McDonald, 'Paullus (2) Macedonicus,' The Oxford Classical Dictionary (2nd ed.; Oxford: The Clarendon Press, 1970), pp.791-92. Klebs, 'L. Aemilius Paullus (114),' Paulys Realencyclopädie der classischen Altertumswissenschaft I, 1 (1893), 576-80. H.G. Gundel, 'L. Ae. Paullus (Macedonicus) (22), ' Der Kleine

Pauly 1 (1964), 92-3.
2. E.g., H.H. Scullard, Roman Politics: 220-150 B.C. (2nd ed.; Oxford: The Clarendon Press, 1973), chiefly pp.207-19. Also, J. Briscoe, 'Q. Marcius Philippus and Nova Sapientia,' Journal of Roman Studies 54 (1964), 66ff. And, J. Briscoe, 'Eastern Policy and Senatorial Politics; 168-146 B.C.,' Historia 18 (1969), 49 ff. I intend to discuss the problem of the prosopography of this period as it arises.
3. The scholars whose works are to be surveyed are intended to be representative. Obviously, a great deal of selectivity has been employed in the choices, and, obviously, other names could easily be added.
4. Machiavelli, Discourses III.16.4: Paullus' virtue and ability; III.25.4: Paullus' poverty; III.35.5: defeat of Perseus and that king's evil.
5. Machiavelli, Discourses I.4.1: comment on discipline; II.1: consideration of virtue and fortune; III.25.4: virtue of poverty.
6. Charles Rollin, Ancient History, Vol. I (New York: Derby and Jackson, 1857), pp.xxii-xxv.
7. Ibid., p.xxvii.
8. Ibid., Vol. II, pp.215-27.
9. Ibid. Vol. II, p.227.
10. Ibid.
11. B.G. Niebuhr, The History of Rome from the First Punic War to the Death of Constantine, Vol. IV, ed. and trans. by L. Schmitz (London: Taylor and Walton, 1844), pp.280-81.
12. See the analysis by E. Badian, Titus Quinctius Flamininus: Philhellenism and Realpolitik (Cincinnati: University of Cincinnati, 1970), pp.10-11.
13. See the old but convenient edition of Niebuhr's letters, B.G. Niebuhr, The Life and Letters of Barthold George Niebuhr, translator unnamed (New York: Harper & Brothers, 1854). For a few examples, see letter 277 (Rome, Aug. 11, 1821), p.410; letter 333 (Bonn, May 12, 1825), p.490; letter 339 (Bonn, May 21, 1826), p.494; letter 340 (Bonn, June 21, 1826), pp.495-6; letter 352 (Bonn, March 14, 1828), p.506; letter 353 (Bonn, April 20, 1828), p.507.
14. J. Michelet, History of the Roman Republic, trans. William Hazlitt (London: David Bogue, 1847), p.8.
15. Ibid., p.231.
16. Ibid., p.232.
17. F.A. Eckstein, 'Lucius Ämilius Paullus (4),' Allgemeine Encyclopädie der Wissenschaften und Kunste III,

Introduction

14 (1840), 176-82.
18. Eckstein, 'Paullus,' 182.
19. Eckstein, 'Paullus,' 181.
20. Eckstein, 'Paullus,' 182.
21. Theodor Mommsen, The History of Rome, Vol. II, trans. W.P. Dickson (New York: Charles Scribner's Sons, n.d.), p.355.
22. Ibid., p.359.
23. Ibid., pp.365-67.
24. Victor Duruy, History of Rome and of the Roman People, II, 1 trans. M.M. Ripley and W.J. Clarke, ed. J.P. Mahaffy (Boston: Dana Estes and Charles E. Lauriot, 1884), pp.167-68.
25. Ibid., p.179.
26. Klebs, R.E. I, 1, 678-79.
27. Benedictus Niese, Geschichte der Griechischen und Makedonischen Staaten seit der Schlacht bei Chaeronea, Vol. III (Darmstadt: Wissenschaftliche Buchgesellschaft, 1963 reprint), p.152.
28. Ibid., p.179. See pp.181-82 for more praises.
29. Ibid., p.186.
30. Ibid., p.187, n.2.
31. G. Colin, Rome et la Grece: de 200 a 146 avant J.C. (Paris, 1905), pp.443-4.
32. Ibid., p.444, n.3.
33. Tenny Frank, Roman Imperialism (New York: The MacMillan Co., 1914), e.g. pp.208 and 218.
34. Ibid., p.213.
35. A.H. McDonald, 'Paullus (4) Macedonicus, Lucius Aemilius,' Oxford Classical Dictionary (Oxford: Clarendon Press, 1949), p.656. See the same article in the second edition of the O.C.D., 1970, pp.791-2.
36. Scullard, Roman Politics, p.198. The praises are oft repeated - see, e.g. p.205.
37. Ibid., p.208.
38. Ibid., p.212.
39. Ibid., p.213. For an expanded version see, H.H. Scullard, 'Charops and Roman Policy in Epirus,' Journal of Roman Studies 35 (1945), 58-64. It might be pointed out at this point that another proponent of prosopography, Briscoe, also has a favorable opinion of Paullus. Briscoe, J.R.S., 54, 76, n.107 discounts the reality of a plebeian-patrician quarrel, and even, indeed, wonders aloud (p.75) 'how much apology for Paullus' actions our sources contain.' Yet, in a later article, Historia, 18, 60-9, Briscoe forgets his curiosity

Introduction

over the sources which excuse Paullus, and bases his conclusions on the belief that Aemilius headed a faction which was sympathetic toward the East and opposed the more aggressive Fulvian group. This holds no more water than Scullard's thesis.

40. Piero Meloni, Perseo e la fine della Monarchia Macedone (Rome, 1953), pp.320-21.
41. Ibid., p.408, n.2.
42. Stanley, 'Paullus,' (Unpublished Ph.D. dissertation), often follows Scullard blindly, and is rarely critical. See, e.g. p.151: 'Thus Paullus (was) the general of the older Roman tradition ... and the last of those philhellenes who championed the freedom of Greece ...'
43. S.I. Oost, Roman Policy in Epirus and Acarnania in the Age of the Roman Conquest of Greece (Dallas, 1954), pp.83-6; and p.133, nn.106 and 112.
44. E. Badian, Foreign Clientelae (264-70 B.C.) (Oxford: The Clarendon Press, 1972), p.98, and n.2.
45. H.E. Stier, Roms Aufstieg zur Weltmacht und die griechische Welt (Koln: Westdeutscher Verlag, 1957).
46. Ibid., e.g., pp.186, 188, 189, 190, 192.
47. H.G. Gundel, 'L. Ae. Paullus (Macedonicus) 22,' Der Kleine Pauly, Vol. I (1964), 92-93.
48. Ibid., 93.
49. E. Will, Histoire Politique du Monde Hellenistique (323-20 av. J.C.) Vol. II (Nancy, 1967).
50. Ibid., p.228 for Paullus' moral and military discipline; also see pp.234, 238, 240.
51. Ibid., p.239.
52. Rosanna Vianoli, 'Carattere e tendenza della tradizione su L. Emilio Paolo,' Contributi dell' Istituto di storia antica I (1972), 78-90. Note the comments on Paullus' military qualities, 83; his honesty, 84; his love of Greek culture, 85; and his humanity toward conquered enemies, especially Perseus, 85-6.
53. Vianoli, 88-9.
54. Vianoli, 89-90.
55. Nels W. Forde, Cato the Censor (Boston: Twayne Publishers, 1975).
56. Ibid., p.8.
57. Ibid.
58. Ibid., p.232.
59. Ibid., e.g., pp.232-34. But all American authors are not like Forde. For a more sober, but briefer, estimation of Paullus, see T.W. Africa, The Immense Majesty (New

York: Thomas Y. Crowell, 1974), pp.133-4.
   60.   Forde, Cato, p.8.

Chapter Two

POLYBIUS AND THE IMAGE

A. BACKGROUND

The historian Polybius is the fountainhead of the tradition concerning Paullus and it is from him that both Livy and Plutarch drew the majority of their own accounts. Like so many other ancient historians, Polybius was an exile, forced from his homeland with one thousand of his countrymen to serve as Roman hostages. (1) Polybius' activities during the Third Macedonian War had been suspect in Roman eyes; Roman reprisal had been swift and merciless, and he and the others found themselves in custody from 167 to 150 B.C. (2) Such treatment would have hardened most men against their captors, but for Polybius the cage was gilded. Soon after reaching Rome, Polybius fell into the company of Scipio Aemilianus and Quintus Fabius, the sons of Paullus. It seems that the historian was in need of some books and Paullus' sons were kind enough to let him use theirs. (3) This, as Polybius is eager to tell, led to deep conversations concerning the books, and, within a short space of time, he became an intimate friend of the brothers and a tutor of Scipio. (4) Not only was the relationship with Scipio pleasurable, for 'they came to regard each other with an affection like that of father and son or near relations,' (5) but it was also profitable. When the rest of the Achaean hostages were removed from the city of Rome to outlying parts of Italy, Paullus and his sons exerted enough influence to overrule the order and keep Polybius in Rome. (6) The historian was obviously in a favored position. He enjoyed Paullus' patronage, the freedom of his house, and even the use of Paullus' hunting preserves where he often went with

Scipio. (7) With all this in mind, it is not surprising that Polybius wrote of Paullus and Scipio with the highest approval. For example, Polybius never hesitates to praise the virtues and high character of Scipio; he was graced with moderation, generosity, financial integrity, and courage in war. (8) In each case, Polybius goes on to state specifically or to imply that these virtues were to a large degree imparted to Scipio by his father Paullus. Thus Paullus was exceedingly moderate in dealing with the vast Macedonian treasures after Perseus' defeat; (9) his generosity was such that he did not covet any of the booty but gave it to the Roman state; (10) in financial matters there was none better; (11) and, finally, he instructed his son in war and in hunting, 'the best training and amusement for the young.' (12) There is no doubt that Polybius was quite taken with his benefactors. He embraced them and the Roman state which they represented with all the fervor and enthusiasm of a convert. The virtue of Paullus is vividly contrasted with the baseness of bribe-taking Greeks, and even Aristeides of Athens and the great Epaminondas pale before Paullus. (13) Romans of earlier times had naturally possessed this merit and Paullus (and Scipio too) enjoyed its beneficial influence. (14) Still, all Polybius' approbation remains, by itself, insignificant and superficial. His characterization of Paullus goes deeper than a few polite remarks and must be seen in the context of Roman history (as presented by Polybius, of course) and especially within the framework of the Third Macedonian War.

Certainly Rome's devastating victory over the Macedonians in 168/7 B.C. had raised many questions in Polybius' mind as to how a secondary Italian city could, within a relatively short period of time, come to dominate nearly all the known world. The accomplishment was quite extraordinary, being both unexpected and greater than anything which had been done by earlier peoples or previous empires. (15) Cities and monarchies had sought world domination long before Rome had conceived of the idea, but none of the older hegemonies had approached what Rome had done. The Roman conquest was an event unique in history and, therefore, worthy of the most detailed investigation and analysis. Consequently it is to this question that Polybius addresses his great work:

> For who is so worthless or indolent as not to wish to know by what means and under what system of polity

the Romans in less than fifty-three years have succeeded in subjecting nearly the whole inhabited world to their sole government - a thing unique in history. (16)

Such an ambitious goal called for a daring plan of attack. One could not depend on a small, limited monograph-type treatment of this grand declaration of purpose; rather, nothing less than an universal chronicle encompassing the history of the entire world would suffice. No land or people was unaffected in those fifty-three years, nor could the history of one be separated from the others. Everything was interrelated and thus unintelligible by itself: 'the how, when, and wherefore of the subjection of the known parts of the world to the dominion of Rome should be treated as a single whole.' (17) By describing 'the how, when, and wherefore' within the seemingly limitless bounds of a universal history men would come to understand the greatness and inevitability of the Roman achievement. More importantly, Polybius' Histories furnished Greek statesmen and men of politics with desperately needed information about the Romans, thereby better equipping the Greeks to deal with the new ruling power. Polybius set for himself the didactic task of informing those peoples under Roman control, chiefly his own countrymen, the Greeks, of the character and constitution of their masters in the hope that they would accept Rome and avoid the fate which the historian himself had suffered. The difficulties which presented themselves were considerable, but so were the rewards. In the description of the Roman drive to supremacy Polybius concentrated his sights on probing the form of Rome's constitution, the significance of which is attested to by Polybius' statement of purpose, and the collective and individual morality of the Roman people, this being the source of any nation's underlying strength. And to these analyses is added a grander notion, that Rome's conquests were inevitable and inexorable.

In the historian's scheme of things, even though the Roman polity occupies the chief area of interest, it is only part of a much larger discussion on the nature of political systems in general. The constitutions of all states tended to operate in fixed and observable stages of development which closely corresponded, in Polybius' opinion, to the birth, growth, and decay of living organisms. Nature had dictated that both humans and governments should follow a similar path, and that, as is natural, 'everything in them is at its best when they are in their prime.' (18) This simplistic way of looking at governments serves the historian well, for he is not only able to set down his ideas on constitutions within it, but he is also able to claim that the future of these states can be reliably predicted. For if states follow nature's organically prescribed course and if one knew exactly where the government was in that course, then any astute person should be able to predict where the state will be going next. The Greeks were especially vulnerable to this formula; their pasts were open for all to see and, through study, one could presage their futures. (19) Divination is promised over and over again to those who follow Polybius. Indeed, the process takes on the overtones of revealed knowledge, 'for he alone who has seen how each form (of government) naturally arises and develops, will be able to see when, how, and where the growth, perfection, change, and end of each are likely to occur again.' (20) There are few exceptions to this dictum. By equating biological and political growth, Polybius constructed a doctrine of cyclical political development, a cycle of constitutions. In this vast cosmic circle states had their births, their periods of development, decay, and then rebirth, again, at which point the cycle begins once more: 'Such is the cycle of political revolution, the course appointed by nature in which constitutions change, disappear, and finally return to the point from which they started. (21) Polybius harbored no qualms or doubts over his system. Its greatest utility was clearly for the Greek statesmen to whom he was writing; for if they could discover where their own states stood in the cycle, then, perhaps, action could be taken to keep the polity from degenerating.

The cycle begins (or ends, depending on how one views it) with a cataclysm of immense proportions which destroys all civilized arts and after which mankind must start anew. (22) Given time, men come together in the fashion of animal herds and live under the rule of the strongest member, the monarch. The monarchy exists until men formulate noble aspirations, a sense of duty, and finally, justice - the monarch is now exchanged for a king who bases his rule, not on strength, but rather on justice and the approval of all. His descendants, however, soon begin to misuse their powers. From noble kingship the cycle carries the polity into tyranny, a most base and wretched form of government. Next is aristocracy and when this corrupts itself, democracy emerges. And finally, as the circle nears completion, democracy descends to mob-rule with all its accompanying violence and destruction. Chaos returns and the cycle is renewed. In the normal course of events there is no way out of the circle; from a time of savagery man progresses into a system where the satisfactory types of government, i.e, kingship, aristocracy, and democracy are paralleled with three objectionable forms, tyranny, oligarchy, and mob-rule. (23) It is indeed a pessimistic outlook, allowing for little or no change, and the inevitability of disaster and ruin. Yet this gloomy vision is precisely the way that Polybius viewed the majority of Greek history. Athens, the 'school of Hellas', along with Thebes, is given short shrift by Polybius. They were able to manage their affairs only when notable men the likes of Themistocles, (24) and Epaminondas, and Pelopidas (25) were in charge of the state; but without these men, the constitutions of Athens and Thebes sank to base levels and were dominated 'by the uncurbed impulse of a mob in the one case (Athens) exceptionally headstrong and ill-tempered, and in the other (Thebes) brought up in an atmosphere of violence and passion.' (26) The final major example of a Greek constitution which falls prey to Polybius' analysis is the polity of Crete. Other writers - Ephorus, Xenophon, Callisthenes, and Plato (27) - had long held that Crete's constitution, similar to the famous Spartan one, was of the highest merit. Polybius sets the matter straight for his readers. For how could a state where the population possessed a 'sordid love of gain and lust for wealth' and for whom neither custom nor law held meaning deserve any favorable recognition? (28) Clearly the writers of old were wrong in Polybius' eyes. The picture remains pessimistic and predictable with the examples of Athens, Thebes, and Crete helping to prove the rule.

Nevertheless, Polybius is not completely dogmatic. There is a way to halt the cycle of constitutions, a way which, if intelligently applied, could allow a state to avoid the problems of the above-mentioned examples. The formula for escape calls foir the mixing of the elements found in kingship, aristocracy, and democracy, 'for it is evident that we must regard as the best constitution a combination of all these three varieties, since we have had proof of this not only theoretically but by actual experience ...' (29) The result is a 'mixed constitution' employing the best aspects of each component while, at the same time, maintaining strict safeguards of checks and balances to insure that none of the branches acquires more than its share of power. (30) Stability takes hold. By keeping watch on that portion of the government representing kingship, tyranny could be avoided, and so on with the other branches, each section watching over the other. Thus <u>stasis</u> is removed, leaving harmony (or better, perhaps, a controlled tension) between the ruling partners. The cycle is halted; but, if the delicate balance is ever upset, nature's course will resume. As proof Polybius is able to adduce three instances of mixed constitutions, Lycurgan Sparta, Carthage, and Rome. These are states which, according to the historian, have risen to heights rarely achieved and are, therefore, mandatory study for students of politics.

Of the mixed constitutions the best and most glorious is that of the Romans. It was formed by the state as a whole with the experience gained through the weathering of great adversity, not being the product of any one man or of any master plan. (31) Its uniqueness can be seen, according to Polybius, by examination of the marvelous way in which Rome was able to combine the best features of kingship, aristocracy, and democracy. All shared in the government and all balanced each other. The Roman consuls, because of the greatness of their powers, resembled kingship; the Senate, as an exclusive body of respected men, constituted the aristocratic element; and the popular assemblies were obviously related to democracy. (32) With this established, Polybius launches into an extensive explanation of the powers of each branch, how they interact, and how they check and balance each other. (33) The conclusion that Rome, because of its mixed constitution, possessed vitality, stabilty, and 'an irresistible power of attaining every object upon which it is resolved' serves to account, at least in part, for the extraordinary rise of Rome to the status of world empire. (34) That the mixed constitution was at its zenith during the Hannibalic War lends even more evidence to the notion that Roman might sprang from its form of government - how else could a state totally defeated at Cannae unite to persevere and finally crush the mighty Hannibal?' (35) Moreover, the Hannibalic War marks the beginning of Rome's conscious drive towards world domination; (36) it was only during that conflict that the mixed constitution came to maturity together with a desire to rule the world. (37) The disaster at Cannae marks, in a sense, the beginning of the march to empire; the defeat hardened the Roman spirit in its determination to overcome all foes. From Cannae, which was Rome's darkest hour, that city revived itself and went on to capture the world at Pydna.

In the historian's eyes the very fact of Roman success in carving out an empire validated his interpretation of the importance of Rome's mixed constitution. If skeptics, however, doubted his theories, there remained additional proof, since both Lycurgan Sparta and Carthage also had similar polities and could be compared with Rome. Sparta, for instance, benefited greatly from Lycurgus' reforms; he had devised a mixed constitution with institutions so perfect that they seemed more divine than human. (38) They were, in fact, equal to Rome but for one fatal flaw since

> if anyone is ambitious of greater things, and esteems it finer and more glorious ... to be the leader of many men and to rule and lord it over many and have the eyes of all the world turned to him, it must be admitted that from this point of view the Laconian constitution is defective, while that of Rome is superior and better framed for the attainment of power ... (39)

Walbank's comment on the historian's opinion of Sparta, that 'it is less well adapted to foreign conquest, and therefore, in view of Polybius' general standpoint in his Histories, inferior' is well taken and to the point. (40) Carthage is also dealt with swiftly. In the past the Carthaginians had enjoyed a very fine mixed constitution, 'but at the time when they entered on the Hannibalic War, the Carthaginian constitution had degenerated, and that of Rome was better.' (41) Little more need be said on the point.

The supremacy of Rome's mixed constitution stands unassailed. It had removed Rome from the cyclical progression of governments and was, furthermore, the device through which the Romans were able to muster their collective strength. Polybius was, nevertheless, not so mechanistic as to say that Roman grandeur rested only on their constitution and nothing else. To the concept of the mixed constitution, which was peculiarly Greek, Polybius welded a variation, the idea of which was singularly Roman. This view, acquired no doubt while the historian was at Paullus' house, held that the underlying reason for Rome's greatness was the high character and virtue which existed as an integral part of the Roman spirit. The quality, which the Romans called virtus, had long been lauded by the Romans themselves as the reason for their eminence. Virtus as possessed by an individual signified virtue, moral excellence, and martial prowess, and, indeed, in the days of old every Roman had supposedly held such nobility; virtus in the Roman state expressed the idea that Rome was superior to all other peoples, morally as well as militarily. It was the force of and the adherence to hereditary manners, laws, and customs that molded the great men of Rome and gave them virtus. There is no doubt that the early Roman poets viewed the state as resting upon the virtue of men schooled in the ways of the ancestors, the mos maiorum. One need only remember Ennius' famous line: 'on antique morals and men stands the Roman state.' (42) The message is clear. Polybius did not avoid it nor would he have wanted to. The explanation of Roman conquest using the mixed constitution was a stroke of genius; one could comprehend it intellectually and thus admire it from a political point of view. But one could never respect it morally. By itself the mixed constitution was too cold, too inhuman - it lacked a sense of justice which a state should have, and, above all, the historian implicitly believed that a conqueror must be just. He, therefore, took the concept of Roman virtus and joined it to the theory of the mixed constitution. The polity was envisioned as the mechanism through which the collective Roman might was exerted, but the basis of the constitution, the substance which gave it meaning and upon which it stood, was traditional Roman rectitude and propriety. Polybius is emphatic on the intimate connection between the moral fiber of a people and the worthiness of their constitution: 'In my opinion there are two fundamental things in every state, by virtue of which its principle and constitution is either desirable or the reverse. I mean customs and laws.' (43) Good customs and laws breed good citizens, and they in turn are the basis of a good and just state. They cannot be separated without violence being done to one or the other.

Polybius' most fruitful example of the primacy of law and custom in Rome occurs in an extensive digression on Roman funeral rites. (44) The ceremony is not one of mere interment - it is, instead, a recommitment to the ideals of the past and an affirmation of ancestral virtue. The Romans were in the habit of making death masks of deceased family members of distinction and these masks, or images, were placed in a conspicuous part of the house. And when an illustrious man died, the dead came alive, as it were, to accept him into their midst. The dead man led the funeral procession, not reclining, but in an upright position, and after him came the ancestoral death masks, each worn by a man whose general appearance was like that of the ancestor. They were dressed and decked out in the precise ceremonial accouterment which belonged to them while living. All rode in chariots attended by the insignia and trappings of offices held; and at the funeral itself they sat on ivory chairs in order to show respect to the newly dead and to hear the eulogy pronounced by the eldest son. It was a mystical affair of immense proportions - what better way to acquire the virtues of bygone ages than to see the dead come alive?

> There could not easily be a more ennobling spectacle for a young man who aspires to fame and virtue. For who would not be inspired by the sight of the images of men renowned for their excellence, all together and as if alive and breathing? What spectacle could be more glorious than this? (45)

Besides this, the historian continues, the Romans were scrupulously honest in financing matters (unlike the bribe-taking Carthaginians and Greeks), (46) careful in their use of religion to placate the masses, (47) and in general much more honest in government than their Greek counterparts. (48) Everything mentioned stems from strict observance of law and custom; it demonstrated to Polybius, and to his readers, that Rome was worthy of a mixed constitution.

Thus far, Polybius' account involved a very rationalistic approach to the problem originally posed in the thesis. By using Greek political speculation he had shown that not only was the Roman constitution suited for the acquisition of empire, but it had also, at least for the time being, given Rome stability and had halted the cyclical progression of governments. It allowed Rome to escape from the miseries of internal strife which attended the cycle and enabled the Romans to concentrate on the suppression of external foes. To this is added the Roman observance of beneficial customs and laws, a crucial feature in determining whether or not a state is just. But Polybius has not yet finished spinning his web. The amalgamation of Greek political theory in the form of the mixed constitution, and the Roman belief in national and individual <u>virtus</u>, is merged into a higher theme involving metaphysics and transcendentalism.

Beyond the rational, and yet still intimately connected with it, the claim was made that 'Tyche (Fortune) has guided all the affairs of the world in one direction and has forced them to incline towards one and the same end,' the empire of Rome. (49) Tyche, which can refer to either what moderns often call 'luck' or 'chance', (50) or else as in this case, a divine being who can operate as a motive and directive force in the lives of men and states, was a Hellenistic concept which was seen by Polybius as influencing the rise of Rome. (51) Who could have foreseen, Polybius asks himself and his readers, that the world empire of the Macedonians would be toppled in a mere fifty-three years? (52) To understand so mind-boggling an event the historian looks to the treatise on Fortune by Demetrius of Phalerum who had asked the same question of the establishment of the Macedonian empire and its victory over Persia. Demetrius' answer was that Tyche 'lent them these blessings' of empire. (53) But having lent these blessings, Tyche could take them away from Macedon, 'and this now happened in the time of Perseus. Surely Demetrius, as if by the mouth of some god, uttered those prophetic words.' (54) When the Macedonians became unworthy of Tyche's favor, that most capricious goddess withdrew her blessings and gave them to Rome. The high character, excellence, and virtue of the Romans qualified them for Tyche's recognition. As Walbank has aptly summarized, Polybius

> reconciles the rise of Rome, as seen as the work of Tyche, with the needs of didactic history by insisting that Tyche <u>directed</u> Roman expansion, but that this sprang from <u>Rome's worthiness</u>. This worthiness appears especially in her mixed constitution and her high moral sense ... (55)

There is a direct relationship between Roman <u>virtus</u> (arete) and <u>Fortuna</u> (Tyche). (56) Polybius further implies that when and if Rome becomes immoral or amoral, Tyche will withdraw her good will in the same way that she abandoned Macedon.

Still, the path to empire was littered with victims. Polybius was confronted with the task of explaining the way in which Rome conquered the world. If the record revealed that Rome was cruel and unjust in her conquests, then severe damage would be done to Polybius' elaborate discussion on Roman greatness. Further, and perhaps more to the point, the historian could never expect his fellow Greeks to respect and accept a cold-blooded conqueror. Polybius, therefore, constructed general rules based on historical examples of how a world empire should act in the acquisition and maintenance of its holdings. There are two main steps: (1) moderation, clemency, and acts of kindness must be employed during the actual time of conquest in order to appease the vanquished, and (2) after a time, to secure the authority of the empire, paralyzing terror is used at the first hint of disobedience. (57) Both Philip II and Alexander are said to have won over their victims with moderation and clemency, but were quite willing to raze cities to the ground in order to further their empires. (58) The Romans, too, followed a similar policy. They not only treated subject peoples with kindness, but went so far as to accept them as friends and even citizens. (59) The Romans were, moreover, model conquerors during the Third Macedonian War. (60) When the masses in the Greek cities began to favor Perseus, the Senate redoubled its efforts to win the Greeks to the Roman side. The kindness of Rome, the ability to forgive wayward Greeks, and the virtue, realism, and intelligence shown during the war were extraordinary. Roman actions were so outstanding that they should be looked upon as 'models and patterns for all who strive for empire ...' (61) There is an obvious distaste for excessive violence during the preliminary stages of imperialism, but after a certain unspecified point the picture becomes more sinister:

> Once (Rome) held sway over virtually the whole inhabited world, they confirmed their power by terrorism and by the destruction to the most eminent cities. Corinth they razed to the ground, the Macedonians (Perseus for example) they rooted out, they razed Carthage and the Celtiberian city of Numantia, and there were many whom they cowed by terror. (62)

A balance of terror had to be maintained for the sake of empire.

Did Polybius approve? Or did his insistence on justice make the final episode of empire building repugnant to him? Certainly he had no taste for overt force if it could be avoided. But in his account of the Third Macedonian War down to the destruction of Carthage and Corinth in 146,

Polybius continually shows that he completely accepted the reality of terror and force in Roman foreign policy. (63) The historian saw little of benefit in the older style of Roman conduct that dealt harshly with an enemy while he resisted, but was lenient after his surrender. To this he had a rather cool answer - 'that this is noble conduct everyone will confess, but perhaps it is open to doubt if it is possible under certain circumstances.' (64) When an enemy blocked the path to world empire then it was simply poor policy to be benevolent to him; at this point moderation and clemency can do more harm than good. If a man chose the wrong side in a war, it was proper that he paid for the mistake with his life. (65) And if a state had the audacity to oppose Rome the result would be utter destruction. Polybius had so taken up the Roman cause that he could not comprehend resistance to Rome in any form; thus Perseus was 'bewitched,' (66) and others who favored Perseus were debauched, stupid, and cowardly. (67) Indeed, entire nations could be possessed by lunacy. When the Macedonians, years after Perseus' death, supported a revolt against Rome, Polybius could only describe the uprising as a 'heaven-sent infatuation.' (68) Similarly, when Greece and even Achaea revolted against the ruling power, Polybius can discover no rational reason to explain it and laments that 'the whole country in fact was visited by an unparalleled attack of mental disturbance, people throwing themselves into wells and down precipices ...' (69) The results are frightful and awful to behold, but at the same time the question of justice never enters into consideration. The goal of world dominion justified any action. Polybius knew and accepted this, and continually bombarded his readers with the impression that from the Third Macedonian War on, Rome only resorted to overwhelming force when confronted by madmen who thought they could cast out the ruling power. (70)

Polybius is unrelating in his efforts to convince his readers of the correctness of the interpretation presented here. His fervour allows him to see only one side of the issue. And, indeed, given the fact that the message was aimed mainly at those subject to Roman power it is not ineffective. Tyche, who can either favor or destroy men and states, picked Rome as being worthy of universal domination. The polity of Rome was not encumbered by the dictates of a single lawgiver, but arose naturally in a state where men, schooled in traditional ways and laws, placed community goals ahead of personal profit. These Romans, favored by Tyche and possessing an ideal government, were thus able to overcome all foes. Moreover, their rule was quite beneficial as long as one respected their power; however, in cases of disobedience or open rebellion they employed the natural right of empires to strike terror and fear into the hearts of any and all enemies. The pages of Polybius' Histories provided example after example to further enhance his points. It was useless, even disadvantageous, to resist the might of Rome, and Polybius constantly implores his readers, and in particular statesmen, to recognize the undeniable, learn from history, and not repeat the mistakes of the past. (71)

B. POLYBIUS AND PAULLUS

The life, career, and death of L. Aemilius Paullus presents Polybius with a perfect example of a man of empire. Every facet of Paullus' life is seen as exemplifying the best of what Rome had to offer. The morality shown by Paullus during his public service on behalf of Rome was as impeccable as his private morality, for in each case he far surpassed not only his contemporaries, who had begun to stray from the manners of the ancestors, but especially his counterparts in alien countries. His every deed was an action against inequity and injustice; he was, further, gifted with a wisdom that understood and respected the secrets of life and the contrivances of Tyche. Polybius wove these traits of Paullus into the fabric of the Histories; they do not stand by themselves, but instead form a deftly constructed part of the historical tapestry, serving, when needed, as instances of how great Rome and Paullus were. But taken together, the traits combine to make the whole greater than the sum of the parts - and the whole is the image of Lucius Aemilius Paullus.

One should never forget that Polybius was the client of Paullus and his sons. The historian was the close friend of Scipio Aemilianus and there can be no doubt that he also had personal contact with Paullus - various tales which Paullus himself used to relate in his old age are quoted by Polybius, and there is no reason to believe that the historian was not present to hear the ramblings. (72) The assumption may also be made (and there is absolutely nothing to hinder it) that Polybius questioned Paullus closely on his early life and on his conduct of the Third Macedonian War. Of course,

Polybius and the Image

Polybius himself had lived through that conflict and much of his information comes from his own experiences. But with the actions of Paullus he had no known contact and must have, therefore, depended on either Paullus or his sons (or both) for details of the campaign, etc. (73) Nor did he have any information at all on Paullus' personal life, and would have, therefore, surely questioned his patrons of the subject. This is not to say that other sources of information were lacking. While commenting on Paullus' virtue, Polybius notes that within Rome itself there were those who spoke ill of the great Lucius Aemilius. Such low types, however, along with their slander, deserve no further mention, since 'on inquiry you will find that (the praiseworthy remarks concerning Paullus are) acknowledged to be true by all.' (74) The historian did indeed have other sources which commented on Paullus, but he dismissed them as malicious chatterboxes. Polybius had already persuaded himself of the validity of his account, and the mention that the narrative itself could easily be confirmed by inquiry guaranteed his Greek readers that what he said was the whole truth and nothing but the truth. (75) Within a few years Polybius had gone from being a Greek political exile with little love for Rome, to being an apologist for the Roman empire. He adopted and took to heart the cause of Rome and the values which the Romans held dear.

The most striking example of Paullus' high principle, according to Polybius, encompasses his conduct of all manners of financial affairs. Now, on the surface the concern placed on the handling of money and wealth seems almost trivial and hardly worth mention as a chief quality of the great Paullus. True, frugality and its complement, industriousness are noble traits in ancient as well as modern times, but Polybius has something more in mind when he speaks of Paullus. In addition to frugality and industriousness which Paullus, of course, possessed, Polybius makes it a point to stress, whenever the situation allows, the fact that Paullus never acquired a penny at the expense of either justice or the Roman state, and that he never turned what money he did have to luxury or extravagance but served, even in death, as an example for Romans and others of a man who did not need ostentation to prove his merit. (76) Not only is Paullus able to show virtue in his private life when it comes to such matters, but his character is so high that he never takes the slightest advantage of his public position. Other men had also been able to lead private lives of considerable restraint, yet none of them could be trusted when it came to public finances, for they inevitably would be tempted to fatten their own coffers. (77) And, indeed, any action which smacks of personal profit at the expense of the government is indicative of a constitution which is caught in the throes of great difficulty. This is the verdict of history, says Polybius, and not even a mixed constitution can survive these activities. (78) The famed Lycurgus had left his city with the most perfect of institutions by which the Spartans could direct their private lives and their city. Yet, he neglected to provide for the day that the Spartans would seek higher glory through war and conquest - consequently, that day brought with it the seeds of Spartan failure. (79) Once they left the bounds of Laconia 'they were compelled to be beggars from the Persians, to impose tribute on the islanders, and to exact contributions from all Greeks;' (80) they sold themselves for Persian gold and in doing so, lost their liberty, their mixed constitution, and most of all, their honor - it is a just criticism.

Still, one historical example does not necessarily make a rule. Polybius is quite aware of this. The discussion continues and this time it is Carthage which exhibits disturbing tendencies when it comes to financial integrity. After the Carthaginian polity had declined from its peak owing to the enormous influx of power and prosperity which their empire gave them, (81) graft and bribe-taking became widespread. (82) Nothing which turned a profit at Carthage was regarded as disgraceful, nor was it any secret that political campaigns at the Punic city were bought and sold with bribery. (83) This case, along with the case of Sparta, present strong warnings of what happens in a state where people use public positions to better themselves, and then, worse still, corrupt others with their ill-gotten riches. Moreover, the Greeks of Polybius' own day had not learned these lessons, and the historian comments more than once on how greedy and avaricious his own countrymen are - one can hardly avoid the impression that he is speaking from personal experience. It is a rare thing to find a Greek who can keep his hands off public monies: 'if (Greek politicians) are entrusted with no more than a talent, though they have ten copyists and as many seals and twice as many witnesses, (they) cannot keep their faith.' (84) And again, 'bribery and the notion that no one should do anything gratis were very prevalent in Greece,' (85) so much so that any type of trust was nonexistant. The problem was, it seems, endemic to the Greeks; even the great men of the past could not redeem Greece in this matter. No one would deny that Aristeides and Epaminondas were men of noble character; but even they fall short of the virtue shown by the Romans and, in particular, Paullus. Aristeides and Epaminondas were well known for their ability to reject the payments of those who wished to gain private favors; is it not, therefore, that much nobler to refuse treasures beyond measure as Paullus had done when he entered the Macedonian treasure-vaults? (86) Thus, when compared to Sparta, Carthage, and Greece, Rome is able to manifest its superiority consistently. All because of the strict observance of laws and customs, a theme which Polybius never ceases to stress. (87)

The entire problem of how people behave with their state's money obviously worries Polybius a great deal. It seems to be one of the first symptoms of decline which a nation experiences once it neglects ancient laws and customs, and permits luxury and extravagance to take hold. Not even the Romans are seen as entirely free from the disease. Their state, their polity, and every aspect of their lives had been at a most perfect condition during the Hannibalic War. But since that time Rome had slipped somewhat and was not so pristine as it had been. When speaking of Roman disdain for bribery and graft during the early second century B.C., Polybius must qualify himself slightly: 'If I were dealing with earlier times, I would have confidently asserted about all Romans in general, that not one of them would do such a thing ... At the present time, however, I would not venture to assert this of all ...' (88) There are further words of warning for Rome. In the years after Pydna, when the Romans thought that they had dominion over the world and when the riches of Macedon came flooding into the city, many gave up their former virtue and abandoned themselves to pleasure and indulgence. (89) Men who filled their pockets at the state's expense, sought young boys, courtesans, and various entertainments and banquets were commonplace. (90) 'Many paid a talent for a male favorite and many three hundred drachmas for a jar of caviar.' (91) It is quite literally an infection which could lay low a nation and its people. Wealth, too much power, luxury, and lavishness all have dark overtones and nearly always lead to hideous results. The abandonment of antique virtues leaves a people with no protection against the seductive lure of vice and debauchery. A once powerful state soon finds itself in a wretched plight:

> When a state has weathered many great perils and subsequently attains to supremacy and uncontested sovereignty, it is evident that under the influence of long established prosperity, life will become more extravagant and the citizens more fierce in their rivalry regarding office and other objects than they ought to be. As these defects go on increasing, the beginning of the change will be due to love of office and the disgrace entailed by obscurity, as well as to extravagance and purse-proud display ... When this happens, the state will change its name to the finest sounding of all, freedom and democracy, but will change its nature to the worst thing of all, mob-rule. (92)

The maxim applies to all nations. Yet, fortunately for Rome the excesses of its citizens had not carried the city to this extreme. For all his criticism, Polybius still felt that whatever might happen was still in the future, and that as long as the best men clung to the old-time morality, Rome could maintain itself.

Outstanding among Rome's best men were Scipio Aemilianus and especially his father Aemilius Paullus from whom Scipio learned virtuous and meritorious behavior. Paullus' <u>virtus</u>, which is discussed within two rather extensive digressions on the greatness of the Roman spirit, (93) is held by Polybius as matching the best ever produced by Rome. Paullus' probity showed itself not only in his private life, but, and this is important when one remembers the comments on the scandal-ridden public servants of Greece and Carthage, also in his service for the state against Perseus. None would dare disclaim the assertion, says Polybius, that Paullus behaved magnificently when dealing with Perseus' treasures. (94) He was a model of Roman virtue especially in an age when the Romans themselves were beginning to succumb to the evils of luxury, since he did not take any of the wealth for himself but gave it all to the state. Indeed, though his own private fortune was meager, he coveted nothing and avoided temptation, for he refused to even gaze upon the treasures. (95) But Paullus was never one to be tempted. As a young man, Paullus had first proved his excellence by performing well in Spain and thereafter returning all booty to the state, not keeping one penny for himself. (96) So amazing was Aemilius' performance in Spain and Macedon that Polybius feels compelled to assure his readers of the truth of what he has written:

> If this appears incredible to anyone, I beg him to consider that the present writer is perfectly aware that this work will be perused by Romans above all people ... and that it is impossible either that they should be ignorant of the facts or disposed to pardon any departure from the truth. (97)

This, obviously, was directed at the Greeks; it informed them, whether they believed it or not, that they were indeed fortunate to be under the thumb of the race from which Paullus had sprung.

The ultimate proof of Paullus' worth came after his death. He had so despised the nonvirtuous gain of money while living that he died relatively poor, at least when compared to other Romans. When Scipio and his brother Fabius, after Paullus' death, wished to return to his wife her dowery of twenty-five talents, they found their father's resources so sparse that, in order to raise the money, they were forced to sell Aemilius' slaves, household goods, and some real property. (98) This, as Polybius happily tells his readers, re-emphasizes Paullus' <u>virtus</u> and confirms the earlier claims of how Paullus dealt with captured riches - 'and this we may say is the best proof there can be of virtue.' (99) Thus, even in death, Paullus was able to affect the conduct of others in these matters favorably. He passed on to his son Scipio a strict moral code, a love of temperance, and a scrupulous concern over the proper conduct of financial affairs. (100) As a good father he bestowed on his sons the greatest of gifts, knowledge of right and just deportment; as a faithful servant of Rome, he served as an example of antique behavior upon which his fellow citizens could draw; and, he was the supreme illustration of the ruling power's merit and reputation which the Greeks could behold and respect.

The image of Paullus goes further. His leadership extends beyond the nobility of his public and private life. He was, for Polybius, one of the best men, an aristocrat who, while he stood above the mass of commoners, worked for harmony and order in Rome and in other states. After his election to the consulate and the acquisition of Macedon as a provincia, Paullus harangued the people about their seeming inability to support commanders in the field. (101) They were the ones, Paullus complained, who sat at home and 'directed' the actions of the legions with idle prattle by finding fault with that which they never understood in the first place. Such talk 'was never of any benefit to the public interest, but had frequently and in many respects been most injurious to it.' (102) It is a stern speech, full of both warning and admonition to those who would try to tell Paullus how to conduct his campaign. For Polybius it demonstrated two important ideas: first, Paullus had no desire to court favor with the people, thinking it better to assert his leadership over those who knew no better, and second, the speech is a fine instance of how Paullus strove to achieve harmony and stability within Rome at a time when interference from the plebs was harming the public weal. (103) Paullus' interest in establishing harmony extends beyond Rome, to Greece. His defeat of Perseus and the dismemberment of Macedon removed from Greece a threat which had arisen years before with Philip V. (104) The Macedonians had tried to impose their will on the Greeks, and the end of Perseus marked the end of those efforts; this had special meaning for Polybius since the Achaeans and the Macedonians had long been at each others throats. Futhermore, Polybius avows that Paullus never approved of the hated pro-Roman factions which were left in control of nearly all of Greece after the final settlement of the Third Macedonian War. (105) These Roman puppets were universally loathed - Polybius relates to his readers the repulsive and abhorrent natures of the Roman toadies (indeed, an accusation by one of them, Callicrates, had sent the historian to Rome), and, in doing so, criticizes the Roman policies which supported them. But Paullus is continually said to have followed the just course when it came to such detestable types. He forbade a pro-Roman named Charops from entering his house when that rogue once visited Rome: 'and when this was noised abroad all the Greek residents were filled with joy, recognizing the Roman hatred of iniquity.' (106) The historian conveniently neglects to ask why a creature of Charop's ill-repute would call upon Paullus in the first place. Nevertheless, to the trusting eye another dimension has been added to Paullus' image.

 Nor is this all. Sage and philosophic wisdom is possessed by Paullus, especially when he speaks of the human condition and the vicissitudes of fortune. Paullus knows well enough the 'slings and arrows of outrageous fortune,' (107) and lectures, rather than talks to, his junior officers on the tragic fate of Perseus. With the defeated king standing in their midst, Paullus exhorted those present never to underestimate the instability of Fortune; the example of Perseus evinced the inconstancy of life. Success should be welcomed with moderation, this being the only honorable thing to do - success is momentary, but humility is a lasting virtue. Indeed, truly wise men learn from the misfortunes of others instead of from their own mistakes, and they are thereby better able to guide themselves through life. (108) The speech is in every aspect worthy of Polybius' Paullus. It allows Polybius to depict Paullus as delivering a sermon of moral instruction on how the successful man of politics should behave when confronted by the unforeseen. The fallen Perseus, who acted disgracefully throughout his life, is contrasted with the victorious Paullus who was wise enough to humble himself before the workings of Tyche. (109) All the platitudes, besides adding to Paullus' image, also lend credence to a theme of didacticism which runs throughout the Histories. The historian, it will be remembered, sought to inform the Greeks of the polity and character of the Romans; he further sought to instruct politicians and statesmen in the proper way to lead their lives, telling them 'that the surest and indeed the only method of learning how to bear bravely the vicissitudes of fortune, is to recall the calamities of others.' (110) This statement is almost word for word exactly the same as the one mouthed by Paullus when he speaks to his staff. (111) Paullus, then, as he lectures on the mutability of life and fortune, presents Polybius with the perfect model of how a statesman should face life. Whether Paullus actually said those words or something similar is another question - for Polybius it hardly mattered. He could use the image of Lucius Aemilius Paullus, against the backdrop of the establishment of the world empire of Rome, in order to indicate the correct demeanor for the knowledgeable statesman.

Polybius' skillfully drawn portrait of Paullus begins to take shape. The image of the historian's patron is far from being merely complimentary, taking on, as it does, a decisive part in the plan of the Histories. One could write endlessly on the eminence of the Roman constitution, the dignity of the Roman spirit, and the worthiness shown by Rome in its drive for empire; but in order to fix these

39

qualities in the minds of his readers Polybius needed an instance of such perfection. Particularly impressive, as shown here, was the life of Paullus. (112) He was as virtuous as any man of Rome, past or present, even more so perhaps, since his morality shone both in his private and public lives. As a father, he set his sons on the path to virtus, and as a public servant his activities offered themselves to the Romans for imitation, and to the Greeks for respect. In a word, the Paullus of the Histories stood for the rectitude which made Rome worthy of its mixed constitution. His character was flawless; but, in addition, he understood the dangers inherent when the common masses tried to dominate national affairs. Paullus, therefore, broke them, at least for the time being, of this obnoxious habit by endeavoring to re-establish harmony in the state. Moreover, his victory over Perseus, the dislike of the Greek hirelings of the Romans, and his wisdom expressed concerning Tyche's handiwork singled him out as being the best representative of Rome's worthiness. But the image is not quite complete. If Paullus was indeed the best representative of Roman worthiness, then almost of necessity he would have to play a principal part in the working out of Tyche's vast plan for Rome. Tyche recognized moral greatness, born of the observance of law and custom, as a prerequisite to her gift of empire. Her grace went to Rome as a whole, and, in Polybius' mind, it was only fitting that Tyche grant the honor and glory of establishing the world empire of Rome to that city's most exemplary citizen of the day, Paullus.

C. POLYBIUS, THE HOUSE OF MACEDON, AND PAULLUS

Paullus is the chief human factor in Polybius' equation for imperium. Upon the ashes of a fallen Macedon stands Paullus, fulfilling the inspired prophecy of Demetrius of Phalerum and acting as Tyche's agent in the final stage of the goddess' plan for Rome. Macedon had long stood, shored up and preserved by the qualities of its kings from Philip II to Antigonus Doson. Clemency, moderation, and all manner of princely traits had attended these kings, and they ruled, not through deceit and unbridled power, but with the support of their subjects and the amity of Tyche. It was not until heinous acts of frightfulness were committed by young Philip V against gods and men that Tyche discarded Macedon

Polybius and the Image

in order to support the virtuous Romans. A new order had come to the world during those days, heralded by a new generation of kings and leaders; more importantly, Tyche had begun to draw together the various strands of history into a unity which presaged Roman domination over the world. (113) The rise of Rome and the disintegration of the other states and kings, especially Macedon, here was a theme which Polybius, as a historian and as an Achaean, set for himself. The lines which mark the path to empire all merge with the figure of Paullus and find completion with his deeds.

The tragic end of the House of Macedon offers itself as a unique chance to view the collapse of one world empire and the rise of another. From the very beginning of the reign of Philip V, Polybius carefully traces the metamorphosis of a king into a tyrant, never failing to provide adequate invective to enhance his assertions that upon Philip's shoulders rests the reason for Macedon's destruction. Whatever the historian's motivations (and it is no secret that as an Achaean, Polybius hated Philip and the Macedonians) the result carries Polybius nearly to the door of the so-called 'tragic' historians against whom he rails; the intensity of his feelings against Macedon is converted into violent and harsh commentary, claims of divine intervention by both Tyche and the Furies, and sequences of description which border on the sensational. And not only is Philip V visited by divine justice which exacted punishment for his evil deeds, but the sins of the father were passed on to the son, and Perseus also falls under the onslaught of a Rome guided by Tyche. The establishment of the Roman domain over the world by Aemilius Paullus is the fitting end of what had become the Tyrant House of Macedon.

The first act in the destruction of Macedon coincides with the rise of Philip V to the throne. (114) This is conveniently placed in 220 and is but one example of how in that year Tyche shaped the world anew by raising to power new kings in all areas of the earth. (115) Now the diverse strands of history (which previously had known no unity) begin to come together until by 216 they intertwine into what Polybius views as an organic whole. (116) The year 220 thus denotes not only the commencement of the <u>Histories</u> proper - the preceding material being introductory in nature - but also the start of Rome's fifty-three year rise to empire, and, conversely, Macedon's fall from that position.

Previously to Philip V there is no question in Polybius'

mind that Macedon was worthy of its empire and the grace of Tyche. From the time of the empire's inception the Macedonian kings demonstrated themselves to be deserving of hegemony. Philip II had shown himself knowledgeable of the proper methods to be used in the acquisition of empire, understanding that moderation was required when dealing with vanquished peoples. (117) In every aspect this man served his country well in raising it from a small monarchy to the glorious station of master of Persia and the eastern world. Alexander had, of course, actually carried out the conquests, but it was Philip who had first conceived of the idea and had intended to carry it out; Alexander merely accomplished what his father planned. (118) The mechanistic imposition of causal relationships did not bother Polybius in the slightest; nor does it chafe him when he is forced to whitewash the character and career of Philip II. If one's view of empire is predicated on the belief that its founders were inevitably just men whose acts had earned them Tyche's goodwill, then one can hardly accept criticisms which portray them as monsters and tyrants. Polybius takes several occasions to attack others who wrote against Alexander's father. The historian Theopompus is subjected to a devastating attack for having described Philip in terms suited for Sardanapalus, but ill-becoming a king of Philip's stature. Whereas Theopompus writes that Philip surrounded himself with the most degraded and debauched misfits of Greece and often lent himself to their lewdness, Polybius will have none of this and discredits Theopompus and his charges - indeed, where it concerned Philip and his companions 'one could scarcely find terms adequate to characterize the bravery, industry, and in general the virtue of these men who indisputably by their energy and daring raised Macedonia from the rank of a petty kingdom to that of the greatest and most glorious monarchy in the world.' (119)

Such writing as Theopompus' is bad enough, but the open opposition which some Greeks took against Philip, this was even worse and earned rich condemnation from Polybius. In a striking and personally revealing passage, Polybius informs his readers that the subject of treason and traitors has often caused him much wonder. (120) One should not be classed as a traitor merely for inducing one's country to submit to a dominant power; so long as alien garrisons were not invited into the cities, or fellow citizens not deprived of their laws and rights, or so long as those who realistically supported the stronger power did not try to foster personal aggrandizement, they should not be labelled as traitors but rather as benefactors. (121) Thus when the point is reached after which destruction awaits for those who foolishly resist, the better course of action lies in submission, but not prostration, before the superior force. It is, moreover, a treasonous act not to bow to the inevitable when the outcome is certain annihilation. In this light, Polybius makes the startling claim that Demosthenes, by encouraging the Athenians and the other Greeks to resist Philip, was more of a traitor than were the men who joined Philip and bowed to his might - 'it was not their duty to fight against Philip, but to take every step for their own honour and glory.' (122) From the historian's viewpoint, no resistance to Philip's power could be comprehended, especially since he had behaved with the justice and magnanimity of a king and conqueror; and from the viewpoint of Polybius the man, the analysis of traitors and treason also served to exculpate the historian himself from blame for his defection to Rome, and even, it may be suggested, to excise the familial guilt he felt over the actions of his grandfather, Thearides, who, years before, had sought to 'save' Megalopolis by collaborating with Cleomenes of Sparta. (123)

Alexander, too, receives favorable mention for his role in the establishment of empire, although at times Polybius is ambivalent when commenting on the conqueror's motives and character. In general, however, Polybius treats Alexander in a good light. There was no denying that Alexander crushed Thebes and sold its people into slavery; yet, in a major section, the reader is told that Alexander committed the deed because he was indignant at the Theban's behavior toward him and for no other reason. (124) Moreover, as he razed the city he took especial care to uphold his reverence for the gods by not disturbing any temple or holy place. (125) He might have destroyed Thebes, but he did so only after being offended; and, more importantly, he did so with purity of heart and devotion to the gods. And after Alexander crossed into Persia he wished nothing more than to avenge the ancient wrongs which the Persians had perpetrated against the Greeks - his virtue continued to shine since he 'refrained from injuring anything consecrated to the gods ...' (126) Nevertheless, in a later passage and with a more perspicacious vision, Polybius treats Alexander realistically. This time the ravage of

Thebes is performed in order to frighten the other Greeks into obedience while the conqueror was occupied with Persia. And this time, 'every one pitied the Thebans for the cruel and unjust treatment they suffered, and no one attempted to justify this act of Alexander.' (127) The difference in commentary may be accounted for by examination of Polybius' purpose behind each passage, and not by postulating any basic change in the historian's views on the nature of empires and their founders. The latter section is only one part of the discussion of the horrors that befell the Greeks during 147/6 when they became misguided enough to revolt from Rome. The remark on Alexander's harsh treatment of Thebes takes its place in a catalog of misfortunes which various Greek cities of the past had suffered; (128) yet, what Polybius really wants to point out in this entire chapter is how insignificant past troubles were when compared to those of 147/6. Individual cities had been destroyed in earlier times, but this was as nothing to the present day when the Greeks were so mad as to think they could defeat Rome - the ruin which Greece underwent because of this was far worse than what Alexander had done at Thebes. Thus, Alexander's actions at Thebes are markedly less serious than they appear at first glance. He had devastated only one city and had done so, not as a rude aggressor, but as a world conqueror whose humility to the divine was pronounced in his every deed.

These traits which helped lift Macedon to the position of world empire continued, for the most part, in the monarchy down to the last king before Philip V, Antigonus Doson. Antigonus is praised over and over in the Histories as a good and just king - and why not since he was allied with Polybius' Achaeans against Cleomenes of Sparta? His life was guided by high principles and excellence, while on the battle field he was a true general and prince, and treated his fallen enemies with generosity and humanity. (129) There can be little doubt that because of Antigonus' sterling qualities, Macedon still retained the grace of Tyche. While the Macedonian kings held to the level of conduct exhibited by Philip II, they were able to sustain their empire through Tyche's blessings and the propensity of conquered peoples to respect and obey an equitable overlord. However, when kings lower themselves by immoral or amoral acts brought on either by their own machinations or by the devious influences of unscrupulous underlings, they become debased in the eyes of Tyche and their subjects, and totter on the edge of oblivion. They descend from the noble stance of a king and fall to the hated appellation of tyrant.

Such was the fate of Phliip V upon whose shoulders Polybius lets rest the entire blame for the fall of Macedon. (130) High hopes had attended the young Philip when he first came to the throne after Antigonus' death. His youth worried some, but this mattered little since others saw him as carrying on, or even raising, the standards which the House of Macedon had always abided by. Philip was 'the darling of the whole of Greece,' (131) and so wooed and charmed Macedon's subjects that 'all his hereditary dominions were more submissive and more attached to him than to any king before him ...' (132) It is no wonder that Polybius is able to assure his readers that the prince was 'endowed by nature with the qualities requisite for the attainment of power' and that these qualities were tempered by high character, moral excellence, and courage. (133) Unfortunately, as horses often show increased defects with age, (134) so too did Philip permit unseen flaws in himself to rise to the surface. Although his nature was basically good and well-meaning, he was swayed too easily by perfidious councellors into avenues which neglected virtue and espoused ruthlessness. The theme of the evil councellors figures highly in the <u>Histories</u>; (135) but in Philip's case it is especially significant since their effect contributed to Philip's change from a king to a tyrant, and, ultimately, to the downfall of Macedon. Demetrius of Pharos must take the chief responsibility for corrupting Philip, although Apelles cannot be excused. (136) Apelles had attempted to negate the beneficial judgement which Aratus was imparting to Philip, while Demetrius, the arch-villain in Polybius' opinion, guided the young king into impious acts against god and man. Thus it was that Tyche not only withdrew her blessings from Philip, but actually visited him in later life with divine punishment meant to exact justice for crimes committed.

Philip's new-found cruelty and impiety drove him to the edge of madness. The utter and senseless destruction of Thermum in 218 was beyond the limits of humanity and rationality, and flaunted all laws of war. In retaliation for Aetolian atrocities at Dium and Dodona, Philip sacked Thermum, rivaling the Aetolians in their impiety by doing 'wanton damage to temples, statues, and all such works with absolutely no prospect of any resulting advantage in the war,' thereby proving himself to be a 'frenzied mind at the height of its fury.' (137) To be at war with men and to do everything against them possible, this was acceptable within what Polybius calls the 'laws of war' - but to attack someone in revenge for an offense that they did not commit, or to take out one's fury on things dedicated to the divine is not even remotely just. (138) It is the deed of a tyrant who strives for mastery through hatred and the abuse of his powers; this is precisely how Polybius describes Philip. (139) He turned from kingship to tyranny, losing the respect of the Greeks and the grace of Tyche.

Worse still, barely a year later in 217 with Hannibal seemingly on the verge of victory in the war against Rome, Demetrius persuaded Philip to ignore the present troubles in Greece and turn his eyes on the west and Italy itself. His objective was obvious - 'an expedition ... to Italy was the first step towards the conquest of the world.' (140) For Philip, the time looked right to extent Macedon's domain, but from Polybius' vantage point, and with the benefit of hindsight, Tyche's plan had already begun. The Hannibalic War, it will be remembered, marked both the zenith of Rome's mixed constitution and the time when Tyche first transferred her goodwill to the Romans. Their <u>virtus</u> and the perfection attained by their polity had come into blossom at the same time that Philip proved himself unworthy through his conduct at Thermum. He was unworthy of Philip II and Alexander (141) and was, further, unfit in Tyche's estimation. In this fashion, Tyche had artfully drawn together the still divergent lines of history - into the mind of Philip was put the idea that he should make war against Rome, a war which he could never win.

The characteristics of the tyrant became more pronounced in Philip as time went on. The barbarism he loosed at Messene was unthinkable. (142) And the narrative presents him, in constantly increasing ferocity, as an ambitious man puffed up with an audacity fed by deceit, lust, infamy, and every manner of disgraceful act. The height of Philip's perversity comes in 203/2 when he allied himself with Antiochus against Ptolemy Epiphanes. (143) Their conspiracy against the young Ptolemy was marked by unbounded impiety, savagery, and covetousness. (144) It ended when Tyche could stand no more - 'this last outrage ... was avenged by Tyche doubly, immediately, in that she raised up the Romans against Philip and Antiochus and forced them both within a short time to pay tribute to her, and then again afterwards, by re-establishing the dynasty of

Ptolemy, while those of his enemies sank in ruin.' (145) Finally, even the very countenance of Philip changed. He took to leading the life of a wolf, preying on whomever he could find. To some he cringed in order to accomplish his ends, but to others who refused him, he growled and concocted plots to use against them. (146) Redemption was beyond hope, for Philip had learned too well from Demetrius of Pharos and Apelles - the student soon surpassed his masters.

The historian's panoramic presentation of Macedon's history of empire, from the glorious days of Philip II and Alexander down to Philip V's mutation into a vulpine tyrant who trusted no one and betrayed every friend, has, in a most ambitious manner, uncovered for the reader a historical example with which the Roman experience could be compared. Intended mainly for Greek consumption, the story enabled Polybius' audience to glimpse the nature of a conqueror, and, in turn, the relationship between victor and vanquished. If the notion that Tyche's power lay behind the sudden and unexpected expansion of peoples to the status of world dominion was to have any meaning (as Demetrius of Phalerum had claimed when he surveyed Macedon's achievement), and if the goddess' grace was dependent on moral worth, then, of necessity, Philip II and Alexander must have been good kings; otherwise, they could not have accomplished what they did. This type of reasoning is quite strained - it forces Polybius to evade a vast body of evidence and tortuously rehabilitate the characters of the kings in order for them to fit his scheme. Theopompus' unflattering description of Philip II is dismissed on specious grounds; and in Alexander's case, murderous brutality is justified with an assurance that Alexander never offended the gods - Polybius' gods obviously cared little for human suffering. The historian was relentlessly mechanistic in his imposition of this maxim once he decided that Tyche always guided the rise of a world empire and that the empire had to be just in order to earn the goddess' recognition. The reasoning behind this imposition combines both moral edification and historical didacticism. The message for the people subjected to the empire's expansion counselled resignation; there was no chance of successful resistance, nor were hopeless efforts along that line commendable. Those who refused to accept the power of the overlords blinded themselves to the workings of Tyche and, in bringing down destruction on their cities, deserved the name of traitor. It was far wiser to see that nothing could be done to stop the inevitable and to bow to the new master. Polybius' readers were provided with numerous examples of how one should deal with a ruling power backed by Tyche's omnipotence. And on a wholly different level, one could easily see the degeneration of an empire and king from benevolence to a most foul tyranny. Against such corruption it was right and proper that former subjects revolt. No Greek state was under any obligation to remain loyal to Philip V after the destruction at Thermum; had Demosthenes lived during this time Polybius, no doubt, would have hailed him as a visionary instead of a traitor. It was the will of Tyche and the verdict of history that as a tyrant Philip V could not long survive, and it was likewise the will of Tyche and the verdict of history that the Roman hegemony was inevitable and should not be resisted. In Polybius' equation for empire, as the founders of the Macedonian world monarchy were just and merciful, so too did the Romans have to be likewise. And since they were superior, it was unwise, both morally and politically, to resist the Romans. This proves to be doubly true as Polybius chronicles the final ruin of the tyrant-house, and the Roman establishment of empire.

Polybius' narrative of Philip V's final years is cloaked in high drama. Tyche had drawn the lines of history even closer together, deciding, chiefly because of the alliance with Antiochus against Ptolemy, to ruin Philip by first tempting him to plan war against Rome, and, then, to murder his own son, Demetrius. (147) Although large portions of the Polybian narrative must be gleaned from Livy, (148) enough remains in the Histories to demonstrate the dramatic manner in which Polybius treated the entire episode.

> For it was now that Tyche, as if she meant to punish him at one and the same time for all the wicked and criminal acts he had committed in his life, sent to haunt him a host of the furies, tormentors and avenging spirits of his victims, phantoms that never leaving him by day or by night, tortured him so terribly up to the day of his death that all men acknowledged that, as the proverb says, 'Justice (Dike) has an eye' and we who are but men should never scorn her. (149)

To achieve her ends, Tyche first infatuated Philip with the notion that he should make war on Rome, and that, to ready

Macedon for war he should engage in the forced movements of populations; secondly, that he ought to imprison or kill all anti-Macedonian leaders; and thirdly, Tyche brought to the surface a deadly conflict between Demetrius and Perseus. (150)

The minute details are not crucial to the present study, especially since they have been so brilliantly analyzed by Walbank; (151) but what is of interest is the manner in which Polybius handled the material. The historian's dramatization is not sensational, although it borders closely on it. Polybius does not seek to involve the reader emotionally in the proceedings, but instead wishes to impart a moral lesson to his audience. (152) With the benefit of hindsight and the need to assure his readers that 'Dike has an eye' and that Tyche would punish such an abomination as Philip, Polybius views the historical events as retribution for Philip's crimes, and as further proof of Tyche's grand plan for Rome. Philip's war preparations, his orders to transfer populations and exterminate any opposition, and the deadly conflict between Perseus and Demetrius are shrouded in terms and descriptions which suit a tragedy but not 'scientific' history - as Walbank has pointed out, 'these factors make Polybius' account of these last years of Philip one of the least satisfying in his whole work.' (153) Historical details serve more to illuminate the moral to be drawn - i.e., the consequences of the changeover from king to tyrant - than to explain the reasons behind what happened. And in order to answer the question of causation, Polybius again brings forward Tyche. It was she who took revenge on Philip and forced him to conjure up a war against the people destined to rule the world. The war itself was passed on to Perseus who had also shown himself to be an implacable enemy of Rome with his opposition to Demetrius, the favorite of the Romans. (154) The fact that actual hostility did not break out until years later under entirely different circumstances did not hinder Polybius. Tyche again rears her head. Long before, it will be remembered, when Philip and Antiochus conspired against Ptolemy, Tyche had vowed to re-establish the Ptolemies on the ruin of Macedon and the disgrace of Antiochus. (155) Perseus was fated to carry out the war planned by his father, and he was fated to fail. Coming when it did, Perseus' defeat allowed the Romans to expel Antiochus from Egypt: 'Tyche having so directed the matter of Perseus and Macedonia that when the position of Alexander and the whole of Egypt was almost desperate, all was again set right simply owing to the fact that the fate of Perseus had been decided.' (156) Thus, Tyche plays a critical role in Polybius' interpretation of Philip's end and in the fate of the unfortunate Perseus, the last king of Macedon.

Perseus himself suffers mightily at the hands of Polybius. He is pictured as a rather sad individual whose misfortunes are to be pitied, but whose life is to be despised. Polybius, to his discredit, makes absolutely no effort either to understand Perseus or to fathom the policies with which Perseus desperately tried to save his kingdom. But then one should not really expect the historian to change his ways and treat Perseus objectively - after all, the record had been slanted in order to portray the Macedonian kings in the manner best suited to complement the scheme of the Histories, and there is no reason to imagine Polybius taking a different tack for Perseus. In order to justify the Roman position in the war against Perseus, Polybius strives to vilify the king and show that the final Roman victory and establishment of empire was the best of all possible outcomes. Perseus' every move showed indecision and cowardice; he acted as if he lived in a fantasy world, directed by unreality and motivated by hopeless illogic. Perseus was 'bewitched', compelled to follow the policies of his father, and caught in the spinning of Tyche's web. It is around those two themes that Polybius will narrate the melancholy history of the last king of Macedon.

Underneath everything, Perseus was not a bad sort. According to the historian, Perseus was a capable man both mentally and physically, not to mention the fact that he was composed in his demeanor, moderate in his desires, and, in general, 'he also showed in the rest of his behavior true royal dignity.' (157) But such auspicious qualities were quickly clouded by a nefarious move designed by Perseus to win the Greek masses over to his cause. At the very outset of his reign, Perseus declared an amnesty for all debtors in Macedon, recalled those who had been exiled, and set free all who were charged with offenses against the crown. (158) Seen objectively, Perseus' actions are easily interpreted as being normal for a new ruler who was trying to solidify his position. There were, however, different connotations for Polybius. The cancellation of debts, the recall of exiles, and the other programs all smacked of the qualities of a social revolutionary. Polybius placed no trust in the motives of the earlier Spartan kings who had fostered similar policies, (159) and the figure of Perseus was surely envisioned as continuing in the Spartans' footsteps. Polybius, the Achaean aristrocrat, was suspicious and close-minded over anything which remotely portended a change in the status quo. By beginning his reign in the way he did, Perseus (at least in Polybius' eyes) invoked the specters of other kings who appealed to the desperation of the poor for their support. (160)

Yet, what galls Polybius all the more is that Perseus succeeded in winning the support of much of the Greek speaking world. (161) The majority of the Greek populace became so enamored of Perseus, especially after he won several initial victories over the Romans in the Third Macedonian War, that the historian is forced to undertake an extended defence of why his countrymen had deluded themselves into turning to Macedon and away from Rome. According to Polybius, the love of the Greeks for Perseus was not due to any intelligent and objective assessment of the situation at hand, but was instead an example of how people instinctively lend their succor to the underdog of a fight. (162) The phenomenon, as described by Polybius, most often occurs at a boxing match; for when an inferior man was brought up against one who was clearly better, the crowd would naturally favor the lesser man, cheering him on when he chanced to land a blow and doing all they could to rattle his opponent. But, says Polybius, if one pointed out to the crowd their error in backing the inferior boxer, then they would immediately turn around and cheer for the better man. Thus, the masses, by favoring Perseus against Rome, were guided by an unreflecting impulse; but if one took the time and asked them to consider which party they would rather see win the war Polybius has no doubt that the people would come to their senses in an instant and side with Rome. The Greeks were like innocent bystanders watching a conflict beyond their ken, and although he condemns their stupidity he still wishes to save them from later retribution: 'I have been led to speak of this matter at such length lest anyone, in ignorance of what is inherent in human nature, may unjustly reproach the Greeks with ingratitude for being in this state of mind at the time.' (163)

Perseus' true colors show themselves more clearly through his actions in the Third Macedonian War. The king's relations with allies or potential allies are repeatedly described in derisive langauge and are cast into the worst possible light. Polybius makes little or no attempt to understand Perseus' position or policies; and what is not

Polybius and the Image

understood is slanted against the king, or worse, used in a concerted endeavor to libel Perseus. For example, when Perseus fails to work out an alliance with Genthius in the opening stages of war it is because the Macdeonian king is either thoughtless or bewitched; and Polybius is certain that 'it is rather bewitchment (daimonoblabeia).' (164) The implication is that Perseus was not in full control of his faculties. He is deluding himself into believing that it is more important to hold onto his wealth (which his father Philip had amassed) then to use it, even sparingly, to help the war effort. Moreover, Perseus is not merely deluding himself, but he is being deluded. Polybius sees no rhyme or reason behind what Perseus does, and therefore describes it as 'daimonoblabeia', which is more than mere bewitchment - it is rather a heaven-sent affliction (165) over which Perseus has no control. There can be little doubt that Tyche lay behind Perseus' infatuation, and that this was all part of her plan to destroy Macedon. The king's bewitchment soon becomes synonymous with avarice and stinginess. As Perseus' position in the war deteriorated, he is alleged to have undertaken secret negotiations with Eumenes in the hope that Eumenes could persuade the Romans to end the war, or, failing that, to withdraw his own forces from the conflict (166) - 'as it was a match between two princes, one of whom (Eumenes) had the reputation of being most unprincipled and the other (Perseus) most avaricious, the contest proved very ridiculous.' (167) Eumenes is condemned for considering such an adventure, but Perseus suffers the most at Polybius' hands. Why Perseus would not pay Eumenes the money demanded is beyond conception; if he had, the results would have been beneficial. Yet, 'to save giving (Eumenes any gold, Perseus) was ready to suffer any disaster and shut his eyes to all consequences. (168) It was Tyche who blurred the king's vision. And not only was Perseus helplessly manipulated by Tyche, but he was also compelled to carry out his father's policies, policies which he did not understand, and, therefore, which he could not pursue with vigor and forcefulness.

With the necessary vilification complete, Polybius reaches a highly significant section in the Histories, that is, the fulfillment of Demetrius of Phalerum's prophecy on the end of Macedon. In the very beginning of his work, Polybius had commented on the 'unexpectedness' of Rome's sudden and dramatic achievement; and when the seemingly impossible finally became reality, Polybius makes it plain

Polybius and the Image

that he was frankly amazed and that he wished to dwell on the Roman accomplishment. (169) Indeed, it would be surprising if Polybius had given the event no more than passing notice. The historian proceeds by employing elements of high drama and vivid description, this being done so that the reader might gain a proper understanding of Rome's conquest together with the culmination of Tyche's plans. Nor is the use of such techniques that unusual for Polybius. In numerous other situations of momentous import (170) the historian resorted to like methods; in fact, the use of 'a more declamatory and ambitious manner' to express historical narrative is perfectly acceptable if the occasion warrants it. (171) It is not sensationalism for its own sake; Phylarchus had been scathingly condemned for trying to involve his readers emotionally in a scene. (172) The high drama and tragic development of occurrences is used by Polybius to enhance and highlight the moral which the episode has called to his mind. Furthermore, it can be demonstrated that even when the descriptions border on the sensational, the historian is relying on the best evidence available, and is never indulging in flights of fancy.

The period from the battle of Pydna to the capture of Perseus constitutes the main area of interest. Here the figures of Paullus and Perseus come into direct conflict on both a historical and moral level. Unfortunately, the part of the Histories which develops the theme is in a most fragmentary state, but with the help of Livy and Plutarch who both drew on Polybius, the dramatization may be uncovered. Nissen long ago recognized that the detailed accounts in Livy and Plutarch describing parts of Pydna, the flight of Perseus, his desperate attempts at escape, his capture, and his meeting with Paullus are of Polybian origin, and that, allowing for some amplification by Livy and Plutarch, they are a faithful reproduction. (173) Minor details might, of course, have been added or given more emphasis than they deserved, but no overt distortion can be discovered between the full narrative of Livy and Plutarch and what fragments of Polybius have survived.

Neither man nor god lent succor to Perseus in his last days. Before Pydna the moon herself portended the eclipse of a king and a kingdom, and at the battle, Perseus' prayers were ignored when the cowardly monarch tried to invoke the aid of Heracles - for Heracles had already given his divine aid to Paullus and the Romans. (174) In his flight from the battlefield in terror, Perseus was accompanied by a large

53

number of cavalry, but many of the horsemen, and nearly all of his 'friends', forsook him so that only the royal pages and those who sought the king's money remained. (175) From Pella where he first fled, he went to Amphipolis, and, when the townspeople would have no more of him, Perseus threw himself at the gods' mercy and became a supplicant at a temple in Samothrace. (176) There he again proved himself the most wicked of men. For when the populace called for the trial of a certain Evander, the man accused of trying to kill Eumenes at Delphi, it occurred to Perseus that he himself should do away with Evander. (177) Little did Perseus realize that by killing Evander he not only had polluted the temple with blood, but had also brought down on himself the guilt that Evander suffered from the violence done at Delphi; at Perseus' sole instigation two of the holiest shrines had been profaned with human blood. (178) Perseus' monstrous evil was now doubly repaid; his remaining friends deserted to the Romans and the Cretans who were supposed to help him escape, robbed him and left. He had planned carefully, but had neglected to remember Cretan perfidy - with the money loaded on the ship, Perseus waited until midnight, then with a few companions, he left by the back door of his house, scrambled with difficulty over a wall, and went to the shore. But the Cretans had long since left, and after wandering about for a time, Perseus returned to the temple at dawn and hid in a corner. (179) Now, bereft of everything but his overweening pride he surrendered to the Romans, railing at his fortune and at the gods who failed to protect him. (180)

A great crowd awaited Perseus' arrival at the Roman headquarters. In previous wars, minor kings had been led into Roman camps, but none came close to Perseus since, through him, the glory of Philip II and Alexander shone. (181) Dressed in dark clothing and with no one but his son to share his grief, Perseus entered the camp. The press of the crowd was so fierce that Paullus' lictors were sent to make way. And when Paullus finally saw the pitiable king, the consul rose, took a few steps toward Perseus, raised him from his supplicant position and escorted him into the council tent. (182) There, Paullus twice asked him why he had been driven to wage war against the Roman people, especially since they had kept the strictest faith with him and his father - to the questions Perseus could find no answer and could only gaze at the ground and weep. (183) But, bidding Perseus to take heart and trust in Roman generosity, (184) 'Aemilius, now speaking in Latin, exhorted those present at the council to learn from what they now witnessed - showing them Perseus who was present - never to boast unduly of achievements and never be overbearing and merciless in their conduct to anyone, in fact never place any reliance on present prosperity.' (185) Whenever men or nations, the consul continued, are too successful, they should always remember the opposite extremity of fortune, for only fools learn by their own mistakes, while wise men profit from the misfortunes of others. (186) Thus it was that Tyche brought Perseus and Macedon to their knees as quickly and as unexpectedly as she had made Alexander master over the Persians one hundred and fifty years before. (187)

Perseus is the tragic hero of the piece. His error which haunted him in the Third Macedonian War was his all-consuming hatred of his brother Demetrius and, through Demetrius, of Rome itself. (188) Because of this (and because of the earlier pact between Philip V and Antiochus against Ptolemy), Perseus was manipulated by Tyche into carrying out his father's plans for war with Rome. He was a man stricken with a heaven-sent infatuation which blinded him to the consequences of his actions. His deeds were so bewildering that when they failed, Perseus, unable to see that he was the cause of the failure, vented his rage on his 'friends' and blamed them instead. And as they deserted him, so too did the gods against whom he repeatedly sinned. Finally, when confronted by Paullus, Perseus realizes his absurdity and witnesses the correct moral behavior of a representative of the new world order.

The writing is highly dramatic and at times very descriptive. Polybius had employed these devices to develop the moral that history should train statesmen in life's vicissitudes, and, further, to celebrate a solemn moment in history. Moreover, one cannot assume that Polybius invented any part of the story; there were many 'friends' of the king who defected to the Romans at various times after Pydna, (189) and up until Perseus' surrender there remained with him a number of Royal Pages (190) who could have easily provided the historian with details of Perseus' flight, etc. Although Polybius couched his account in the cloak of a tragedy, he did so, not for pure sensationalism, but to enhance a moral which he saw embedded in information provided by first-hand sources.

At the apex stands Paullus, dignified in his carriage, yet

Polybius and the Image

always aware of the mutability of life and fortune - the perfect statesman/conqueror. His supposed sermons on the fate of Perseus and the instability of life in general surely warmed Polybius' heart; but at the same time the historian was conscious of the need to make Paullus and his activities after the formal end of the war conform to the description of the just overlord. In Polybius' opinion, Paullus did not let irrational rage take its toll on the Greek cities, nor did he punish the masses for their support of Perseus. (191) The vast majority of Greece was treated with a moderation and clemency that befitted the majesty of Rome. Perseus himself was the prime example of Roman magnanimity, his treatment being far better than what he should expect. (192) Paullus' interest in religious shrines as he toured Greece also marked him with the necessary qualities of the founder of an empire. (193) He was also a realistic conqueror who knew how to use force when there was no alternative. When an enemy proved himself intransigent or when that enemy betrayed Rome's trust at a critical time, then no mercy could be hoped for. Thus, because of Perseus' uncompromising enmity toward Rome, the best course for Paullus was to dismember Macedon and to give the parts their 'freedom'; a 'free' and disjointed Macedon, the kingship of which had been exterminated, would constitute no problem for the ruling power. And, although there remains in the Histories no comment on the later sack of Epirus, in all probability it too was excused on the grounds that the Epirotes, who had been Rome's allies during the early part of the war, later turned on Rome, and, therefore, deserved what they got. (194) The velvet glove slipped, displaying an iron fist.

Mention must be made of one final aspect of Paullus' image. When Polybius first conceived of his Histories he wished only to cover the fifty-three year period which ended with the fall of Macedon. (195) Later, however, he decided to expand the work to include the years down to 146. Polybius had become concerned with the policies and methods which the Romans employed in their universal rule; judgements concerning the Roman imperium could not be made without surveying the fates of the peoples under Rome's control. The Histories were, therefore, continued in order

> that contemporaries will thus be able to see clearly whether the Roman rule is acceptable or the reverse,

and future generations whether their government (i.e., the Roman) should be considered to have been worthy of praise and admiration or rather of blame. (196)

The two-fold thesis questions whether Roman rule was politically acceptable and beneficial, and whether it was acceptable on a moral level. The criterion for judgement was to be the conditions of the subject peoples throughout Rome's new empire. (197) But while Polybius propounds the problem, as Walbank has pointed out, he 'never makes any attempt to answer it' (198) - at least not directly. The historian's coverage of 168/67-146 never directly pursues an answer to this thesis, and, seemingly, Polybius himself did not arrive at an answer. (199) Yet, it may be suggested that Polybius had no real intention of conclusively answering the question; but what he did try to do was to allow the reader to come to a conclusion himself. The Histories had already laid out in great detail a model of empire and a pattern of conduct by which men of authority must abide. An abundance of examples existed by which a person could judge the qualities of a master. In the case of Macedon, there was no real trouble until the reign of Philip V; and in the case of the Romans, they too would enjoy hegemony until a time when they corrupted themselves. This was still in the future, although disturbing signs of both laxity and depravity were evident in the present. If Rome was to survive and, more importantly, if Roman rule was to be politically and morally acceptable, then characteristics such as those exhibited by none other than Aemilius Paullus must be retained by the rulers of the state. There is an interesting passage in Diodorus (surely taken from Polybius since Polybian fragments bracket and complement it) commenting on Paullus' conduct in the Third Macedonian War and what it meant - Aemilius was the standard of perfection, and 'since there were others also who affected a similar attitude, Rome's worldwide rule brought her no odium so long as she had such men to direct her empire.' (200) If any verdict is to be rendered, it is to be done using the life and career of Paullus as the rule. Polybius answered the question of Roman sovereignty, but he did so indirectly by saying that as long as the Romans followed Paullus' example, their dominion would be welcomed and beneficial. It was lucky for Scipio Aemilianus and Rome that he inherited the 'virtues' of his esteemed father, Paullus.

NOTES

1. Livy 45.31.9; Polyb. 30.13.1-11 and 32.1-2; Pausanias 7.10.11.
2. Cf. F.W. Walbank, Polybius (Berkeley: University of California Press, 1972), p.7. On Polybius' release, see Polyb. 30.6, and Pausanias 7.10.12. For a consideration of Polybius during his exile, see P. Pedech, 'Un Grec a la decouverte de Rome: l'exil de Polybe (167-150 av. J.C.),' Orpheus 11 (1964), 123-40.
3. Polyb. 31.23.4; cf. Plutarch Aem. 28.
4. Polyb. 31.24.5; 31.24.9.
5. Polyb. 31.25.1.
6. Polyb. 31.23.5.
7. Polyb. 31.29.8.
8. Polyb. 31.25.2; 31.25.9; 31.29.1. Cf. Walbank, Polybius, p.173.
9. Polyb. 18.35.4; 31.22.3-5.
10. In general, the same passages as in note 9. The point is that Paullus' high virtue extended from his private to his public life, and that he considered the good of the state to outweigh personal profit.
11. Polyb. 31.25.9-10.
12. Polyb. 31.29.1-5.
13. Polyb. 18.34.7-8 speaks of bribery among the Greeks. This is contrasted in 18.35.4 with Paullus' high character. See 31.22.6-7 for the comparison between Paullus and Aristeides and Epaminondas; also cf. Diod. 31.26.2.
14. Polyb. 18.35.1-3.
15. Polyb. 1.1.3-4; 1.2.1 ff. This unexpectedness is seen as being intimately related to Tyche's plan for Rome - see F.W. Walbank, A Historical Commentary on Polybius, Vol. I (Oxford: The Clarendon Press, 1957), p.40.
16. Polyb. 1.1.5. Cf. Walbank, Commentary, I.40.
17. Polyb. 3.1.4-5.
18. Polyb. 6.51.4. Book Six is, perhaps, the most interesting of all the surviving books of the Histories. It sets down not only Polybius' notions on the nature of constitutions in general, but also provides a rather simplistic analysis (chiefly meant for Greek consumption) of the workings of the Roman polity. In general, see Walbank, Commentary I. 635-746; Walbank, Polybius, pp.130-56; F.W. Walbank, 'Polybius on the Roman Constitution,' Classical Quarterly 37 (1943), 73-89; C.O. Brink and F.W. Walbank, 'The Construction of the Sixth Book of Polybius,' Classical

Quarterly 48 (1954), 97-122; P. Pedech, La Methode Historique de Polybe (Paris: Societe d' Edition 'Les Belles Lettres', 1964), pp. 303-30; K. von Fritz, The Theory of the Mixed Constitution in Antiquity: A Critical Analysis of Polybius' Political Ideas (New York: Columbia University Press, 1954).
19. Polyb. 6.3.1-2.
20. Polyb. 6.4.12. On the cycle of constitutions, the anacyclosis, see Walbank, Commentary I.643-48.
21. Polyb. 6.9.10.
22. Polyb. 6.5.4-9.9. This section covers the overview from which Polybius approached the progression of the different forms of government.
23. Polyb. 6.4.2-10.
24. Polyb. 6.44.2. Athens and Thebes, however, do not seem to conform to the biological pattern of growth - see Walbank, Commentary I.724-25.
25. Polyb. 6.43.6-7.
26. Polyb. 6.44.9.
27. Polyb. 6.45.1. Cf. Walbank, Commentary I. 726-27.
28. Polyb. 6.46.3 for gain; and 6.47.4-6 on the importance of law and custom, i.e. public and private morality. Cf. Walbank, Commentary I.732-33. Also, von Fritz, Mixed Constitution, Appendix III, pp.398-402.
29. Polyb. 6.3.7.
30. The best example of the 'mixed constitution' is that of Rome - Polyb. 6.15.1.-17.9.
31. Polyb. 6.10.13-14. Thus, Polybius contrasts the Roman experience with the constitution of Sparta formulated by Lycurgus; Rome, of course, is favored.
32. Polyb. 6.11.12-13.
33. Polyb. 6.12.1-17.9.
34. Polyb. 6.18.4.
35. Polyb. 6.11.1.
36. Polyb. 3.2.6.
37. Walbank, Polybius, pp.61-2; see Polyb. 3.32.7.
38. Polyb. 6.48.2.
39. Polyb. 6.50.3-4.
40. F.W. Walbank, 'Polybius and the Roman State,' Greek, Roman, and Byzantine Studies 5 (1964), 250.
41. Polyb. 6.51.2-3.
42. Ennius, Annals 467; Moribus antiquis res stat Romana virisque.
43. Polyb. 6.47.1.

44. Polyb. 6.53.1-54.5. See Walbank, Commentary I.737-39. Polybius' description gives one the distinct impression that the historian himself observed a Roman funeral firsthand. Could the funeral have been Paullus'? Note Diodorus' account, 31.25, and surely taken from Polybius since it is bracketed by Polybian fragments, where Paullus' funeral is described. It is possible that the description of Roman funeral rites found in the Histories was based on what the historian actually saw; thus, in a symbolic fashion, Paullus passed on his virtue to his son Scipio. So Pedech, Methode de Polybe, pp.428-29.
45. Polyb. 6.53.9-10.
46. Polyb. 6.56.1-5. See Walbank, Commentary I.741.
47. Polyb. 6.56.6-12.
48. Polyb. 6.56.13-15.
49. Polyb. 1.4.1.
50. Polyb. 36.17.2.
51. Polyb. 1.4.4-5. On Tyche in general, see Walbank, Commentary I.16-26; Walbank, Polybius, pp.58-65; Warde Fowler, 'Polybius' Conception of Tyche' Classical Review 17 (1903), 445-49; P. Shorey, 'Tyche in Polybius,' Classical Philology 16 (1921), 280-3; Pedech, Methode de Polybe, pp.331-54; von Fritz, Mixed Constitution, Appendix II, pp.338-97.
52. Polyb. 29.21
53. Polyb. 29.21.6.
54. Polyb. 29.21.7.
55. F.W. Walbank, 'Polybius and the Growth of Rome,' (summary in the) Classical Association Proceedings 43 (1946), 11.
56. L.R. Lind, 'Concept, Action, and Character: The Reasons for Rome's Greatness,' Transactions and Proceedings of the American Philological Association 103 (1972), 255 n.82.
57. See Diod. 32.2, and 32.4.1-5. This section of Diodorus certainly comes from Polybius. M. Gelzer, Kleine Schriften II, 64-5, has argued thusly, and he is supported by Walbank, GRBS 5, 254. Compare Diodorus with strikingly similar passages in Polyb. 5.10.1-8; 10.36.5 (cf. Walbank, Commentary II.246).
58. Diod. 32.4.1-3.
59. Diod. 32.4.4. For all his talk of the mixed constitution, and Roman virtus, etc., Polybius in this passage appears to recognize some of the more substantial reasons for Roman success. As the historian notes here, it is

Roman willingness to extend their rights and privileges to others that helped Rome acquire and maintain its empire.

60. Diod. 30.8. This section must surely derive from Polybius. (1) It is bracketed by sections for which Polybian fragments are parallels. (2) The tone and message of the passage fits, as I show, into Polybius' scheme for empire building. (3) The only other author known to have covered the Third Macedonian War in any detail (besides the Roman annalists who never felt the need to justify Roman treatment of Greece) was the mysterious Poseidonius quoted only by Plutarch Aem. 19.7-10; 20.6; 21.7. Poseidonius wrote a history favorable to Perseus; but this passage in Diodorus is of the opposite nature and praises the Romans.

61. Diod. 30.8. Cf. Polyb. 36.9.7. Greeks of a later time saw the Third Macedonian War as the beginning of a new Roman policy of destroying an enemy totally.

62. Diod. 32.4.5. For similar thoughts concerning Roman conquests, see ad Herennium, 4.27.37.

63. See F.W. Walbank, 'Political Morality and the Friends of Scipio,' Journal of Roman Studies 55 (1965), chiefly 10-12.

64. Polyb. 27.8.9.

65. Polyb. 30.6.3-4.

66. Polyb. 28.9.4. The word is daimonoblabeia - cf. 36.17.15.

67. See Polyb. 29.13.1; 30.9.1.

68. Polyb. 36.17.13-15.

69. Polyb. 38.16.7.

70. Cf. Polyb. 36.9.12-17. The Carthaginian situation was slightly different. The Punic city was not gripped by the insanity that attacked Greece and Macedon - its end is justified in another way. In this case, Polybius seems to support the argument that since Carthage had surrendered to Rome, then Rome had every legal right to treat that city as it saw fit, especially if Carthage refused to comply with Roman commands. The ultimate destruction of Carthage 'was not even of the nature of an injustice.' For a more complete discussion, see Walbank, Polybius, pp.175-6; and Walbank, J.R.S. 55, 9-10.

71. E.g., the sentiments expressed at Polyb. 1.1.2; 30.9.20-21; 38.4.7-8.

72. On Paullus' terror upon seeing Perseus' phalanxes at Pydna, see Polyb. 29.17.1 and Livy 44.41.1. On Paullus' saying about his ability to throw a good party, see Polyb. 30.14 and Livy 45.32.11.

73. Polybius nowhere cites Paullus or his sons as a source, but everything suggests that they were questioned. There were also writers who composed monographs concerning Philip V, Perseus, and their wars against Rome - see Polyb. 8.8.5; 22.18.5; 3.32.8; Livy 40.55.7; and Felix Jacoby, Die Fragmente der griechischen Historiker (Leiden: E.J. Brill, 1963), II A, 83; II B, 893. Polybius also used the letter of Scipio Nasica for the events surrounding Pydna - see Walbank, Commentary I.31; P. Pedech, Methode de Polybe, chiefly pp.370-1; and G.A. Legmann, 'Die Endphase des Perseuskriegs im Augenzeugenbericht des P. Cornelius Scipio Nasica,' Beiträge zur alten Geschichte (Festschrift Altheim) (Berlin; 1969), 387 ff. But the section in question, Polyb. 29.14.3, comes from Plutarch, Aem. 15, who could have combined versions from Polybius' original and from Nasica's letter. Finally, there are Perseus' 'friends' and the king's Royal Pages, who deserted to the Romans and were used as sources; see e.g., Polyb. 29.8.10; and Pedech, Methode de Polybe, p.361.

74. Polyb. 18.35.8.
75. So Walbank, Polybius, p.3.
76. See Polyb. 31.22; and 18.35.4-6.
77. Polyb. 6.46.9 for Cretans; 6.56.2 for Carthaginians; 6.56.13 for Greeks.
78. Cf. Polyb. 6.57; also 6.56.1-2.
79. Polyb. 6.48.6-8; 6.49.6-10.
80. Polyb. 6.49.10.
81. Polyb. 6.51.5. Walbank, Commentary I.736.
82. Polyb. 6.56.1-4. Walbank, Commentary I.741.
83. Polyb. 6.56.1-4.
84. Polyb. 6.56.13.
85. Polyb. 18.34.7.
86. Polyb. 31.22.6-7.
87. Polyb. 6.56.1.
88. Polyb. 18.35.1-2. F.W. Walbank, A Historical Commentary on Polybius vol. II (Oxford: The Clarendon Press, 1967), 594.
89. Polyb. 31.25.6-7. Yet, one should note that there had been decline even before Pydna, although after Pydna things turned for the worse. It seems that Polybius sees some sort of military decline after the time of the First Punic War, 1.64.1-2. Also, cf. 18.35 where, in praising Paullus, Polybius saw decline among other Romans. Also see, Brink and Walbank, C.Q. 48, 105-7; Walbank, G.R.B.S. 5, 255.

90. Polyb. 31.25.6-7. For a similar statement concerning Carthage, see 6.51.3-6. Cf. Walbank, C.Q. 37, 82.
91. Polyb. 31.25.5.
92. Polyb. 6.57.5-10. On this passage see, Walbank, G.R.B.S. 5, 251-2. On the process of a polity's decay and the stages of that decay, see Walbank, Commentary I.754.
93. Polyb. 18.35; and 31.22-30 for Paullus and Scipio.
94. Polyb. 18.35.4.
95. Polyb. 18.35.5.
96. Polyb. 31.22.3.
97. Polyb. 31.22.8-10.
98. Polyb. 18.35.6.
99. Polyb. 31.22.1.
100. Chiefly, Polyb. 31.25.9-10. Every one of these virtues was held by Paullus.
101. Polyb. 29.1.1-3. Cf. Livy 44.22.8; but Livy expands Paullus' speech in order to transform Paullus into a man who has molded his life around the mos maiorum.
102. Polyb. 29.1.2.
103. On the importance of harmony in the state, see Walbank, Polybius, p.173. Indeed, the most important qualities for a state to possess are: (1) political stability in the face of internal or external threats (cf. Polyb. 6.56.1-2), and (2) the capacity to build an empire (Polyb. 6.50.3-6) - see Walbank, J.R.S. 55, 8.
104. Cf. Polyb. 27.10.3.
105. See Polyb. 30.13.11; and 32.6.5.
106. Polyb. 32.6.6.
107. Shakespeare, Hamlet III.58.
108. Polyb. 29.20.1-4.
109. Paullus further humbles himself when, after his triumph, he speaks of the deaths of his sons. I have not included mention of this within the narrative because all traces of this speech have vanished from the pages of Polybius; but there is no question that the account originally stems from Polybius. Paullus sought no pity or sympathy by the speech, but simply informed his fellow citizens of his achievements against Perseus, and then commented on the fickleness of Tyche. Paullus had accomplished too much, his fortune had been too good to last - and knowing that Tyche allows no one to propser for long, he prayed that the goddess should inflict him, rather than the entire state, with ill. See Appian, Mac. 19; Diod. 31.11.1-2; Plutarch Aem. 35-36; Livy 45.40-1. Also see the comments of Walbank, Polybius, pp.62-

3; and Massimiliano Pavan, 'Duo Discoursi di Lucio Emilio Paolo,' Studi Romani 9 (1961), 593-613.
110. Polyb. 1.1.2; cf. 39.8.2.
111. Polyb. 29.20.4.
112. Other examples which could serve a similar purpose were the lives of Scipio Africanus Maior and Scipio Aemilianus. For Scipio Africanus, see Polyb. 10.2-5; for Aemilianus, see chiefly 31.22-30. Also note F.W. Walbank, 'The Scipionic Legend,' Cambridge Philological Society Proceedings 93 (1967), 54-69.
113. Polyb. 4.2.4-11.
114. See F.W. Walbank, 'Polybius and Macedonia,' Ancient Macedonia: Papers Read at the First International Symposium Held in Thessaloniki, 26-29 August 1968, 291-307 for an illuminating study of Polybius' portrayal of relations between Achaea and Macedon from the time of Philip II down to Philip V with emphasis given to an examination of the historian's blatant prejudices. Walbank does not, however, consider the problem in the way it is approached here.
115. See Polyb. 4.2.4-11; 3.1.9-11; 1.3.1-4; 2.71.9-10; 39.8.4-6.
116. For a summary, see Polyb. 5.105.4-10.
117. He is praised chiefly for his conduct towards Athens after the battle of Chaeronea; note Polyb. 5.10.1-5 and 22.16.1. Compare Diod. 32.4.1-2. And see Walbank, Commentary I.548.
118. So Polyb. 3.6.1-14; 22.18.10.
119. Polyb. 8.10.5-6. On Theopompus, see 8.9.
120. Polyb. 18.13-15. See Walbank, Commentary II.564-70; and Walbank, Polybius pp.84-6.
121. Polyb. 18.13.10-14.15.
122. Polyb. 18.14.8.
123. See Thomas W. Africa, Phylarchus and the Spartan Revolution (Berkeley: University of California Press, 1961), pp.32-3; and p.79 n.111-14.
124. Polyb. 5.10.6.
125. Polyb. 5.10.6-7.
126. Polyb. 5.10.8.
127. Polyb. 38.2.13-14; cf. 4.23.8.
128. See Polyb. 38.2-3.
129. High principles and excellence: Polyb. 2.70.7; general and prince: 2.64.6; generosity and humanity: 2.70.1.
130. On Polybius' treatment of Philip V and the fall of the House of Macedon, see the brilliant article by F.W.

Walbank, 'Philippos Tragodoumenos: A Polybian Experiment,' Journal of Hellenic Studies 58 (1938), 55-68.
131. Polyb. 7.11.8.
132. Polyb. 7.11.4.
133. Polyb. 4.77.1-3.
134. Polyb. 10.26.8. Cf. Walbank, Commentary II.231.
135. See Walbank, Polybius, pp.93-4. And Pedech, Methode de Polybe, p.234.
136. Apelles is clearly not the chief villain - cf. Polyb. 4.76.1-7; 4.82.2; 4.84.1 (his effort to diminish Aratus' influence with Philip); 4.87.1-11. Demetrius of Pharos is far worse - note the contrast between Demetrius and Aratus, 5.12.5-8; 5.101.7-10; and especially, 7.14.3.
137. For the action at Thermum, see Polyb. 5.9-12; 11.7.
138. See Polyb. 5.11.3-9; 11.7.2-3; 7.14.3.
139. Polyb. 5.11.6.
140. Polyb. 5.101.10. Cf. Appian Mac. 1.1.
141. Polyb. 5.10.10.
142. Polyb. 7.11-13. Walbank, Commentary II.56-7.
143. Polyb. 15.20. See Walbank, J.H.S. 58, 63.
144. Polyb. 15.20.4.
145. Walbank, J.H.S., 58, 63.
146. Polyb. 16.24.1-8.
147. See chiefly Walbank, J.H.S. 58, 63. On the conflict between Philip's sons, see C.F. Edson, 'Perseus and Demetrius,' Harvard Studies in Classical Philology 46 (1935), 191-202.
148. See H. Nissen, Kritische Untersuchungen über die Quellen der vierten und fünften Dekade des Livius (Berlin: Weidmannsche Buchhandlung, 1863), pp.234-5. Also Walbank, J.H.S. 58, 61. Livy 40.3-16.3 are Polybian.
149. Polyb. 23.10.2-3.
150. Walbank, J.H.S. 58, 63 and 67.
151. See the entire article by Walbank, J.H.S. 58.
152. Sensational writing is one of Phylarchus' habits which Polybius severely criticizes because it obscured the nature of the cause and effect which lay behind events. See Polyb. 2.56.60; especially 2.58.12 and 2.61.1. On Phylarchus and Polybius' criticism of him, see Africa, Phylarchus, chiefly pp.29-35.
153. Walbank, J.H.S. 58, 67.
154. Polyb. 20.18. As Philip II had planned the war which Alexander carried out, so did Philip V plan the war against Rome which Perseus undertook.

155. Polyb. 15.20.8.
156. Polyb. 29.27.12.
157. Polyb. 25.3.5-7. On Perseus, see Piero Meloni, Perseo e la fine della Monarchia Macedone (Roma, 1953). One may also note the striking point concerning the vilification of Perseus by the sources, made by Edson, H.S.C.P. 46, 202: 'We hate none so much as those we have wronged, and the vilification of Perseus in our tradition shows only what desperate expedients the Roman and Romanizing historians were forced to adopt in order to justify Rome's attack on Macedon in 172.'
158. Polyb. 25.3.1-4. Cf. Diod. 29.33.
159. E.g., Nabis, whose social outrages and crimes are catalogued in Polyb. 13.6-8; and Cleomenes, whom Polybius loathed as a tyrant and revolutionary - see Polyb. 2.47.3; 4.81.12-14; 9.23.3. Note the discussion by Africa, Phylarchus, pp.23-27.
160. It has been generally assumed that a large portion of the Greek populace supported Perseus; also, that the upper classes favored Rome against Macedon - cf. e.g. Frank, Roman Imperialism, pp.201-3; and R.M. Errington, Dawn of Empire: Rome's Rise to World Power (Ithaca: Cornell University Press, 1972), p.202. Recently, however, E.S. Gruen, 'Class Conflict and the Third Macedonian War,' American Journal of Anicent History 1 (1976), 29-60, at e.g., 46-8, denies the validity of such an over-simplified view. Unfortunately, Gruen goes too far in the opposite direction and claims that there is no evidence that the Greek masses favored Perseus. Perseus clearly had vast support among the Greeks; cf. this case with that of Antiochus III, Livy 35.33-34; also Africa, Phylarchus, p.70 n.117. Note the more complete discussion and criticism in Chapter 5.
161. Perseus' favorable relationships with many of his fellow kings are fairly well attested. Seleucus' daughter, Laodice, was married to Perseus, and she was transported to Macedon by a Rhodian fleet; Polyb. 25.4.8. In return, Perseus refitted the Rhodian navy and presented the sailors with gifts; Polyb. 25.4.9-10. Perseus also felt confident enough to inform much of the Greek world of his exact position to Rome after the meeting with Philippus in 172 and the subsequent 'truce'; cf. Polyb. 27.4. The king's popularity in Greece, and especially Boeotia, is well attested; see Polyb. 27.2.7; 27.5; 27.9-10. Furthermore, Perseus gave his sister in marriage to Prusias.

162. Polyb. 27.9-10.
163. Polyb. 27.10.5.
164. Polyb. 28.9.4. Cf. Diod. 30.9.2 and 30.21.2, where Perseus is simply 'mad'. Also see Walbank, Commentary I.24.
165. See Polyb. 36.17.15. Cf. Walbank, Polybius, pp. 176-7; and Walbank, Commentary I.24.
166. Polyb. 29.5-9.
167. Polyb. 29.8.2. Cf. Livy 44.26.1-3.
168. Polyb. 29.9.12.
169. Concerning 'unexpectedness', see Polyb. 1.1.4; on the Roman achievement and Polybius' amazement, see 29.21.8-9.
170. Walbank, Polybius, pp.39-40 provides a convenient list of the passages, but he does not include the fall of Perseus. E.g., see Hasdrubal's end, Polyb. 38.20; the ruin of Greece in 146, 38.1-4 and 16.7; and the capture of Corinth, 39.2.
171. Polyb. 38.4.1.
172. Walbank, J.H.S. 58, 56-7.
173. For what remains of Polybius, see 29.14-21. Cf. Livy beginning at (conveniently) 44.36-46 and 45.4.2-9.7; and Plutarch Aem. chiefly 17-27. See Nissen, Untersuchungen, chiefly pp.264-271, and 273. That Livy depended only on Polybius and did not use the letter of Scipio Nasica has, beyond a doubt, been shown by Nissen, pp.267-9.
174. Polyb. 29.16: story of eclipse of the moon, and the reactions of the Romans and Macedonians. 29.17.3-4: Perseus' cowardliness and flight from Pydna. 29.18: Perseus' flight and his offerings to Heracles. Plutarch Aem. 17.7-13: eclipse of moon; reactions of Romans and Macedonians; Paullus' sacrifices to the moon and to Heracles; Paullus' precautionary piety. Aem. 19.4-5: Perseus' cowardliness at Pydna, his flight, and his offerings to Heracles. Aem. 19.6: Heracles favors Paullus. Livy 44.37.12: Paullus' sacrifices to Heracles. 44.42.2: flight of Perseus to Pella.
175. Livy 44.43: Perseus has now sunk so low as to put his trust in 500 Cretans, people infamous for their cupidity and treachery. Plutarch Aem. 23; basically the same account as Livy, except in 23.1-5 where Plutarch enlarges on the details of Perseus' flight; or else he has copied Polybius more faithfully than Livy.
176. Plutarch, Aem. 23. Livy 44.43; 44.45; 45.4. 2-7.
177. Livy 45.5.3-8.
178. Livy 45.5.9-12. Cf. Diod. 29.25 where the crime against Demetrius had already invalidated Perseus' claims as

Polybius and the Image

a supplicant.
 179. Livy 45.6.1-6.
 180. Livy 45.6.10-12.
 181. Livy 45.7.1-4.
 182. Livy 45.7.4-5. Cf. Diod. 30.23.
 183. Livy 45.8.1-5. Cf. Diod. 30.23.
 184. Livy 45.8.5.
 185. Polyb. 29.20.1. Cf. Plutarch Aem. 27.2-6; Livy 45.8.6-7; Diod. 30.23.
 186. Polyb. 29.20.2-4.
 187. Polyb. 29.21. Cf. Livy 45.9.7; Diod. 31.10.
 188. Note the definition of the tragic hero and his fatal error by Aristotle, Poetics 1453a.15-16. Perseus fits this mold.
 189. At e.g., Livy 45.6.1.
 190. Livy 44.43.1; 45.6.7.
 191. Cf. Diod. 30.8.
 192. Diod. 31.8.2.
 193. Polyb. 30.10.
 194. This is, of course, conjecture, but it is based on what one might expect from Polybius. Polybius 30.15 does no more than mention Paullus' deed in Epirus - there is no further comment in this fragment. But there is evidence to suggest that Polybius could have seen the Epirus incident in the manner described here. Cephalus, who was a Molottian, had originally backed Rome (Polyb. 27.15.10-12) until, sometime during or after 170 (see 27.16.3), the accusations against him by Charops forced him to switch sides and back Perseus (27.15.13-16). Thus, Cephalus took the Molottians into the Macedonian camp at an especially crucial and gloomy time for Rome (30.7.2). And it was against the Molottians that Paullus later struck. See Oost, Roman Policy, pp.83-6; Gruen A.J.A.H. 1, 41; and the extended discussion in Chapter 5.
 195. Polyb. 3.4.1.
 196. Polyb. 3.4.7.
 197. Polyb. 3.4.12.
 198. Walbank, Polybius, p.181. Also, Walbank. J.R.S. 55, 12; and H. Strasburger, 'Poseidonius on Problems of the Roman Empire,' Journal of Roman Studies 55 (1965), 46.
 199. See note 198.
 200. Diod. 30.23.2.

Chapter Three

LIVY AND THE IMAGE

A. LIVY, PAULLUS, AND THE THIRD MACEDONIAN WAR

For Livy, the patriot-historian, Rome's past was a storehouse of useful examples upon which he could draw in order to demonstrate the nobility of Rome and of the men who were that city's faithful servants. The <u>Ab Urbe Condita</u> is, above all else, a glorification of the Roman achievement from its earliest beginnings in the distant and mythical past, down to the time of the historian's patron, Augustus. Livy's theme, which is carried throughout his monumental work, invites the reader to consider 'the kind of lives our ancestors lived, of who were the men, and what the means both in politics and war by which Rome's power was first acquired and subsequently expanded.' (1) The kinds of lives led by venerable ancients, and the ways in which they acquired glory and dominion for Rome, this was the stuff of history for Livy. With it he constantly strives to impress his audience with the majesty and greatness of the men of the past, men who lived in better, simpler times and who were themselves guided by unclouded virtue. This idealization of Roman morality is contrasted with a darker side of the Roman experience; for when antique wisdom was allowed to lapse, Rome underwent a moral decline of alarming proportions which extended to Livy's own day 'when we can neither endure our vices nor face the remedies needed to cure them.' (2) But history, according to Livy, is the best medicine for such ills, since it contains both fine models for emulation and examples of wretched and disreputable behavior which should be avoided. (3) Corruption can be erased, infections cleaned out - in Livy's eyes his times were indeed debased, but with the knowledge provided by the history of Rome's exalted past and the heroes who upheld the grandeur of their state, present day men could renew themselves. (4) Bygone ages and men comforted Livy; he could understand them better and find escape through their deeds. Yet, he was still a creature of his epoch when 'Augustus Caesar brought peace to the world ...' (5) A new age dawned with the Augustan hegemony, an age in which the past was revered and in which Rome itself was given a new lease on life. The didacticism so evident in Livy's <u>Ab Urbe Condita</u> was intended to impart to Rome the forgotten spirit of ancient morality; this would allow the brilliance of a new age to shine even brighter.

Livy's idealized rendering of Rome's past was conditioned by more than the historian's quite obvious patriotism. He will, whenever the need arises, never hesitate to change or modify any occurrence which tends to repudiate his account of Roman nobility and purity. Livy is constantly on guard to protect the names and reputations of his beloved heroes of Rome's past, and, in numerous instances, the historian falsifies history or alters the record to minimize, or even remove entirely any less-than-noble action. As Walsh has summarized, 'Livy has allowed his pursuit of edifying examples to take precedence over a truthful account, not merely by distortion of emphasis, but even by the suppression of unpalatable facts.' (6) In an age which prided itself on the belief that Augustus had brought peace to a war-torn world, it would be, on the most immediate level, poor public relations to have Rome's official historian remind people of the ruthless campaigns which were conducted against nearly every nation of the known world. Not only would the bald record of such wars belie the historian's claims of Roman virtue, dignity, piety, etc., but it would, in a very real sense, damage the credibility of the Augustan propaganda which attempted to foster the notion that Rome was returning to an observance of what was imagined to be the pristine qualities of the early Republic. Wars of conquest now became wars of liberation. Where a chronicle of horror or deceit existed, it was modified, altered, or ignored. Livy was a perceptive and sensitive man who had no taste for many of the acts his beloved ancestors inflicted upon their enemies. And being perceptive, he carefully censored and sanitized his record of Roman imperialism. Furthermore, under the aegis of the

Livy and the Image

Princeps, clemency was accorded the position of one of the most honored Roman virtues, and Livy is always alert for an opportunity to impose this trait on Roman adventures. (7) Thus, the continual use of these devices - i.e., the suppression of the uncomfortable facts and the exaltation of clemency - in the re-interpreting of much of Rome's history, and in particular the wars of conquest against Greece and Asia, convicts Livy of consciously distorting what he knew to be true in order to protect the images he held dear, and in order to serve the purposes of his patron, the emperor Augustus.

Livy's treatment of the time between the ascension of Perseus and the splendid triumph of Aemilius Paullus in 167 is a notable example of how the historian seeks to alter the picture so that Rome is favored over and above all others. The period encompasses the last extant pentad of the Ab Urbe Condita (books 41-45); its major emphasis is the Third Macedonian War, and its major figures are Perseus and Paullus, that war's chief contestants. The theme of the pentad, the magnificent Roman victory over the last of the Macedonian kings, nicely complements the major thrust of the entire work by showing that Rome's conquests were achieved only by men who clung to antique morals, who were virtuous in their conduct, and who excelled in dignity and nobility - there is no question that Livy concentrates these qualities on the hero of the piece, Lucius Aemilius Paullus. (8) Indeed, were it not for Paullus, Livy implies that Rome might never have beaten Macedon. The consuls before Paullus are uniformly maligned for abandoning integrity and justice, and, instead, clinging to the ruinous teachings of what the historian terms 'the new and over-sly wisdom.' (9) Nevertheless, Livy still takes care, even when dealing with the consuls before Paullus, to remove, minimize, or distort any act which could reflect against Rome as a whole. Roman support and use of many political factions in Greece to their own ends in furthering the war effort is a subject on which Livy is quite touchy; often he will neglect to mention such matters altogether, and where he is virtually forced to include the pro-Roman factions, he will characterize the position of the Romans themselves as aloof and disinterested in what is seen as petty Greek squabbles. Furthermore, Livy will go out of his way to justify the Roman treatment of Perseus and Macedon, and especially of Rhodes. Shifting the blame for the war onto Perseus is not at all difficult for a man of Livy's abilities, but it takes

Livy and the Image

every bit of his talent to exonerate what was perpetrated against Rhodes. To have admitted Rome's ruthlessness in either situation was more than Livy's blind patriotism could have handled. Thus, in the last remaining pentad of his history, the main threads to be followed in uncovering Livy's not-so-subtle distortion of the record concern the Roman pursuit of the Third Macedonian War before and after the consulship of Paullus, Rome's relations with its supportive Greek factions, and the vilification which both Perseus and Rhodes suffer. Selective use of annalistic sources, together with a careful revision of Polybius, are employed by Livy in reaching these ends.

The annalists upon whom Livy drew for a good deal of Books 41-45, Q. Claudius Quadrigarius and Valerius Antias, (10) are wretched sources. They were chiefly used when Livy dealt with material which was beyond the scope of Polybius; that is, events in Spain, Italy, and, most importantly, politics in Rome itself. (11) What little remains of the annalistic writers shows that they were more interested in writing history for entertainment and show, than for accuracy and instruction. Both Claudius and Antias were not above inventing pure fiction to enhance or supplement events which seemed too dry by themselves; (12) the writers were clearly disinterested in the workings of politics and politicians, this being vividly shown by the confused account of the Scipionic trials; (13) their writings took on such a senatorial bent, that, at least in Antias' case, plebeian consuls are defamed in order to protect the patricians; (14) and finally, 'it may be regarded as certain that Claudius and Valerius ... are responsible ... for the presentation of all Roman wars as just and all Roman dealings as honourable (even where the reverse is clear to us) that marks so much of Livy.' (15) Livy was, of course, not unsympathetic to any of this. (16) Great care must be exercised when confronting the annalistic sections of Livy; this is as true for Books 41-45 as it is for any other section of the Ab Urbe Condita. Thus, when Livy's narrative carries him away from Roman affairs in the East (where Polybius is the source), he is forced to use Claudius and Valerius whose annals were largely constructed around what Badian has termed 'plausibly detailed mendacity.' (17) The annalistic account, for instance, which is used by Livy for several sections dealing with Perseus and Rhodes must be treated with skepticism, for it seeks out every opportunity (and even invents some) to cast the best possible light on Rome and the worst on Perseus and the unfortunate Rhodians. Furthermore, and more important, nearly the whole of Livy's version of the internal Roman politics of the Third Macedonian War era stems from the annalistic sources; the outline which emerges is crucial in understanding Livy's treatment of the war. The political quarrels, so beloved of prosopographers who see in them the dynamics of vicious factional politics, (18) are pictured as a struggle between the plebeian magistrates who directed the Roman armies against Perseus and other foes, and a noble, humanitarian Senate.

Who were the chief men of the Third Macedonian War, and by what means both in politics and war did they strive for power? The question is significant for Livy and for the theme of his entire work. If the most powerful men of the state flaunted the traditional mores of the Roman people and were so blinded by their own sense of glory and pride that they were insolent toward the collective national wisdom of the Senate, then the well being of the commonwealth was jeopardized both at home and abroad. The consuls from 173 to 169 were of this misshapen mold. Not every one of them was evil; indeed, some opposed their ambitious colleagues. But the rest were twisted men who abided by their own brand of conduct - and they were all plebeians. In the year 173, the consul Marcus Popillius waged war in Liguria, chiefly against the Statellates whose town he razed and whom he sold into slavery. (19) Such unbridled violence shocked the Senate, which censured Popillius, and in a spasm of clemency, ordered the consul to restore the Ligurians to their freedom and homes. (20) But Popillius, a most unprincipled man, displayed a ferocia animi toward the patres, and demanded that they vote him thanksgivings and honors. (21) Nor were further troubles to be avoided. The very next year Gaius Popillius was elected consul, and he too, like his brother Marcus, was at odds with the Senate. The question of honorable treatment of the Ligurians continued to be the issue. (22) On the one hand, there stood a harmonious Senate, desirous of according dignity and freedom to the Ligurians, (23) while on the other stood Marcus and Gaius Popillius who supported an unjust war, contra ius ac fas. (24) The confrontation continued until, at last and by unscrupulous means, M. Popillius escaped condemnation. (25)

Livy's purpose behind this first example of plebeian-Senate conflict is fairly obvious. He knows perfectly well of

Roman incompetence during the opening years of the Third Macedonian War, and, by devising a clash of wills between plebeian consuls and the Senate, he is thus able to lay the blame for this at the feet of the consuls. The insolent refusal of the consuls to obey the guardian of Rome's traditional ways opened the door to the military fiasco which was the Roman war effort against Perseus. The Senate is envisioned as nobly standing up to the machinations and undisciplined tactics of the consuls: religious observances are strictly maintained, (26) <u>ius</u> is not depreciated before gain, (27) and, finally, the Ligurians were restored. (28) Livy's artistry is quite effective in this, his opening volley against the plebeian consuls. He is almost convincing, until one realizes that the discord between the senatorials and the consuls was hardly based on moralistic principles. The underlying factor was not justice or humanity, but what was useful to the national interests of Rome at the time. Had the Senate actually turned kindhearted at this time, campaigns against the Ligurians would not have been resumed in 167 immediately after the defeat of Perseus. (29) In other words, a policy of benevolence towards Liguria, a policy which was unheard of until 173 and which was ended in 167, (30) was not based on virtuous motives, but was a calculated maneuver to keep the Ligurians quiet while Rome was occupied with Perseus. And Livy, although he writes on blissfully unaware, confirms this: 'It was considered more useful to the state that the thoroughly aroused Ligurians should be restrained and calmed.' (31) One must compliment the senators on their foresight - once the policy was firmly in place, it worked well. (32) The differences between the Senate and its consuls were not over humanitarian principles; more realistically they should be viewed as disagreements over how the war should be pursued. The Popillii clearly wished to continue the effort to subdue Liguria, while the Senate thought it better to occupy only one front at a time. That the differences between the two were not irreconcilable is shown by the fact that Gaius Popillius held numerous official positions throughout the Third Macedonian War. (33)

But for Livy the only thing of importance was the debilitating effects which such morality would have on Rome. Yet, the actions of the Popillii were not nearly so ominous as the underhanded trickery practiced by Q. Marcius Philippus against Perseus in 172. Philippus had been instrumental in deceiving Perseus, through the promise of peace, into delaying the king's war preparation; in the meantime, the Romans strengthened their positions in Greece. (34) The ploy was astoundingly successful, since Perseus was seeking any way he could to avoid war with Rome. In fact, a large part of the Senate heartily approved of Philippus' methods and his accomplishment. (35) They saw nothing wrong with the use of fraud and subterfuge. In the eyes of Livy, however, this was most disturbing; now, even some senators had drifted away from the mos maiorum. There remained, nevertheless, older men in the Senate, who, 'mindful of ancient custom,' did not recognize in Philippus' 'diplomacy' the ways of Rome. (36) They would have nothing to do with this nova ac nimis callida sapientia, (37) and for this they earned Livy's understanding and sympathy. Romans of older days, the senators complained, never waged war with deceit, but only with virtus and fides; to do anything less was to descend to the level of the Carthaginians and Greeks. (38) The only way to conquer a foe was 'by the hand-to-hand clash of force in a proper and righteous war,' (39) and this excluded Philippus and the others like him who ignored ancient, tried and true methods. As long as commanders in the field arrogantly flaunted their powers contrary to antique customs, Rome would never be able to fulfill its divinely bestowed role in the world. Only when men returned to old-fashioned discipline would Rome regain its footing on the path to empire. Such was the warning of the senators who despised the foul habits of Philippus' new wisdom; and such were the fears of Livy when he surveyed the acts of the Roman magistrates who directed the opening years of the Third Macedonian War.

In ever increasing numbers, charges of cruelty, avarice, laxity, foolishness, etc. are hurled at the chief Roman commanders. In Greece, P. Licinius, consul 171, and G. Lucretius, praetor of the same year, conducted their campaigns crudelius avariusque. (40) And G. Cassius, the other consul for 171, is also condemned for having tried to lead his army into Macedonia. (41) Failure and disgrace follow the Roman effort against Perseus into 170. A. Hostilius, the consul, who was defeated by the Macedonian armies, is blamed for diminishing the effectiveness of his office and command by currying political favor through gifts of leaves of absence. (42) More serious, however, was the unbridled ferocity of L. Hortensius, the praetor of 170, who sacked the city of Abdera, and pillaged the city of Chalcis with arrogance, greed, and cruelty. (43) Specific details do not concern the discussion here; the men and their deeds are swept together into the pattern which Livy imposes on the first years of the war. They (the men and their actions) are symptoms of a decline in the moral fiber of Rome, and are therefore denunciated in the strongest of terms:

> ... no one could be unaware that these things had been done and were being done without the consent of the Senate, - no one, that is, who knew that the Roman People had declared war on Perseus and previously on Philip, his father, to preserve the freedom of Greece, and not to inflict on allies and friends such injuries from Roman officers. (44)

The Senate, Livy informs his readers, was not a party to, nor did it lend its authority to, the inglorious suppression of Greek cities.

This smacks of special pleading, and need not be believed; one wonders if Livy himself was so credulous. The active support which Rome gave to its Greek puppets, and the control over much of the internal politics of Greek cities which Rome gained through aiding friendly factions, shatters the myth that the Romans had only noble principles in mind when they warred with Perseus. Senatorial policies were not based on morality. In place of Livy's confused narrative may be seen a policy of placating the Greeks during a stage of the war in which Perseus was rapidly gaining support through a series of victories over the Romans. (45) To the profusion of foreign embassies that cluttered the Senate chambers during 171/70, some seeking Roman aid, some complaining of offenses committed against them by Romans, the Senate was conciliatory and, in some cases, humble. (46) With a large portion of the Greeks leaning towards Perseus, the Senate was especially careful to assume the stance of disapproving of certain activities of the consuls and praetors which might drive neutrals or even friends into Perseus' camp. One may note in conclusion, that with the defeat of Perseus, the Senate was no longer obliged to indulge the lamentations of the Greeks - reprisals and massacres, supposedly ordered by the Senate, more than compensate for the 'humility' shown in the war's darker days. (47)

In one final effort to cast aspersion on Roman handling of the war prior to Paullus, Livy carefully disparages the consulship of Q. Marcius Philippus, the author of the 'new wisdom'. Although Philippus very nearly made an end of the war by his daring invasion of Macedon (the account of which is hopelessly confused by Livy (48)), he is criticized for pulling back his forces while Perseus was at his mercy. (49) Moreover, the consul's rashness placed the army in a most difficult position, for Perseus controlled all avenues of possible retreat; had it not been for the king's indecision and 'madness' the Romans might have been boxed in and destroyed. Indeed, when a commission is sent to inquire as to the progress of the war, the allegations against Philippus grow more serious: the consul foolishly disregarded obvious dangers, he refused to offer battle, the soldiery sought only idleness and were ill-equipped, etc. (50) With the likes of Philippus and the magistrates before him, Roman defeat was staved off only because the delirium of Perseus prevented him from seizing the opportunities offered.

The situation, mood, and atmosphere changes drastically with the election of Paullus as consul for 168. Livy builds up a sense of great expectation that something extraordinarily favorable for Rome will attend the new consul. (51) Preparations for war are said to have occupied Paullus' every thought, day and night; (52) and when Livy comes to report Paullus' speech before the Senate, vows of precautionary piety, claims of prophecy, and a comparison between Paullus and a great military hero of the past are all emphasized. (53) None of this is to be found in the other recorded versions of the speech; (54) Livy has chosen to add moralistic touches, thereby glorifying the character of Paullus. Not only would Paullus conduct himself in a manner befitting the mos maiorum in a moral and religious sense, but he would also restore military discipline to the level of the ancients. The laxity which previous consuls had condoned was now vigorously opposed and forbidden. Although the troops had for so long abandoned the rigor of the camp, Paulus fired within them a new spirit - 'throughout the army even the veterans admitted that they, like raw recruits, had for the first time learned how military matters should be handled.' (55) Livy is even able to confirm that 'soon you could have seen no one idle in the whole camp,' for they were now engaged in readying themselves and their weapons for the coming battle. (56) The notion that Paullus was able to re-instill old-fashioned military discipline into the army is a theme to which Livy returns again and again; Paullus did things according to the ways of the ancestors, always remembering that strength without

Livy and the Image

piety was worthless. (57) This is but one part of the personality of the man whom Livy saw as mirroring the best of Rome's customs and traditions. In the historian's scheme, Paullus is diametrically opposed to the crafty plebeian exploiters of the 'new wisdom'. And unlike the men of Livy's own age, Paullus had the fortitude and sage understanding to endure the remedy for the vices of his day - for this, Livy respected and honored him.

Nor would it do for Paullus and those associated with him to pursue the war with anything less than clemency and justice. Thus, while Paullus and the praetor Anicius are in Greece and surrounding areas, Livy judiciously tailors his account to demonstrate that these men did nothing more than strive to free the Greeks. Anicius won over the cities of Illyria with his clementia and iustitia, (58) and when Genthius, the Illyrian king surrendered to the praetor, Anicius wined and dined the fallen monarch. (59) Livy then states that Genthius was merely put under guard; however, Appian makes it plain that Anicius' lictors cast Genthius into prison for safe keeping until the time when he was to be led in triumph. (60) It is no accident that Livy covers up this matter. Paullus, too, is given his share of praise. The consul saw to it that in the days following Pydna, no wrong was done to the conquered. (61) And to Perseus himself, Paullus advised that he should trust in fidem et clementiam populi Romani, and surrender; (62) the last of the Antigonids knew enough to attempt flight. (63) Later, after the capture of Perseus, Livy describes Paullus' grand tour of Greece as nothing more than a sight-seeing holiday during which the consul raised 'no question as to how either any individual or any state had felt about the war with Perseus, so as not to trouble the minds of the allies by any fear.' (64) A noble gesture, worthy of a cultured and virtuous gentleman. Yet, considerable doubt is placed on Livy's notice of the 'goodwill' tour; Plutarch, who is also exceedingly favorable to Paullus, maintains that Paullus restored a number of governments (obviously those loyal to Rome) during his excursion. (65) Again, Livy has subtly altered the account in order to exaggerate the image of Paullus. Indeed, Livy's artiface reaches new heights during his description of the ceremony of the formal settlement of Macedon and the war. Here the reader is allowed to catch the emotional feelings of the Greeks who first viewed the awe-full presence of Paullus - 'the ceremonial of a new master was frightening as it met their eyes' - and here, Paullus is endowed with the

Livy and the Image

greatness of Rome, the maiestas of the Roman people. (66) Nothing is allowed to interfere with this vision of Paullus; the stark reality of the aftermath of the Third Macedonian War is thrust into the background or explained away. The sacking of several cities after they had already surrendered, the support of a massacre in Aetolia, various and widespread purges of all pro-Macedonians, the wholesale banishing of political prisoners to Italy, and the frightful sack of Epirus are all justified in one way or another. (67) Livy's Paullus would surely not sully himself with such matters.

The Senate is not to be forgotten in this orgy of righteousness. The settlement of Macedon was outlined and considered from the point of view that it should not diminish the clementia and gravitas of the Roman people. (68) The senators' excellence compelled them to respect the position of the vanquished 'so that it should be clear to all nations that the forces of the Roman People brought not slavery to free people, but on the contrary, freedom to the enslaved.' (69) A nice complement to the grandeur of Paullus. Now, in the last pages of the pentad, Livy artfully combines the images of the two.

The stage is dominated by the figure of Paullus. Around him cluster the best and wisest men of the state, the senators, and against them are set a vindictive military tribune and the ungrateful troops whom Paullus had just commanded. The scene is the debate over the ex-consul's triumph; and the issue is the lack of booty which Paullus' troops had received. Paullus 'had held the soldiers to antiqua disciplina; he had given them less of the booty than they had hoped for from such lavish royal resources, though had he given rein to their greed, they would have left nothing to be deposited in the public treasury.' (70) Livy takes every advantage of the high drama of the episode, first to glorify Paullus, second to once again evince the primacy of the old ways against the turpitude of depraved men and manners, and third to use the incident as a capstone to the pentad and the Roman achievement. The tribune, M. Servius Galba 'suddenly' rises to openly oppose Paullus, the soldiers were 'roused by (his) utterances'; and the senators 'hastened' to support Paullus, 'crying out' that he should not be robbed of the triumph. (71) Backed by the collective auctoritas of the Senate, (72) the aged M. Servilius spoke. In grand fashion, Servilius' speech recounted the various themes which Livy has already invoked. Paullus was a general of the old mold, one who allowed no breach of discipline. (73) Great military

79

Livy and the Image

heroes of the past are conjured in Paullus' behalf - Quintus Fabius Maximus, G. Lutatius, Camillus, and Scipio Africanus all make an appearance. (74) And if the populace dared to deprive Paullus of his triumph, the gods themselves would be slighted. (75) Servilius' admonitions were successful; and Paullus finally triumphed, resplendent in dignitas and clothed in lordly maiestas. (76) Even the deaths of two of his sons were borne with unflinching manliness. (77)

The image is complete, and thanks to Livy's artistry it is highly effective, especially if one is drawn to the idealized hero who forms his life according to the precepts of ancestral virtues. Where Polybius sees Paullus as a noble man of empire who established the new world hegemony of Rome with justice and magnanimity, Livy's Paullus conforms in every way to what Livy saw as traditional Roman moral and martial rectitude. Paullus was as the generals of old had been, pious to the gods, dutiful to the state, and lenient to vanquished foes. He saw the vices of his age and had the courage to despise them; Livy's grand theme finds an excellent representative in Paullus. If the record had to be altered, so be it. The historian would see to it that his history was sugar coated - such medicine was easier to swallow.

B. LIVY AND ROMAN FOREIGN POLICIES

The theme of the conflict between the 'new wisdom' of the nefarious plebeian magistrates who practiced it, and the old Roman virtues of the Senate and Aemilius Paullus is, of course, the framework around which Livy builds his version of the Third Macedonian War. His highly critical characterizations of the men who conducted the early years of the war help to explain (or excuse) the Roman inability to make any headway against Perseus. From Livy's viewpoint, even the hint that the behavior of the plebian commanders was less than proper was enough to warrant condemnation. Not until Paullus gained the consulship did the Roman war machine reach its full potential and crush the Macedonians. So much is obvious, yet there remains more to tell. For, as previously mentioned, there are areas of Roman foreign policy which were so deceitful and unjust that to have included them in the historical narrative would have demonstrated, even to the most disinterested reader, the ruthlessness of Roman motives in the Third Macedonian

Livy and the Image

War. The full story of the open support which was given to the pro-Roman factions in the Greek cities, or an unbiased account of Perseus' position and the stance of Rhodes in the war would have exposed the absurdity of the claim that Rome's only goal was to free the Greeks. These policies reflected against Rome as a whole in a way which threatened to make a mockery of the historian's account. Thus, acting as his own censor, Livy wrote the official version of the Third Macedonian War carefully ignoring or explaining away the support given to the pro-Roman factions, and also carefully slandering the respective positions of Perseus and Rhodes.

The significance of the pro-Roman factions to Roman foreign policy cannot be doubted. Polybius, even though his later books are in a most fragmentary state, constantly reminds his readers of the bitter and sometimes bloody duels which raged between the political factions of the varoius Greek cities. (78) And when the opportunity permitted, the Romans eagerly grasped the chance of aiding their friends and, conversely, of ousting those who favored Macedon. Indeed, as the Third Macedonian War progressed, no middle ground was allowed - one was either for the Romans or against them, and to be neutral was to be an enemy. (79) As for the pro-Roman factions, they were highly beneficial to the Roman effort in that they strived to keep their cities in Rome's sphere of influence, thereby allowing Rome to control affairs through them. Finally, although a discussion of the causes of the war with Perseus does not properly belong in this section, it may be stated that a major reason for war was the complaints made against the Macedonian king by Rome's aristocratic backers in Greece.

Yet, when one reads Livy only vague hints and shadowy inferences concerning these matters are able to be gleaned from the narrative. If a certain instance strikes Livy as too outrageous, he will edit it out; or if the passage seems too important (or insignificant) to ignore, then the historian will hold that the Romans favored neither faction, but, instead, served as rather aloof peacemakers who always rendered a fair verdict after hearing both sides. Livy keeps examples of direct Roman interference into Greek internal politics to an absolute minimum. And, as a comparison with the surviving fragments of Polybius shows, this pattern is most rigid and rarely deviated from - Livy took the job of cleansing his chronicle of Roman policies very seriously. His first mention of Callicrates, the Achaean politician who was strongly pro-

Livy and the Image

Roman, gives no indication that this man was supported by Rome. (80) Livy admits that Callicrates favored Rome over Macedon, but Callicrates did so because he 'believed that the safety of the state depended on whether the treaty with the Romans were preserved inviolate.' (81) The reader is left with the impression that Callicrates' policy of approval toward Rome was independent of outside encouragement; Polybius knew better. (82) In a similar vein, Livy gives the impression that only Rome could possibly bring peace to Greece, especially since the people there seemed bent on self-destruction. (83) The frenzy of the Aetolians and of the Cretans was so intense that although Roman envoys struggled to establish harmony, peace was not to be had. Peace, Livy intimates, was the only Roman objective. Again, when the Greek states threatened to bring ruin down upon themselves, new Roman envoys were sent to restore peace. In Thessaly the leaders of both factions were reproved, and in Aetolia the factions were asked 'to refrain from their warfare and to end their quarrels in forgetfulness of the past.' (84) This shining altruism may, however, be doubted since in the very next section Livy goes on to tell how the same envoy who tried to pacify the Aetolians called a meeting of the Achaean assembly and cautioned them not to back Perseus in the war. (85) The calling of such an assembly by a Roman official was not only illegal, (86) but was also highly arrogant; it clearly points to the Roman encouragement given to Callicrates and his followers. Unfortunately, time has dealt harshly with the corresponding passages in Polybius - their nonexistence precludes any direct proof that Livy consciously altered the account.

Nevertheless, when Livy's narrative reaches the Third Macedonian War, and when Polybian fragments again reappear, there is more than ample evidence with which to indict Livy. The break-up of the Boeotian League, orchestrated in 172 by Q. Marcius Philippus to keep various cities out of Perseus' hands, was a maneuver which seems to have offended Livy. (87) Polybius knew full well that the cities involved were forced to hand over their sovereignty to Rome, but it would never do for Livy to admit that uncomfortable fact. Thus, while Polybius writes that the Greeks were ordered to go to Rome to announce the submission of their cities, (88) Livy makes a notable change and says that the envoys went to Rome to renew ties of <u>amicitia</u>. (89) Moreover, although Livy does concede the fact that the Roman envoys condemned the pro-Macedonian leaders in Boeotia, he leaves it at that, without relating that two of the most important anti-Romans were jailed and later committed suicide. (90) The alterations are slight, but significant. More noticeable yet is Livy's account of the aftermath of the major battle of 171 in which Perseus soundly defeated the consul P. Licinius Crassus. Livy (42.60.8-10) relates that blame for the defeat fell on the cowardly Aetolians, and that because of this, five Aetolian chiefs were sent to Rome as punishment; Polybius (27.15.14), however, directly contradicts Livy by explicitly stating that the charges against the Aetolians had nothing to do with the battle, but were trumped up by a certain Lyciscus, the pro-Roman leader in Aetolia itself. Politics, not a charge of cowardliness, lay behind the Roman decision to deport the Aetolian hostages to Rome.

The most damning piece of Livian editing occurs when the historian recounts yet another Roman embassy to the Greek cities, this one headed by G. Popillius and Gn. Octavius. (91) The embassy, taking place as it did during a dark period of the war for the Romans (the year 169), was unmistakably intended to firm up faltering Roman factions. Furthermore, the envoys moved cautiously taking care not to arouse any more anti-Roman sentiment than was already present. Their first concern, as Polybius makes evident, was to aid their friends; secondly, and equally important, they were judicious in their handling of the highly volatile predicament. Little of this is to be found in Livy's version; one might, indeed, on a quick reading, imagine Livy and Polybius to be speaking of two different Roman missions. At Achaea, Livy (43.17.4) assures his readers that the envoys spoke kindly and were heard in a like manner, and that after they left, there remained great feelings of hope in the city. Polybius (28.3.7-10), who certainly had reason to remember Popillius and Octavius, writes with no Augustan prejudices - the Romans had almost accused Lycortas, Archon, and Polybius himself before the Achaean assembly on charges of being opponents to Callicrates and the pro-Romans, and were only dissuaded from doing so because of insufficient evidence. Aetolia, the perennial favorite of Roman legates, is next on the envoys' list. And here again, as he has done many times in the past, Livy (43.17.5-6) suppresses all references to Lyciscus, the pro-Roman. In the version of the Ab Urbe Condita, the Aetolians are suspected of planning a revolution, and for this reason hostages are requested of them by the Romans. Livy is so brief as to be obscure, even incomprehensible. The real issue, clarified by Polybius (28.4) was whether or not more opponents of Lyciscus should be given as hostages and deported to Rome. The only stumbling block was the violent reaction which the proposal met; this heated response (Livy's revolt?) is said by Polybius to have been the reason why the envoys left without reaching their goals. Livy's pattern of distortion continues to hold true to form when he covers the legates' activities at their last stop, Acarnania (43.17.7-9). With an almost monotonous predictability, Livy excludes any mention of the pro-Roman faction, leaving, instead, the impression that the Romans were wholly disinterested in the politics of Acarnania. (92) And, predictably, Polybius (28.5) exposes the intrigues of the pro-Romans, and their attempt to have garrisons introduced as a deterrent to those who favored Macedon; only opposition from the populace thwarted the plan. (93)

Only when the evidence of Rome's assistance to its supportive factions becomes overwhelming does Livy falter. The aftermath of the war and the resulting extensive purges of pro-Macedonians in Greece and Asia leave Livy with very few excuses for Roman conduct. The utter and total defeat of Macedon permitted the Romans to abandon their momentary virtue of placating the wavering Greek states. No longer was there any need to play the game of conciliation. Now, anyone who had lent comfort in any form to Perseus, or, in fact, anyone who stood in opposition to the pro-Roman factions, was marked for execution or exile. Livy has the nearly impossible task of justifying such barbarity. Still, the historian strives mightily to protect his ancestors. Concerning Paullus, Livy claims that the consul's 'tour' of Greece was only for sight-seeing, with no questions being asked or accusations made, this 'so as not to trouble the minds of the allies by any fear.' (94) Yet, as previously discussed, Plutarch has a somewhat different view of the tour. In any case, Livy continues with assurances that Paullus was generous to the Greeks and to Perseus himself, that a grant of freedom was given to those who had been Perseus' subjects, that the Roman officer who was involved in a massacre of Aetolians was condemned by Paullus, and that Paullus deported all Macedonians of consequence only because they were 'haughty tyrants.' (95) But when it comes to the actions of other Romans in Greece at the same time, the best argument that Livy can muster is that they were duped by the perfidious cleverness of those Greeks who saw their own positions heightened by the Roman victory, men who 'filled the ears' of the Romans with stories calculated to do away with their hapless opponents. (96) And the Romans believed them. This was the reason why the Roman legates were sent to hunt down those who were pro-Macedonian. (97) Greek craft and deception played on Roman gullibility to achieve its ends. These arguments suffice only if one approaches the actual events with a preconceived notion of Roman nobility. If accountability is to be assigned, then Paullus and the other Romans cannot be excused. They were far too shrewd to be manipulated by unscrupulous Greeks. The Romans used the Greeks, not the other way around. The careful reader will note that Livy admits that Paullus approved of the Aetolian massacre (except, of course, for the fact that a Roman had personally been involved), that the consul deported those whose names had been furnished to him by pro-Roman leaders, that two pro-Macedonians were beheaded on Paullus' order, and that the sack of Epirus was accomplished with cold-blooded precision. (98) Indeed, while these instances are sufficient to disprove Livy's patriotic declarations, one could easily add to the list of deeds of frightfulness. (99) So rampant are the Roman operations of a deceitful nature that Livy's own narrative exposes the cruelty in all its nakedness.

Add to these difficulties the justification of the action taken against Rhodes at the war's end. Throughout the war, as Polybius relates, (100) and, indeed, for a number of years before, Rhodes had been a firm friend to Rome. Unfortunately for the island state, their wavering economic situation, adversely affected by the war, led them to try and mediate a peace between Perseus and Rome. And the result was that the Senate viewed this offer as a hostile act, and very nearly sent its armies against Rhodes; luckily, Rome's once loyal friend suffered only economic desolation and political extinction. (101) A client should never advise a patron in matters of war and peace. Livy could hardly allow the truth to reach his pages. Therefore, the Rhodians are vilified throughout the last pentad. The historian's object is a simple one; namely, to show that the Rhodians got what they richly deserved.

Thus, they are charged with unspeakable cruelty against innocent men, women, and children. (102) Accusations are made of a conspiracy between Perseus and Rhodes against Eumenes, and of a growing attachment between Perseus and

Rhodes against Rome. (103) Still, nothing is more damaging to the island state than a lengthy section which Livy eagerly snatched from the annalists Quadrigarius and Antias. (104) For Livy it hardly mattered that the annalistic report was both confused and misdated, and that when the same event is later found by Livy in Polybius, it is re-introduced into the Ab Urbe Condita. What does matter is that the Rhodian envoys to Rome are said to have spoken haughtily to the Senate and to have made a veiled threat to enter the war on Macedon's side. Such shocking behavior called forth bitter editorial comment from Livy: 'I feel sure that even now these statements cannot be read or heard without indignation; from this one can judge what the Senate's state of mind was as they listened.' (105) The account, dubious as it is, offers Livy his chance to understand, and, therefore, vindicate the Senate of the measures taken against these 'unfaithful' Rhodians. The historian's unshakeable belief now carries him through the rest of the pentad; with it he is able to ignore any and all contradictory statements, and with it he is able to save the memory of his ancestors. (106)

Moreover, the image of Perseus is blackened by a barrage of calumnies. Livy's motives and tactics in the effort to defame Perseus are very like those of Polybius. That is, to justify the blatant Roman aggression against Macedon, the most expedient method is to cast Perseus in the part of the implacable enemy against whom Rome had no other choice but to fight. Livy accepts Polybius' basic notion that Perseus was carrying out a war already planned by his father, (107) although in Livy's chronicle the figure of Tyche or Fortune is largely absent and seems to have nothing to do with the war. This points to the major difference between the accounts of Livy and Polybius; for while Polybius' Perseus is a confused individual whose mind was clouded and bewildered by the contrivances of Tyche, Livy's Perseus is a more cunning and severe man whose merciless character is further heightened by the fact that he is also quite demented. From Livy's viewpoint, Perseus the madman stained the opening of his reign with the infamous murders of countless people, among whom one could count members of the royal family and court - and this does not even include the murder of Demetrius. (108) The attempt to butcher Eumenes at Delphi and the supposed plot to poison every Roman of distinction add still more fuel to the fire. (109) And when a Roman embassy called on Perseus to demand reparations and denounce the treaty

Livy and the Image

between Rome and Macedon, the king behaved in an extraordinarily arrogant fashion, yelling at the envoys, shouting that the Romans were to blame for the trouble between the two countries - the envoys had been precise, legal, and just in their arguments and presentation, but Perseus gave them no sign of hospitality or courtesy in return. (110) In other words, Perseus forced the war by his irreconcilable attitude.   Slurs continue to be hurled at Perseus. (111) It is enough, however, to say that the gods themselves despised Perseus and honored Rome, and that Perseus had lost all control over his senses. (112) This is all that Livy wants to know; he neglects to consider his own statements that Perseus advised his allies not to anger the Romans, and that, on several occasions, Perseus actively sought a peace but was snubbed by Roman commanders. (113)

Livy has approached every aspect and episode of the Third Macedonian War with an eye to having it conform to his preordained beliefs concerning the men who conducted Rome's war and politics, and also concerning the methods they used to acquire an empire. His willingness to impose his conceptional framework on events and men is both disturbing and enlightening; disturbing, because it has fostered a vision of Roman history based on little more than faith and eloquence, and enlightening, because, when cautiously approached, it reveals the mind and prejudices of the historian himself. Old themes dot the landscape of Livy's last extant pentad: there are the plebeian magistrates, artful and shrewd with their new wisdom, against the traditional Roman manners epitomized by the figure of Paullus. History is molded to this motif. Further, there is the just and noble Rome which would never stoop to conquer. How could Rome ever have backed wicked Greek politicians, or forced war on Perseus who only wanted peace, or struck down an old ally and friend, Rhodes? Clearly Rome could not have done such things, especially in the official presentation of history.

NOTES

1. Livy *Preface* 9.
2. Livy *Preface* 9.
3. Livy *Preface* 10.
4. Livy *Preface* 11; P.G. Walsh, *Livy* (Cambridge:

The University Press, 1961), p.40.
   5.   Livy 1.19.3.
   6.   Walsh, Livy, p.109.
   7.   Ibid., p.74. Also see, Ronald Syme, The Roman Revolution (Oxford: Oxford University Press, 1968), pp.299 and 442. Augustus himself brags of his clemency after Actium, Res Gestae 4.
   8.   F.W. Walbank, 'The Fourth and Fifth Decades,' in Livy, ed. by T.A. Dorey (London: Routledge and Kegan Paul, 1971), p.62.
   9.   Livy 42.47.9 (P). Where a passage from Livy is noted, I will indicate the source from which Livy drew - (A): annalistic source; and (P): Polybian.
   10. Concerning the historians, see E. Badian, 'Early Historians,' in Latin Historians, ed. by T.A. Dorey (New York: Basic Books, Inc., 1966), pp.18-22. Walsh, Livy, pp.120-122, and 133-135. Walbank, 'Decades,' p.50. Nissen, Untersuchungen, pp.39-41, and 43-46. Scullard, Roman Politics, Appendix I, p.250.
   11. Cf. Walsh, Livy, p.135; and Walbank, 'Decades,' pp.56-9.
   12. Cf. Badian, 'Early Historians,' pp.19 and 21; Walbank, 'Decades,' p.58.
   13. For the trials, see chiefly Livy 38.40.4-60.10 (A). On specific source problems even noted by Livy, see 38.56 (A). Valerius Antias appears to be the source which caused Livy so much trouble. A. Klotz, 'Zu den Quellen der vierten und fünften Dekade des Livius,' Hermes 50 (1915), 481-536, sees the Scipionic trials as a turning point in Livy's use of Valerius; prior to this, Livy depended chiefly on Valerius, but after this, he turned more to Claudius. Klotz correctly notes Livy's confusion concerning which annalist to follow - neither seems to satisfy him - but there are problems in Klotz's mechanistic approach to the problem. For criticism, see Walsh, Livy, pp.133-34; Walbank, 'Decades,' p.50; and M.L.W. Laistner, The Greater Roman Historians (Berkeley: University of California Press, 1971), p.84.
   14. For example, the vilification of Terentius Varro. Livy follows Valerius in placing the blame for deciding to fight at Cannae squarely on Varro at, e.g. 22.43.7-9 (A), and 22.45.5 (A), contra Polybius 3.107 where it is the decision of the Senate to fight. Also see Walsh, Livy, p.72. Claudius, it should be noted, is known to have translated (and perhaps used as a source) the history of Acilius, a senator/historian associated with the so-called Scipionic Circle, and also a

'philhellene'; see Livy Per. 53; and Walsh, Livy, p.120.
 15. Badian, 'Early Historians`' p.19; Walsh, Livy, p.153 ff.
 16. Livy, indeed, will criticize Valerius - e.g. 36.19; 36.38; 38.23.11; 39.41.6; 39.43.1; 42.11.1; 44.13.12; 45.43.8, all (A) - but this never stops him from using that annalist.
 17. Badian, 'Early Historians,' p.21.
 18. The major prosopographical studies of this period are, F. Münzer, Römische Adelsparteien und Adelsfamilien (Stuttgart: Metzler, 1963 reprint), chiefly pp.198-233. Scullard, Roman Politics, chiefly pp.190-219. Briscoe, Historia 18, 49-70. Briscoe, J.R.S. 54, 66-77.
 19. Livy 42.7.3-9.6 (A)
 20. Livy 42.8.7-8 (A).
 21. Livy 42.9.1 (A).
 22. Livy 42.10.10-12 (A); 42.21.1-5 (A); 42.22.1 (A); 42.22.5. (A).
 23. Livy 42.21.4 (A).
 24. Livy 42.21.2-3 (A); cf. 42.28.2-3 (A).
 25. Livy 42.22.7 (A).
 26. Livy 42.20.2-6 (A); 42.28.7 (A); 42.30.8-9 (A).
 27. Livy 42.24.7 (A).
 28. Livy 42.22.5 (A).
 29. See T.R.S. Broughton, The Magistrates of the Roman Republic Vol. I (The American Philological Association, 1951), 432. Also see, I. 437. This work hereafter cited as, M.R.R.
 30. E.g.: 180: Both consuls assigned to Liguria, M.R.R. I.367.
179: Both consuls assigned to Liguria - Fulvius celebrates a triumph, M.R.R. I 391-92.
178: One consul assigned to Liguria, M.R.R. I.395.
177: One consul sent to Istria; campaigned in Liguria and celebrated a triumph, M.R.R. I. 397-8.
176: One consul assigned to Liguria, M.R.R. I.400.
175: Both consuls assigned to Liguria, and both triumph, M.R.R. I. 401-2.
174: Uncertain.
167: One consul assigned to Liguria, M.R.R I.432.
166: One consul assigned to Liguria, the other campaigned against the Alpine Gauls; both triumph, M.R.R. I.437.
 31. Livy 42.26.1 (A).
 32. A. Atilius, cos. 170, spent an uneventful and quiet year in Liguria; Livy 43.9.1-3 and 11.3 (A).
 33. 170: Popillius was fighting against Perseus - Livy

43.22.2-3 (P).
169: Popillius sent as an envoy to various Greek cities to make sure that they still supported Rome - Polyb. 28.3-5; Livy 43.17.2-10 (P).
168: As an envoy to Egypt, it was Popillius who ordered Antiochus to withdraw - Polyb. 29.2.1-4 and 29.27; Livy 44.19.13 (A); Livy 44.29.1-5 (P); Livy 45.10-12.8 (P) and 13.1 (A).

34. Cf. M.R.R. 1.413. Also see, F.W. Walbank, 'A Note on the Embassy of Q. Marcius Philippus, 172 B.C.,' Journal of Roman Studies 31 (1941), 82-93. Briscoe, J.R.S. 54, 66-77. U. Kahrstedt, 'Zum Ausbruch des dritten römisch-makedonischen Krieges,' Klio 11 (1911), 415-30.

35. Livy 42.47.4 and 9 (P).
36. Livy 42.47.4. (P).
37. Livy 42.47.9 (P).
38. Livy 42.47.5-8 (P) gives the sentiment of the 'older' senators; also see Diod. 30.7.1. Notice of this 'new Wisdom' certainly comes from Polybius, but we are not entitled to think that Polybius himself disapproved of such diplomacy - on this, see Walbank, J.R.S. 55, 7.
39. Livy 42.47.8 (P).
40. Livy 43.4.5 (A). For Licinius and Lucretius in general, see M.R.R. I.416. It is unclear as to exactly what misdeeds Licinius did, but he might have been involved in the taking of Coronea in Boeotia, Livy 43.4.11 (A); also, Summary Bk. 43. As for Lucretius, he took the cities of Haliartus and Thisbe (note that Livy is being careless when he thinks that Lucretius took Thebes) 43.63.3-12 (P). It must be asked why Lucretius is condemned when Haliartus, Thisbe, and Coronea are all allies of Perseus. Note the clearness of senatorial motives in the decrees favoring pro-Romans placed on Thisbe and Coronea - R.K. Sherk, Roman Documents from the Greek East. Senatus consulta and epistulae to the Age of Augustus (Baltimore: Johns Hopkins Press, 1969), n.2 for Thisbe, and n. 3 for Coronea. Also see extended discussion in Chapter 5. Lucretius is also blamed for cruelty against Chalcis, 43.7.8-10 (A); on his trial, see 43.8 (A). The expediency of the Senate's 'humanitarianism' (aside from the decrees imposed on Coronea and Thisbe) is blatantly obvious when one remembers that immediately after the war, Haliartus was given to Athens by the Senate as a present for remaining loyal - Polyb. 30.20, who does not approve.
41. Livy 43.1.4-12 (A); 43.5 (A). The problem here

seems to be that Cassius, by leaving his area of concern, left Italy open to possible attack by northern tribes - cf. 43.1.9 (A). That this was indeed a worry is seen by the fact that envoys from the Gauls, Carians, Histrians, and Iapydes all showed up in Rome to complain about Cassius, and were placated by the Senate - cf. 43.5 (A).

42. On the defeat, see Livy 43.11.9 (A); 44.36.10 (P); 44.36.10 (P). On the favors, see Livy 43.11.9-10 (A).

43. Hortensius is portrayed as surpassing the inhumanity of his predecessor, Lucretius. On Abdera, see Livy 43.4.8-13 (A); and on Chalcis, see 43.7.5-8.7 (A).

44. Livy 43.8.5-6 (A).

45. E. Badian, Foreign Clientelae (264-70 B.C.) (Oxford: The Clarendon Press, 1958), pp.96, and 99-100 makes this same general point. This work hereafter cited as F.C.

46. One may note that Livy makes an attempt to contrast the clemency and justice shown by certain Romans (among whom was Paullus) towards Spain with the dishonorable acts committed in Greece. Cf. the plea of the Spaniards for advocates to speak their case, Livy 43.2 (A) (but note the outcome of the case, 43.2.11 (A)); the lenitas mentioned in 43.4.5 (A) is contrasted with what Licinius and Lucretius did. On embassies and complaints from Greece, see 43.4.8-13 (A) for Abdera; 43.5 (A) for envoys of Cincibilus, king of the Gauls; 43.6.1-3 (A) for Athens; and especially 43.7.5-11 (A) for Micythion, the envoy from Chalcis. In every case, the Senate was extremely careful to soothe hostile feelings and promise relief. Perhaps there is an echo of this policy in Polybius' idealized portrayal on the Senate's actions during the Third Macedonian War in Diod. 30.8. Nearly all the passages in Livy commenting on the ruthlessness of the Roman generals, the foreign embassies, and the Senate's reactions are of annalistic origin and are, therefore, already suspect because of the pro-senatorial biases of the annalists.

47. Cf. Badian, F.C., p.96.

48. Livy 44.5 (P).

49. Livy 44.6.4-5 (P); 44.8.4-5 (P).

50. This is the commission sent by Paullus - Livy 44.20.2-7 (A).

51. Cf. Livy 44.17.1 (A); 44.17.6 (A); 44.18.1 (A).

52. Livy 44.18.1-5 (A).

53. Livy 44.22 (P). Laistner, Roman Historians, p.88 is quite taken with Paullus' speech and its 'message'; 'There is

Livy and the Image

a timeless quality about these observations which make them appropriate in any age and not least in our own.'
54. Polyb. 29.1; Plutarch Aem. 10.
55. Livy 44.34.6 (P).
56. Livy 44.34.7-9 (P); cf. 44.40.1 (P).
57. This theme is present in several of Paullus' numerous speeches. On piety, see Livy 44.38.7 (P). On ancestoral discipline, see 44.39.2 (P).
58. Livy 44.31.1 (P). Cf. Walsh, Livy, p.73.
59. Livy 44.31.13-15 (P).
60. Appian, Illyrian Wars 2.9.
61. Livy 44.46.1 (P).
62. Livy 45.4.7 (P); 45.8.5 (P).
63. The fact that Perseus was mistreated after surrendering under a pledge of faith becomes to later people a supreme example of Roman treachery. See, Sallust, Letter of Mithridates, 7.
64. Livy 45.28.6 (P). But cf. 45.32.8 (P) where Livy virtually admits Paullus' contacts with the pro-Roman factions during the tour.
65. Plutarch Aem. 28.2.
66. Livy 45.29.1-3 (P). The phrase maiestas populi Romani is not found in the text, but it is clearly implied. Paullus will not speak to the Greeks directly, but rather has his commands translated from Latin to Greek. The importance of this is attested by Valerius Maximus 2.2.2 who states that it was contrary to the maiestas of the Roman people to answer the Greeks except in Latin.
67. For the sack of Aeginium, Agassae, and Aenia, supposedly to punish them for their misdeeds, see Livy 45.27.1-4 (P). Paullus is at first disassociated with the Aetolian massacre, 45.28.6-8 (P), but later, 45.31.1-2 (P), supports what had been done. On extensive witch-hunts for pro-Macedonians in Greece and Asia, see 45.31.7-15 (P); Paullus executed two of the more important enemies. On the banishing of political prisoners with Paullus' permission (contra Polyb. 30.13.11, but arguing from later events) see 45.31.9-32.8 (P) - the Macedonian prisoners are described as 'haughty tyrants.' Paullus' sack of an Illyrian city, and the infamous attack on Epirus (as 'ordered by the Senate'), is described at 45.33.8-34.6 (P).
68. Livy 45.17.7 (A).
69. Livy 45.18.1-2 (A).
70. Livy 45.35.7 (A).
71. Livy 45.35.8-36.5 (A); 45.36.6 (A); 45.36.7-8 (A);

Livy and the Image

45.36.10. (A).
72. Livy 45.37.1-2 and 11 (A).
73. Livy 45.37.12-38.10 (A).
74. Livy 45.37.12 (A); 45.38.4-8 (A).
75. Livy 45.39.10. (A).
76. Livy 45.40.4 (A).
77. Livy 45.40.6-42.1 (P). In a sense, Paullus asked to devote his family in order to protect the state. On devotio, see Livy 8.9.4-10 (A); 8.10.11-12 (A).
78. Polybius, being a high official of the Achaean League, was himself caught up in numerous factional disputes concerning what stance Achaea should take with respect to Rome. A major turning point in the relations between Rome and the Greek factions which supported her came with Callicrates' speech to the Senate in 180 when he advised Rome to intervene directly in the affairs of Greece - Polyb. 24.8.1-8, and especially 24.8.9-10.15 for Callicrates' speech and the Senate's favorable reaction to it. Polybius finds it necessary to apologize for Roman support of Callicrates - 24.10.11. A list of every instance of support given to pro-Roman factions is not needed; suffice it to say that Roman policies backing these groups continued throughout the 160s - cf. Polyb. 30.32. See the discussion in Chapter 5.
79. Note the fate of Cephalus who was supposedly neutral, but on account of the accusations made by Charops, was forced to switch sides to Perseus - Polyb. 28.15.8-16. Polybius himself, at least ideally, thought that neutrality was best - Polyb. 30.6.6.
80. Livy 41.23.5-18 (P) for Callicrates' speech. The occasion was a letter from Perseus wishing to normalize relations between Macedon and Achaea, and, of course, Callicrates was against this. He is opposed by Archon who spoke on behalf of restoring relations, 41.24 (P). Both speeches are highly significant for what they reveal of current Greek knowledge of the position of Macedon. See Walbank, J.H.S 58, 65-66 n.51; and, Badian, F.C., p.94 n.1.
81. Livy 41.23.5 (P).
82. See n.78.
83. Livy 41.25 (P); cf. 42.2.1-3 (A).
84. Appius Claudius was sent to Thessaly, and Marcus Marcellus to Aetolia and then to Achaea - Livy 42.5.8-6.2 (P).
85. Livy 42.6.1-3 (P).
86. Cf. Livy 39.33.8 (P); Badian, F.C., pp.89-90.

87. Broughton, M.R.R. I.413 for references.
88. Polyb. 27.2.6.
89. Livy 42.44.5. (P).
90. Polyb. 27.2.8-9; and Livy 42.44.6 (P).
91. Broughton, M.R.R. I.426 for references.
92. On the mission to Acarnania, see Oost, Roman Policy, pp.78-79.
93. Oost, pp.78-79 recognizes the precarious position of this state (and others) because of Rome's apparent weakness and Perseus' strength, and notes that the Romans did nothing to push the Greeks into the Macedonian camp. On the other hand, Badian, F.C., p.96, views this embassy as 'a genuine attempt to heal discord within the states;' Badian does qualify himself, but is still too generous to Roman policies in this particular instance.
94. Livy 45.28.6 (P).
95. Generosity: Livy 45.28.9-11 (P). Freedom: 45.29.12. (P). Massacre: 45.28.6-8 (P). Condemnation: 45.31.1-2 (P).
96. Livy 45.31.6 (P). Livy 45.31.6-9 (P) characterizes the three main groups of Greek politicans: two groups were bad, one because it fawned on Roman power, and the other because it fawned on the friendship of kings. Only one group, that which pursued a policy of neutrality, was good. Cf. 42.30.1-7 (P) for similar views. The notion of the three groups of politicans was adapted from Polyb. 30.6-8; in these sections Polybius is primarily concerned with justifying his own policy regarding Rome - he contrasts his own policy with others who followed different paths. Polybius' three groups consisted of those who favored neutrality, those who wished Perseus well (but who could not provide any actual aid), and those who openly supported Perseus. And since Polybius' differentiations meant nothing to Livy, Livy changed them to fit his own pattern - another example of Livian distortion of Polybius.
97. Roman envoys were either sent to, or had names provided to them by politicians from Achaea, Epirus, Acarnania, and Boeotia - Livy 45.31.9-15 (P); cf. Polyb. 30.13.6-11.
98. Massacre: Livy 45.31.1-2 (P). Deportation: 45.31.9 (P). Executions: 45.31.15. (P). Sack of Epirus: 45.34.1-6 (P).
99. E.g., the actions breaking up the Acarnanian League, Livy 45.31.12 (P); actions against suspected 'enemies' in Asia and the islands, 45.31.13-15 (P). But for a

supreme example of Livy's cover-up, note that the historian fails to record that, having failed to seduce Attalus away from Eumenes with a gift of Aenus and Maronea, the Senate reneged on its promised gift and took back the towns - Polyb. 30.3.

100. E.g., Polyb. 28.2.5-8; 28.17.

101. This, of course, was caused by the opening of Delos as a free port.

102. Livy 41.6.8-12 (A); see Polyb. 25.4-5 for a different picture.

103. Against Eumenes: Livy 42.14.10 (P). Against Rome: Livy 42.26.8-9 (A). The accusation of a conspiracy against Rome comes from the report of a Roman embassy which is nothing more than an annalistic invention - see Scullard, Roman Politics, p.200 n.1; and Broughton, M.R.R. I.412.

104. Livy 44.14.8-15.8 (A). Claudius is mentioned at 44.15.1, and 'other historians,' surely Antias, at 44.15.3. On the second part of the doublet, see Livy 45.3.3-8; also see Polyb. 29.19.2-11.

105. Livy 44.14.13; this is Livy's own observation.

106. For other examples of how Livy distorts the Rhodian position, see 44.23.10 (P) where Metrodorus, Dinon, and Polyaratus, the leaders of the pro-Macedonian faction, are called the leaders of Rhodes. Also Livy 44.29 (P) for a distortion of Polyb. 29.16.

107. Livy 39.23.5 (P); 42.5.1 (P); 42.52.3 (P).

108. Cf. Livy 42.5.4-7 (P). This is rife with anti-Perseus propaganda and seeks to compare the evil Perseus with the good Eumenes.

109. Livy 42.15-17 (P).

110. Livy 42.25.1-13 (A). This embassy and notices of several others of the year 172 are annalistic inventions - see Nissen, Untersuchungen, p.246 ff.; Broughton, M.R.R I.412-15, and nn. 4 and 8; Scullard, Roman Politics, p.200 n.1.

111. Again from an annalist, Livy 42.36.4-8 (A) falsely charges Perseus with: (1) the capture of Perrhaebia (but at 42.53.8 (P) Perseus takes it again); (2) the capture of several Thessalian cities (but in 41.22.6. (P) and 41.23.14 (P) there is no mention of this - in 42.67.9-11 (P) there are several cities which were allied to Perseus, but certainly not captured). Livy can also be very careless, if not stupid; see 42.46.7-10 (P) where he has only one embassy from Perseus, instead of the two which Polyb. 27.5.1 records. Livy also has Thebes, instead of Thisbe, as an ally to Perseus - also cf.

Livy and the Image

Livy 42.63.12 (P).
    112. Gods: Livy 44.1.10-11 (P). Madness: 44.2.12 (P), and 44.6.14-17 (P).
    113. Advice to allies: Livy 42.46.10 (P). Peace offers: 42.62.10 (P), and 44.25.3 (P).

Chapter Four

PLUTARCH AND THE IMAGE

Time wore lightly on the image of Aemilius Paullus. His character and virtues entranced those who, by temperament or inclination, favored men of the past over present company. The years had smoothed out the wrinkles in the facade; indeed, Paullus came to be seen as the epitome, the embodiment of republican nobility. And this is precisely the manner in which Plutarch approached the famous Lucius Aemilius. No longer will Paullus be under the constraints of history; no longer will he be confined by the mundane restrictions placed on men of ordinary mien for Plutarch lifts him out of the historical scene and gives him a world unto himself, a world attuned only to the virtues and deeds of Paullus. From Plutarch's hand emerges a Paullus who is, by design, ahistorical; he is, as Plutarch freely admits, (1) no more than a reflection of reality, a stylized and formalized representative of public and private propriety. His prime function is edification, for in him Plutarch has found a sterling example of moral excellence and integrity.

That Plutarch never had any intention of writing a history of Paullus' life, or for that matter of any of the men whose lives are so honored, is abundantly clear. Plutarch is not interested in the cataclysmatic effects of war on a people, as was Thycydides; he is not trying to understand the rise of a nation to world dominion, after the fashion of Polybius; nor is he endeavoring to record the history of an entire people, as Livy had done. Each _Life_ which Plutarch wrote is an entity by itself; it does not depend on other writings to introduce it, nor does it form a part of a larger continuous narrative. The result is a series of biographies of famous men of action, men in whose lives Plutarch has seen either virtue worthy of imitation, or turpitude to be avoided at all costs. The Lives were written from the point of view of a moralist who desired to remember the deeds of eminent men, and who, more than all else, hoped that those deeds would favorably influence the lives and manners of his audience. (2) Plutarch is frank about his purpose, for in the opening chapter of the Alexander he reminds his readers not to expect detailed examinations of every important event. (3) He is writing biography, not history, and prefers to concentrate on those small actions which clearly reveal a man's soul. (4) And Plutarch truly loved his work. He began writing so that others might learn of and share in the dignity of conduct which the study of illustrious men offered; but he continued for his own benefit 'using history as a mirror and endeavoring in a manner to fashion and adorn my life in conformity with the virtues therein depicted.' (5) While he worked on a specific Life it was as if the subject himself had entered Plutarch's home as a guest, where, upon associating with him over a period of time, the moralist carefully chose from the man's life what was finest to know and to learn from. (6) So beneficial was the observance of merit and worth that one eventually came to repel instinctively anything which smacked of baseness or ill-repute.. (7) This type of study could hardly be effective in a history where the examination of a man's character was most often relegated to a digression. Thus it was that Plutarch focused exclusively on the moralistic consideration of his subject's life. All was subordinate to Plutarch's didacticism and to the affection which Plutarch felt for many of those about whom he wrote.

Few men of the past can claim so much of Plutarch's favor as Aemilius Paullus. Although he was not a man of philosophic predilection, he was a man who abided by the ancient laws and customs of his land and who thereby gained a just and incorruptible personality. (8) Naturally, Paullus was of good character to begin with, and this was the impetus that led to his rigid adhesion to righteous behavior. The Life itself is constructed entirely around the moralist's purpose of highlighting Paullus' virtues; and, indeed, there is no one particular trait for which Paullus is singled out, since he is one of those rare individuals who, in Plutarch's eyes, possesses every variety of nobility of conduct. (9) History has little meaning here - the Life, as previously mentioned, is painstakingly attuned to representing Paullus in the best possible light. His career is not related during the course of describing a period of time; rather, Paullus' career is used to magnify the virtues of the man. Confrontations with enemies, both Roman and alien, are cleverly employed to heighten the figure of Paullus. Periods of crisis show him at his best, and even minor occurrences demonstrate his worth. Both publicly and privately - whether dealing with religion, his family, politics, or war - there are few men who match Paullus. (10) To further this notion, Plutarch introduces Perseus as a foil to the noble Paullus; the conflict between these two men is nothing less than a contest between the good and meritorius Paullus and the depraved and wicked eastern potentate, Perseus. It is an agon, a competition, between the finest representative of Rome, and the most evil example of monarchy. So stereotyped is this agon of morality which Plutarch artificially sets up between the two men, that Paullus and Perseus are reduced to stick-figures who do little more than depict extremes of behavior. In no estimation can Paullus, the paragon of virtue, and Perseus, the creature of monstrous corruption, be seen as anything more than personifications of the good and bad in men. Again, the agon is intended to applaud Paullus, and to show the reader the correct way to order his own life.

The sources upon which Plutarch drew for his Life of Paullus are curiously mixed. (11) Polybius is, as one might expect, the chief source which Plutarch depended on. The account of Paullus from the Histories fits well into the moralist's preconceptions of how a man of greatness should act; and the traducement of Perseus by Polybius was also of great use to Plutarch. Roman annalistic writings can also be found in the Life, although it is not at all certain whether Plutarch consulted the annalists themselves or whether he discovered a convenient summary of Paullus' life which was originally drawn from Quadrigarius or Antias. Other, more obscure sources were also used; there is a letter by Scipio Nasica to an unnamed king telling of Scipio's exploits during the last campaign against Perseus, and also a history written by a certain Poseidonius in defense of the Macedonian king. (12) Thus it is clear that Plutarch had at his command a variety of sources from which he could have extracted a detailed and balanced account of Paullus, Perseus, and the Third Macedonian War. But this was not, unfortunately, his purpose. In Polybius and the annalists, Plutarch found little to worry about - they were open in their praise of Paullus. Nasica and Poseidonius are a different matter however;

99

while he does specifically cite these authors, Plutarch ingeniously manipulates their writings, choosing precisely those incidents which help to further his own vision of Paullus. Plutarch allows Nasica to describe his own deeds, but at a crucial point just before Pydna, Plutarch has Paullus lecture Nasica and the others who wished an immediate engagement, telling them to cool their warlike spirits and await a more opportune time for battle. (13) Nasica is used to glorify Paullus' wisdom and moderation. In a similar vein, the passages taken from Poseidonius tend to extol the Roman victory, even though it is clear that they are torn out of context and served no such purpose in the original. (14) The Life of Paullus is not sloppily done, for around a preconceived notion of what Aemilius was like, Plutarch built a coherent and flowing narrative. The 'scissors and paste' method is not evident here. Every source, even the one which was potentially hostile, is carefully screened so that Paullus stands forth as the personification of Roman virtus which Plutarch imagined. (15)

The beginning of the Life itself shows that Paullus' early years could hardly have been more worthy. His pedigree was flawless, for the reader is assured by Plutarch that in all probability the pater familias of the Aemilii was none other than Mamercus, the son of Pythagoras the philosopher. (16) Not only that: Paullus himself, born in an age of men of the highest repute, did not follow the normal avenues of success, such as pleading cases and courting favors, but surpassed all his fellows in the noble pursuits of courage, justice, and trustworthiness. (17) The moralist has set the necessary background; the lineage extending back to Pythagoras, the greatness of Paullus' ancestry, and the fact that Paullus was a model of rectitude in an age which abounded in that virtue surely warmed Plutarch to his subject. But there is more yet - Plutarch has barely begun. As an augur, Paullus was an example of exceptional piety for others of the profession who craved the position more for their own glory than for the good of religion. So fastidious was Paullus in his duties that he raised augury to a higher art, confirming the dictum of philosophers that religion was the science of worshipping the gods. (18) The notice of the philosophers' saying is undoubtedly a bit of Plutarch's own philosophizing. In any case, the real importance behind the keeping of religious minutiae is political, since Plutarch states that one who keeps faith with seemingly insignificant details would never neglect the larger obligations due the state - 'for no man begins at once with a great deed of lawlessness to disturb the civil polity, but those who remit their strictness in small matters break down also the guard that has been set over greater matters.' (19) Paullus was, moreover, strict in the maintenance of military customs and discipline. No soldier was courted, no rule bent; Plutarch sternly notes that by training his fellow citizens in the rigors of war, Paullus restored Rome to the greatness she had known in the distant past. (20) The purpose of all these remarks, the moralist's laudatory proclamations, is to introduce Paullus as a man whose outstanding virtues are evident in both his public and private lives: while others sought success, he followed justice and bravery; in religious activities he abided by the ways of ancient custom and by the precepts of philosphers; and as a general, laxity was repudiated and citizens were trained in antiqua disciplina. These traits have a familiar ring about them. But unlike Polybius who saw Paullus as a representative of the new world order, and unlike Livy who viewed Paullus as a man molded by ancient ways and customs, Plutarch is mainly concerned with instructing his audience by using what he sees as the greatness surrounding every aspect of Paullus' life and career.

The search for peace and harmony is a major characteristic to be found in Paullus' public duties. Plutarch relates that Spain was left in peace after Paullus had been sent there as a praetor. (21) Equally noteworthy, Paullus did not profit by one penny from his Spanish campaign; this is singled out for especial praise since Plutarch, throughout his Lives, always notes the right and wrong use of wealth as the mark of a man's worth. (22) The frugality of Paullus' private life obviously extended to his public services. Later, during his first consulship, he was both humane and conciliatory toward the defeated Ligurians, to the point where they put their faith in Paullus and trusted him completely. (23) The establishment of peace, the maintenance of concord, these were his only objectives. At Rome itself, Aemilius assumed the consulship for a second time only when it became evident that the state required his services to defeat Perseus - the cries of the mob did not sway him in his decision. (24) And when he came to address the people, he warned them not to interfere in his campaign by their idle chatter and inane 'advice'. He owed them nothing, but he owed the state victory, and the people, after having been reproved, were inspired with love and respect for Paullus. (25) Plutarch's rendition of the image of Paullus is well underway.

The conduct of Paullus' personal life leaves little to be desired. The divorce of his first wife was not done maliciously, but rather on account of simple incompatibility. (26) Moreover, his fatherly abilities made him the most respected parent in all Rome. The education of his children was marked by strict training in the mos maiorum, and by intensive study of all things Greek. Philosophers, grammarians, artists, and huntsmen filled Paullus' house educating his sons in Greek learning. (27) Thus, the private side of this man of extraordinary virtue.

Enter Perseus, a man of disgusting and loathsome nature, who stands as Paullus' antagonist in war and opposite in morality. The agon commences under Plutarch's direction, although there is never any question as to which man will win. Passions, chief among which was unthinking avarice, ruled Perseus. Indeed, there was the rumor that he was not an heir of Philip at all, but was only the son of a common sempstress. (28) Perseus was the most contemptible of kings. Although he could have easily purchased the arms of the Basternae, he was too miserly, and preferred to risk his kingdom rather than spend his monies. (29) Paullus, the readers are told, scorned Perseus, but admired his army when he first came upon it. (30) The contrast between the two combatants becomes more pronounced as Pydna approaches. The Macedonian is exceedingly fearful and without hope; the Roman, on the other hand, is unswerving in his purpose. (31) And when the final battle began, Paullus stood like the pilot of a ship watching the tides of the struggle, but Perseus, like the coward he was, fled the field, saying that he must sacrifice to Heracles - little did he know that Paullus had already honored that god. (32) Similar scenes of Paullus' virtue and Perseus' baseness are repeated again and again. There is Perseus' disgraceful flight to the sanctuary at Samothrace; to which tales of portents showing divine favor to Aemilius are juxtaposed. (33) The climax of the agon comes with direct confrontation between the cowardly Perseus and the noble Paullus; following his capture, Perseus humbles himself before the consul and shames himself with cries and supplications. And just before the triumph, Perseus begs Paullus not to lead him in the procession. To these ignoble acts Paullus replied that such behavior depreciated the worth of the victory, and that, in any event, Perseus could always choose death instead of humiliation. (34) Plutarch offers no relief to the unfortunate Perseus; there is no hint of pity for the fallen monarch. At the triumph itself, tears flowed for Perseus' children who comprehended little of what was happening to them. But no sympathy is extended to Perseus, and he moved almost unnoticed in the procession except for the fact that his countenance bore the marks of his evil. (35) Such was the inevitable outcome of a miser and a coward who dared pit himself against the virtuous Aemilius, and, for Plutarch's audience, this was the intended message.

Yet the agon's end does not mark the end of Paullus' praise. His celebrated tour of Greece was done so that harmony might be restored to a strife-torn land, and Plutarch notes approvingly that during the 'holiday', Paullus stopped at Greece's two most sacred shrines, Delphi and Olympia. (36) These were acts done, not in the heat of battle or at a moment of great decision when even less gifted men might rise above their normal characters, but during a less pressured moment when defects of behavior could more easily present themselves - and Paullus never falters, nor does his nobility ever lapse. Furthermore, Paullus is commended by the moralist for the way he handles his amusements and banquets, and also for how he treats the guests at these affairs. At his victory celebration Paullus is said to have shown that he was equally adept in directing a banquet and in generaling an army. (37) And when it came to disposing of the vast Macedonian treasures, Paullus would not even look upon the gold and silver, and took nothing for himself but Perseus' library which he gave to his sons. (38) The only kink in Aemilius' flawless character is the attack which he carried out against Epirus. C.P. Jones has stated that Plutarch uses the sack of Epirus as an example of the way in which Rome ruthlessly dealt with her allies; (39), and, indeed, there is no doubt that Plutarch was shocked by the destruction inflicted on Epirus, and comments that the deed was incompatible with Aemilius' just and moderate nature. (40) But if Jones imagines that any overt criticism of Paullus was intended, he is quite wrong. No aspersion is cast on Paullus, nor does Plutarch appear to be reproving Roman policy on account of the sack of Epirus. The episode, horribly unfortunate, was at least in Plutarch's eyes, part of the war, and does not diminish the brilliance of Paullus. This is made abundantly clear when, in the very next chapter, Plutarch dismisses the occurrence at Epirus and proceeds to the controversy surrounding Paullus' triumph. (41) Here again Paullus' virtues shine as the moralist contrasts him with greedy soldiers who found their pay for the Macedonian campaign hardly enough to satiate their appetite for riches. The outcome of the dispute over the triumph reveals a re-establishment of concord within Rome itself, thus showing once more the beneficial effect which Aemilius bestowed on the common weal. The triumph was a magnificent event, lasting three full days, and crowned by the nearly divine figure of Paullus who wore the most glorious trappings of power, a purple robe intertwined with golden thread. (42) No right-thinking man envied the triumphator in his moment of glory. Still, there are forces beyond the human which dog men with misfortune. For those whose successes are too numerous and whose prosperity is too great, an evil daimon and a vengeful Tyche await.

In curious fashion, Plutarch introduces two 'divinities' or 'powers' which torture Paullus because they were jealous of the magnitude of his achievements. So great had Paullus become that both a daimon and Tyche sought to cause him ill. (43) The two 'powers' appear to be synonymous in every feature, except that Tyche's anger is expressed by the word nemesis. (44) Neither 'power' could bear to allow Paullus to continue unmolested. Plutarch, of course, took the concept of Tyche, as it related to the vicissitudes of life, from Polybius. But he took only this particular facet of Polybius' Tyche, having absolutely no use for the wider significance given the goddess by Polybius. Plutarch cared nothing for the fact that Polybius' Tyche could guide the destinies of men and states - what attracted the moralist and what caught his eye was the fact that Tyche was a capricious goddess and that she would never allow men to prosper indefinitely. The daimon appears as Plutarch's own introduction, being little more than a malevolent spirit akin to Tyche. Together both the daimon and Tyche demonstrate to the moralist's audience the instability of life; and together they are used to heighten Paullus' stature still more. For he lost one son before his triumph and one son afterwards, a cruel blow which caused men to shudder at the cruelty of Tyche. (45) Nevertheless, Paullus is said to have put aside his grief so as not to lose sight of the public good. (46) He addressed the people, not as one who wished sympathy and pity, but as a father instructing his children in the mysteries of life. (47) It was far better, he told them, for the daimon and Tyche to inflict misery on him instead of them visiting the state as a whole with retribution; no one would dispute the fact that it was better for a father to lose two sons, than for a state to lose its good fortune. Plutarch has here both the perfect instance with which to demonstrate the uncertainty of existence, and also the perfect model of a man who confronted overwhelming personal tragedy with stoic nobility.

Finally, Paullus' last years are chronicled with as much enthusiasm as the rest of his life. Plutarch is always concerned with how a man of mature years carries himself - Paullus, once again, does not fail the moralist. Paullus continues to disdain the currying of favors with the common people, and in this respect he is said to surpass his famous son, Scipio Aemilianus. (48) Paullus' prudent exercise of power during his censorship proved that he was worthy of Rome's admiration and love. (49) And when his end came, he met it bravely. The way in which one faces death and the memory others retain of a man are important indicators, in Plutarch's opinion, of a person's merit; often one has but to read the death scene of one of the moralist's subjects in order to sense the tenor of the man's entire life, for those who have been 'good' will have a noble finish, while base men will suffer ignoble extinction. Plutarch permits Paullus to shrug off his mortal coil in a befitting manner. Religious duties and pious sacrifices occupied Aemilius to nearly his last breath; and his death and funeral called forth, as his life had done, the admiration of not only his fellow Romans, but even of his former enemies, the Spaniards, Ligurians, and Macedonians. (50) To these aliens, Paullus was a friend and benefactor, and they carried his bier to its final resting place.

Plutarch is the ancient world's last great interpreter of the life and character of Paullus, and in many ways the moralist's version is the most attractive. His image of Paullus' nobility and virtue is always comforting to those desirous of escaping from their own times. It offers a splendid vision of uprightness, of clemency and justice, and of a life well spent in the service of family and nation. And far be it for Plutarch to present a mere history of Lucius Aemilius Paullus - Paullus was too important to have such restrictions placed on him. He had, in a very real sense, become a friend to the moralist, and, in Plutarch's case, the familiarity bred only admiration. Enamored of what he saw in Paullus, Plutarch disregarded any deed which did not contribute to his preconceived vision of Perseus' conqueror. Yet it would be wrong to accuse Plutarch of deliberate and conscious distortion, at least in the Life of Paullus. He simply refused to believe anything bad of his beloved Paullus, and as a moralist, that was his perogative. On the other hand, the historian's blind acceptance of Plutarch's Paullus, the personification of virtus and pietas, is indefensible.

NOTES

1. Plutarch Aem. 1.1.
2. Cf. Plutarch Cimon 2.3-5; Per. 1-2.4; Nic. 1.5; Demosth. 11.7; Aem. 1; Alex. 1; Demetr. 1.1-6; Pomp. 8.7.
3. Plutarch Alex. 1.
4. Plutarch Alex. 1.
5. Plutarch Aem. 1.1
6. Plutarch Aem. 1.2-4.
7. Plutarch Aem. 1.5.
8. Plutarch Comparison: Timoleon and Paullus 2.1.
9. Cf., Alan Wardman, Plutarch's Lives (Berkeley: University of California Press, 1974), p.3. Wardman's book is, in my opinion, the best and most insightful of all works on Plutarch.
10. One should note that while Timoleon is highly favored by Plutarch, on balance, when Paullus and Timoleon are compared, the Roman receives the most praise.
11. I have no intention of providing a detailed study of the sources. This is not my purpose, and it is, in any case, fairly obvious from whom Plutarch draws. For a detailed consideration of the sources, see Nissen, Untersuchungen, pp.298-305. Polybius, Histoires Livre I, trans. P. Pedech (Paris: Societe d'Editions, 1969), p.lxv, who follows Nissen. Christiana Liedmeier, Plutarchus Biographie van Aemilius Paullus: Historische Commentaar (Utrecht: Dekker & van de Vegt N.V., 1935). R.E. Smith, 'Plutarch's Biographical Sources in the Roman Lives,' Classical Quarterly 34 (1940), 1-10. The main point of Liedmeier (e.g., pp.169, 171, 191, and elsewhere) and Smith (pp. 4, 7, 9) is that several sections of the Paullus derive from an existing Biography of Paullus which Plutarch used. This is, of course, possible; however, I prefer the analysis which maintains that Plutarch used a number of separate sources - see note 15.
12. See Plutarch Aem. 15.5 for Nasica; 19.7 for

Plutarch and the Image

Poseidonius.

13. See Plutarch Aem. 17 for Nasica's exploits; 18.1-6 for Paullus' speech.

14. Cf. Plutarch Aem. 20; and especially, 24.1-4.

15. I reproduce here the summary of Plutarch's sources for the Life of Paullus as found in Nissen, Untersuchungen, p.305: Polybius: Chaps. 4-6, 10-15, 19, 23, 28, 29, 35, 36.
Nasica: Chaps. 15-18, 21, 22, 26, 27.
Poseidonius: Chaps. 8, 9, 19, 20, 23, 24, 37?.
Collections of Anecdotes: Chaps. 5, 10, 14, 15, 25, 38.
For precise details Nissen should be consulted. One should recognize, however, that Plutarch appears, in several chapters, to intermix sources. E.g., in chap. 26 Plutarch describes the capture of Perseus in Samothrace - he seems to be following Nasica, although the account in the Life is very close to what is found in Livy 45.6-8 (P). Also cf. Plutarch Aem. 27.2-6 following Nasica, with Polyb. 29.20.

16. Plutarch Aem 2.2.
17. Plutarch Aem. 2.5-6.
18. Plutarch Aem. 3.3
19. Plutarch Aem. 3.5.
20. Plutarch Aem. 3.6-7.
21. Praetor in 191. Plutarch Aem. 4.4.
22. Plutarch Aem. 4.5; cf. 28.10. On Plutarch's opinion of the use and abuse of wealth, see Wardman, Lives, pp.83-5. Cf. Plutarch Cimon 10 and 14.4 for the correct use of money; and Crassus 12.3, and Luc. 41.7 for abuses of wealth.
23. Plutarch Aem. 6.4-7.
24. Plutarch Aem. 10.
25. Plutarch Aem. 11.
26. Plutarch Aem. 5.1-4.
27. Plutarch Aem. 6.8-10.
28. Plutarch Aem. 8.10: avarice; 8.11-12: Perseus' mother.
29. See Plutarch Aem. 12.3-12. Perseus is unfavorably compared with Philip II and Alexander who are said to have been more concerned with empire than with treasure. Cf. Wardman, Lives, p.33.
30. Plutarch Aem. 13.4.
31. Plutarch Aem. 16.4 for Perseus' fear; 13.6 for Paullus' purpose.
32. Pilot: Plutarch Aem. 18.3. Perseus' cowardice: 19.4-6. Paullus and Heracles: 17.9-11.

33. Perseus' flight: Plutarch Aem. 23. Divine favor to Paullus: 24.3.-6
34. See Plutarch Aem. 26.9-12; and 34.3-4.
35. Plutarch Aem. 33.8
36. Plutarch Aem. 28.1-5. He also establishes harmony in Macedon - 29.1.
37. Plutarch Aem. 28.7-9. Plato Laws i637Af and ii652A notes the importance of man's behavior at symposia - cf. Wardman, Lives, p.8.
38. Plutarch Aem. 28.10-11.
39. C.P. Jones, Plutarch and Rome (Oxford: The Clarendon Press, 1971), p.100.
40. Plutarch Aem. 30.1. For the sack of Epirus, 29.
41. Plutarch Aem. 30.2-31.10.
42. Plutarch Aem. 34.6-7.
43. On Tyche, see Plutarch Aem. 22.9; 27.4; 35.3; 36.1; 36.3; 36.5-6; 36.8. On the daimon, see 34.8; 27.5; 36.5. On nemesis, see 22.9; 36.9. Cf. Wardman, Lives, p.74, although he never mentions that Plutarch borrowed from Polybius.
44. See Plutarch Aem.22.9; 36.9.
45. Plutarch Aem. 35.1-3.
46. Plutarch Aem. 36.1.
47. Plutarch Aem. 36.2-9.
48. Plutarch Aem. 38.2-6.
49. Plutarch Aem. 38.7-9.
50. Plutarch Aem. 39 for the death of Paullus.

Chapter Five

ANOTHER LOOK

A. THE EARLY YEARS

Born about 229/28, (1) Lucius Aemilius Paullus was one of two children of the consul of 219 and 216, Lucius Aemilius Paullus, who died at Cannae. The name of Paullus' mother is unknown, but to her fell the responsibilty of raising both him and his sister Aemilia. Exactly how his mother educated the young Paullus cannot be determined, unless one is willing to believe Plutarch's claim that the youth disdained the normal path of advancement which included law and the cultivation of influential friends, and depended on courage, justice and rectitude to guide him to greatness. (2) In any case, Paullus' mother surely cared for advancement and power; her daughter Aemilia married one of Rome's most renowned generals, Scipio, the conqueror of Hannibal. (3) And Paullus himself, despite what Plutarch says, was groomed for the standard military career which most Romans of nobility pursued. He was a military tribune three times, although when and under whom is unknown. (4) By the year 195 he was a quaestor, but here, too, all details are lacking. (5) In 194 Paullus was one of three men sent out to colonize Croton, (6) and in 193 he was elected curule aedile, an office which he undertook with zeal by directing a modest building program in Rome. (7) From the manner in which Plutarch has constructed his narrative it appears that Paullus gained the augurate in 192; the position, as previously discussed, pleased the moralist because of Aemilius' supposed strict observance of law and custom. (8) Thus far the list of offices is nothing out of the ordinary, nor is one able to draw much information from the bare notice of Paullus' formative years other than the assumption, made because his sister was married to Scipio, that he had powerful friends.

In the elections for 191 Paullus was given his first chance to prove himself, and was elected praetor and assigned the unruly province of Farther Spain. (9) Spain had come to the Romans as booty from the Second Punic War, and Rome had suffered only minor troubles in its control of the area down to 197. (10) Nevertheless, as the Romans began to focus more interest on Spain, and in 197 divided the country into two provinces, they brought down on themselves a major revolt which lasted nearly twenty years. (11) Tied to the provincial organization of 197 was an increased Roman desire to exploit the land economically, and to accomplish this, two more praetors for Spain were elected in that year. (12) When the war broke, even several Phoenician cities joined the uprising and by 195 the situation had become so serious that Rome committed a consular army under Cato to the conflict. Cato's efforts did not end the fighting. (13) It was to this same war that the Senate sent Paullus in 191. He went with considerable powers, for while his title was praetor, he held the insignia and the imperium of a proconsul. (14) Although the sources are both vague and contradictory, it appears that sometime during 190 Paullus suffered a major defeat at the hands of the Lusitanians. Yet, his command was continued, and in early 189 he redeemed himself and won an overwhelming victory for which he acquired the title of imperator, and for which the Senate voted thanksgivings in his honor. (15) Paullus' defeat in his first year in Farther Spain did his reputation no good; but the massive victory over the same enemies a year later erased the stain, and never again in his military career was Paullus to shame himself on the battlefield.

Beyond the mere notice of Paullus' military capabilities, there is a much more interesting problem. an inscription which declares that Paullus set free the slaves of the Hastensians and placed them and their land under the aegis of Rome. (16) Some scholars, including Mommsen, (17) have seen Paullus' decree as part of a deliberate policy on Rome's part to break up local Spanish power-bases and loyalties, substituting in their place ties with Rome. This assertion receives support from Livy's statement that Culchas, one of the Spanish chiefs who revolted in 197, had his holdings reduced from twenty-eight to seventeen cities during the time the Romans had been in Spain. (18) Thus, on the surface at least, Paullus' decree and Culchas' reduction in towns seem to point to a general Roman policy of stripping power from the Spaniards and replacing it with dependence on Rome. Yet, as Badian has noted, (19) it is difficult to know what to make of Culchas' case, especially when Polybius quotes one of the Scipios' letters in which they claim to have strengthened the same Culchas. (20) Moreover, Paullus' order stands isolated, with nothing even remotely resembling it; (21) the circumstances under which it was delivered are unknown, and, as Sutherland states, no generalized deduction can be drawn from it. (22) When these notices are combined with the uncertainty over Livy's comment on Culchas, it would be unwise to formulate any conclusion concerning Roman policy in Spain during these years. At most, one might venture to say that by declaring those people to be free from Hasta, an enemy city which caused Roman commanders much trouble, (23) Paullus sought to weaken Hasta's sphere of influence in the immediate area.

Important as the Spanish campaigns of those years had been, Rome was gambling for far bigger stakes against Antiochus in Asia. Greece had not welcomed its 'liberator' with the enthusiasm that Antiochus had hoped for, and in 191 the king faltered and was forced to retreat to Asia. There he met the formidable genius of P. Scipio (and Scipio's brother, the consul Lucius), and there, in 190, Antiochus' forces were shattered at Magnesia. (24) The Roman victory was decisive, and in some quarters the conviction surfaced that Rome had defeated her last great enemy and was now mistress of the world. (25) But it was not the Scipios who remained to settle the war; factional struggles broke around Antiochus' vanquishers and were ultimately to destroy them. The elections for 189 did not find the Scipionic command against Antiochus prolonged - the Scipios were ordered to hand over their armies to the new consul, Manlius Vulso, and return to Rome. (26) The Scipios had defeated Antiochus and had even arranged the basic terms around which the peace was to be formed; now Manlius stepped in to reap the final glory, a painful slap for Hannibal's victor to endure. Scipio did not meekly submit: Aemilius Paullus, who was in Spain during the opening months of 189, returned to Rome and became one of the ten commissioners sent to assist Manlius in implementing the settlement with Antiochus. (27) There can be little doubt that Paullus was placed on the commission as a friend of Scipio; Paullus had absolutely no familiarity with eastern affairs, and it appears that he was hurried home from Spain for the specific purpose of joining the commission. (28) Indeed, there is evidence to suggest that Manlius and the ten commissioners, others of whom besides Paullus supported the Scipios, (29) were at odds with each other. (30) Their return to Rome was to prove this.

Upon his application for a triumph, Manlius was confronted by the majority of the ten commissioners who launched an effort to block the honor. In particular, Paullus and another politician tried to hinder Manlius on account of what only can be seen as a desire to humble the man who had robbed the Scipios of their rightful glory. Two main charges were lodged against Manlius: (1) that he had neglected proper fetial rites and had made unauthorized war against the Gauls in Asia, and (2) that his generalship was exceedingly poor, since the army was badly mauled during its return to Italy through Thrace. (31) Both charges, if they were made at all and are not some annalistic invention, are of the lowest type of political harassment. Livy's source was, almost certainly, Valerius Antias, (32) and the various speeches in the crucial passage are rife with sensationalism and glaring mistakes in detail; on these grounds alone the entire episode deserves the utmost suspicion. Regarding the first charge - the attack against the destruction of the Asian Gauls by Manlius in 189 - the unnamed speaker maintained that war had not been declared against the Gauls, and that by his attack Manlius had disobeyed time-honored fetial laws. The accusation borders on the ridiculous; not only had the Gauls been allies of Rome's chief enemy, Antiochus, (33) but it was clear that in order to bolster Eumenes' position after the war, the Gauls, who had long terrorized Asia, would have to be eliminated. (34) It is hard to believe that Manlius' command in the East did not include Antiochus' allies, the chief outlaws of the area. Furthermore, by the early second century the fetial laws were hardly as strict as they had been in previous times. As Walbank has noted, by this time it was common for formal procedures to be altered or avoided, or for the real issues to be masked in order to secure the desired vote for war. (35) If Manlius had been so blatant in his actions, then one has to ask why he was not accused of perduellio, and why he was granted his triumph? (36) One may note, finally, a glaring anachronism: Livy, following Antias, the Sullan annalist, writes that the war against the Gauls had not been sanctioned by the authority of the Senate or by a vote of the people. (37) But Livy forgets that Sulla had been the first to decree that the Senate was legally able to declare war (38) and that earlier only the people had the power to decide that question. Antias stupidly imposed the procedures of his own day on to the debate over Manlius' conduct, and Livy followed him; the blind led the blind.

The second charge is slightly more credible, although, as Nissen has pointed out, the wild exaggeration and rhetorical enhancements of the speaker's version of what happened pushed the reality of the situation past recognition. (39) It was claimed that Manlius was a poor general, and that he had led the army into an ambush in Thrace which cost much of the eastern booty and the life of one of the ten commissioners. There is no question that the attack took place; but the blame should be placed on Manlius' over-confidence rather than on any lack of ability. While the Scipios before him had sought the aid of Philip V when passing through hostile territory, Manlius thought the safeguard unnecessary, (40) and the Thracians took good advantage of Philip's absence. (41) Manlius' defeat was real enough, but at the same time his opponents' only motive for advancing their argument was to humiliate the consul before the Senate and to deny him a triumph. Thus, the assault upon Manlius' reputation by Paullus and the other commissioners reveals nothing in the way of foreign policy convictions, cultural preferences, or personal traits; it was no more than a Scipionic maneuver to take revenge on a political foe.

The evidence for the next few years contains practically no mention of Paullus. Sometime, either in 187 or 186, he was a candidate for the consulship and lost. (42) He ran again for office in 185, and, again, he was defeated. (43) It is possible that Paullus' connections with Scipio were hindering him through these years, since the famous Scipionic trials were going on at this time; (44) but it is just as possible that other reasons contributed to Paullus' failures - there is simply no way of knowing. Nevertheless, he did finally acquire the consulship for 182, although one need not follow Scullard's supposition that many voted for Paullus because of their remorse and shame at Scipio's recent death in exile. (45) In any case, he was accorded the area of Liguria where, during 182, he had moderate success against an elusive and dangerous enemy. (46) The year 181 saw Paullus' imperium prorogued. (47) At the very beginning of the spring Paullus set out against the Ligurian Ingauni in a campaign which was to win him a triumph. Unfortunately, Livy's account of the consul's actions comes entirely from an annalistic source (48) which reads like a wild west tale: Ligurian deception had succeeded in catching Paullus unaware, and, in a hotly contested battle, the consul's troops hardly managed to save their fort. Two messengers were sent to get help, but despite great consternation and the herculean efforts of the Senate to send aid, nothing was accomplished; now Aemilius could hold out no longer and, assuming that his messengers had been killed and that no help was on the way, he inspired the troops with a stirring harangue and led them out to crush the Ligurians. Whatever the details, his victory must have been great; it was followed by a formal surrender after which Paullus razed the walls of the Ligurian cities and confiscated all Ligurian pirate vessels. (49) And rather than exterminate the Ligurians, Paullus allowed them to survive as a buffer state between Italy and Rome's hated enemies, the Gauls. (50) Paullus' return to Rome and subsequent triumph marked the high point of his career up to that time; yet after 181, down until the period of the Third Macedonian War, evidence concerning Paullus' activities is almost completely lacking. Plutarch mentions that Aemilius desired another consulship, but, that when he failed to gain it, he returned to his duties as an augur and a father. (51) And, untrustworthy or not, it is the only hint of what happened in what seems to have been a type of retirement.

Specific information on Paullus' private life, outside of conventional laudatory notes, is quite difficult to come by; there remains, nevertheless, the tradition that he conducted himself with nobility of bearing and was, above all else, philhellenic in his cultural tastes. The latter trait is unquestionably true, although one should take care not to draw unwarranted conclusions from it. Paullus' acquaintance with Greek culture is well attested; Plutarch states that while educating his sons, Aemilius filled his home with Greek tutors, from grammarians, philosophers, and rhetoricians, to artists and those men schooled in the art of hunting. (52) Such a notice by Plutarch might be suspect if there were nothing else to confirm it; but the elder Pliny substantiates the moralist's statement by noting that, during Paullus' 'tour' of Greece, he requested that the Athenians provide him with a philosopher to serve as a teacher to his children. (53) Indeed, the fact that Paullus opened his house to Polybius proves that he was not unsympathetic toward

Greek intellectuals. He also knew the Greek language, although it is interesting to observe that he considered it beneath his honor to address the Greeks in their own tongue. (54) When it came to Macedonian booty, it is most often said that Paullus was quick to take Perseus' library for himself and his sons. (55) He was also a connoisseur of Greek art. In Greece he is said to have erected statues of himself at Delphi, (56) and to have requested a victory monument from the Athenians. (57) At Rome he decorated temples and public buildings with captured art treasures. (58) While this cultural philhellenism of Aemilius cannot be seriously doubted, what is striking is the callous way he used the art and culture of Greece. His 'love' of Greek art manifested itself in the egotistical placement of his own likeness at the most sacred shrine of Hellas, and in denuding Macedon of its finery so that Roman tastes could be flattered. Moreover, the knowledge of the Greek language seems to have been more for his own edification than it was to bring him closer to what so many scholars have seen as a 'hellenic disposition' (whatever that might mean). In no way can it be imagined that Paullus' attraction to Greek culture (not at all uncommon in his day) warped his political attitudes to the point where he compromised the national interests of the Roman state. As Colin has observed, while Paullus did indeed sample the culture of Greece he was absolute in his separation of intellectual proclivities and political realities. (59)

The presence of the numerous tutors at Paullus' house also shows that he was a man of considerable means who could pay for such an establishment. This is all the more significant when it is remembered that tradition has pictured Aemilius as a man who lived and died in near-poverty. (60) Polybius, who is followed by all other writers who comment of Paullus' wealth, praises his patron on his nobility of conduct, especially in financial affairs. Polybius assures his audience that of all the money Paullus carried back from Spain and Macedon, he coveted none of it even though he could have used the treasures as he saw fit. (61) The result was that he died so poor that his sons could only repay his wife's dowry by selling a part of the estate, (62) the remainder of which came to somewhat more than sixty talents, a fortune characterized by Polybius as only moderate for a Roman. (63) This was all Polybius needed to convince himself that Paullus had directed both his private and public lives with the utmost virtue and nobility. Yet, it must be remembered that the historian's portrayal of Paullus is quite idealized; one should not be too easily persuaded by Polybius' affirmation of his patron's financial integrity and nobility of action. Perhaps Paullus' financial scruples were a result of a vivid remembrance of the Scipionic trials. It is, moreover, not at all certain that Paullus did not pocket any of the Macedonian booty except for Perseus' library. (64) He gave his son Scipio complete control over the royal hunting preserves and everything connected with them, (65) and there can be little doubt that the festival which Paullus held to celebrate the end of the war and to reward Rome's friends was paid for out of captured wealth. (66) In any case, an estate of more than sixty talents after all debts had been paid was scarcely a paltry sum, (67) and however he acquired it, Paullus should not be considered a man who lived and finally died in simple and beneficial poverty.

If anything, one can easily see Paullus as ignoble in his private life. Plutarch tells his readers that Paullus divorced his first wife, Papiria, the mother of Fabius and Scipio, because of unknown personal reasons. (68) But the moralist does not continue the story, and concludes by tritely saying that minor differences drive apart as many people as do major faults. (69) Polybius, on the other hand, relates more, although he does so only to point out and applaud the filial piety of Scipio Aemilianus for his mother, Papiria. It seems that after Paullus divorced Papiria, he neither returned to her the dowry nor gave to her any money at all. Papiria's lack of means kept her well beneath the level to which she was accustomed, even to the point where she chose not to attend religious celebrations for fear of embarrassment. (70) The wretched conditions continued for a number of years (71) until Aemilia, the wife of Africanus and sister of Paullus, died leaving Scipio a huge fortune which he promptly gave to his impoverished mother. (72) For Polybius, the act is a fine instance of Aemilianus' magnanimity; no comment is made on why Aemilius kept the mother of his famous sons in such a state. Obviously, the historian had no desire to bring attention to a part of Paullus' life which showed him in a less-than-favorable light. To be sure, Paullus clearly disliked the woman. But discovering a more compelling reason for his behavior toward her is not an easy task, and the only evidence which holds any hope of doing so is shaky at best. From the author of <u>de Viris Illustribus</u> one learns that it was Aemilius' licentiam et paupertatem that kept his estate relatively small. (73) Now, the author of this late work is not the most reliable, but the reading quoted here appears fairly certain, and it does offer an interesting explanation for both Paullus' failure to return Papiria's dowry and to support her, and for the size of his estate at his death. Merely because one cannot find a similar statement in the remains of the authors who eulogize Paullus does not preclude the possibility that the later compiler of de Viris Illustribus stumbled across it. If accepted, the note adds another flaw in the armor of the noble image constructed around Paullus' private life.

When evidence concerning Paullus finally becomes more abundant, the year is 171, and the circumstances is a quaestio repetundarum established to hear Spanish grievances against Roman maladministration. (74) In a series of trials, all revolving around the alleged extortion of money and grain from Spanish cities allied to Rome, representatives from the area complained bitterly that at least three Roman praetors had treated them worse than Rome normally treated its enemies. (75) The Spanish were permitted their choice of advocates to plead the case against the praetors; the envoys from Nearer Spain picked Cato and Scipio Nasica, and those from Farther Spain selected C. Sulpicius Gallus and Lucius Aemilius Paullus. (76) There is nothing mysterious about the choices of these men as advocates since all, except Sulpicius, had served in Spain, and the Spaniards were surely familiar with them. Scullard's explanation that the selection of these men 'demonstrates that the Spaniards regarded some of their rulers as men of principle and throws into relief the corruption of the younger generation' is no more than wishful thinking. (77) Moreover, not all the trials were brought to completion; one praetor was acquitted, and the others merely went into voluntary exile. The most telling point is the note that the Roman advocates refused to allow any more accusations against influential men of power, a suspicion heightened by the sudden exit from Rome of the praetor under whom all trials of this type were conducted. (78) Certain reforms were eventually enacted to placate Spanish complaints, (79) but that does not negate the fact that Scullard's 'men of principle' suppressed legitimate accusations. In fact, the move is not that surprising - why let the charges of mere provincials tarnish the names of respectable Romans? What is surprising is what moderns read into the motivations of Paullus and the others.

In Paullus' career thus far, one is obliged to recognize his abilities as a politician and a soldier. His victories in Spain and Liguria marked him as an outstanding commander, while at the same time giving him the glory and honor that always attended an <u>imperator</u> and triumphator, something which he must have indeed sought remembering his father's fate. He was, moreover, an ambitious man; he appears to have cultivated powerful friends, and to have dared, on their behalf, to accuse a man of consular rank of high treason and gross incompetence. It was a deed of no mean courage and daring to attack Manlius Vulso before the Senate, even in the hope of destroying an enemy. Paullus' rewards for his audacity, if any, are unknown; but his ambitions were not satiated until he attained the power and influence of the consulate. So much is obvious. Equally obvious is a harshness of character which the sources ignore as best they can. Whatever the reason for his divorce from Papiria, the reality of her impoverishment after their separation contradicts the conventional laudations which the ancients heap on Paullus' private conduct. And it lends further weight to the observation that whatever the benefits accrued from the study of Greek culture, nothing spilled over into at least this one facet of Paullus' private life.

B. POLICIES OF IMPERIUM

Still, all the preceding is but a prelude to Paullus' victory in the last great war against the successors of Alexander, a war the results of which are best seen by observing the wretched fate of King Perseus, an object lesson for those few monarchs or peoples blind enough not to have accepted the reality of Roman suzerainty. What brought on the Third Macedonian War was not, as the ancients thought, an inevitable progression of events and plans which Philip passed on to his son Perseus, nor was it the product of factional bickering at Rome and the evil desires of villainous plebeian magistrates, a theory some moderns have suggested. Both explanations are too dependent on assumption and presumption. The Roman declaration of war against Macedon, and, indeed, the conduct of most major aspects of the war and its settlement were in concert with long established lines of foreign policy. Such policies, designed to retard the power and sovereignty of Macedon while making Greece subservient to Roman will, were basic to Roman schemes throughout the 180s and 170s, and show no sign of being manipulated by any other principle than national interest. It is in this light that Roman-Macedonian relations must be examined, and it is in the same light that one must see Paullus' participation in the war, for those years find him the faithful exponent of Roman policies, not the shortsighted leader of a political faction.

The roots of the policy which guided Rome through the 170s must be sought in the years following the Treaty of Apamea. For it was during this time that the Senate, not trusting its long-time antagonist Philip V, even though he had aided in the recent war against Antiochus, sought to keep Macedon from expanding its power or borders. (80) From Rome's point of view, an independent and strong Macedon could not be tolerated; Philip was no longer a man to be feared, but he remained a man to be cautious of. Indeed, certain actions by Philip had already made the Senate wary. Philip's failure to protect the consul Manlius and his legions from Thracian bandits gave the appearance that he was, in some manner, party to the deed, and later, when the king decided to move into Thrace itself and annex two important cities there, he gave offense both to Rome's faithful ally, Eumenes, and created the impression that he was attempting to bolster Macedon's power and influence. (81) There was, furthermore, Philip's efforts at rebuilding his country economically, and, finally, a growing tension between the king and the Thessalians over disputed territory in Greece proper. (82) All this, but especially the increased interest in Thrace and Greece, gave pause to Rome. Still, the use of force was unadvisable at this point. The Romans seized on, instead, the policy of using the complaints of others to contain Macedonian power and bring Philip to heel.

During the winter of 186/85 powerful embassies journeyed to Rome to enter a long series of grievances against Philip. (83) Envoys from the Thessalians, the Perrhaebians, and Eumenes presented themselves before a Senate which was all too willing to listen. Charges were made of Philip's expansionist tendencies, the most serious of which was his take-over of the Thracian cities, and, although Macedon's own representatives countered by saying that their king had done nothing without the consent of Roman generals, the Senate was in no mood for excuses and quickly dispatched a commission to Greece in order to hear anyone who wished to speak against Philip. (84) Specifics need not concern the present discussion; it is only important to note the commission's methods and decision. Each and every case was decided against Philip, and the king was not only ordered by the commissioners to withdraw from all disputed areas, but was also compelled to confine himself within the ancient boundaries of Macedon. (85) The harshness of the Romans' order was well calculated; it suppressed any action (such as moving into Thrace) which was thought to be harmful to Eumenes, and, further, forbade any advances into Greece. The Senate soon confirmed its embassy's directive. Now, another commission was sent to keep an eye on Philip and to make sure that he obeyed Rome's decree. (86) It accomplished little more than heightening the tension between Rome and Philip; by 184 the Macedonian king appears to have been convinced that war between the two states was inevitable. (87) From Philip's stance, a policy which continually ruled against him even in the most trivial cases had only one goal, his ruin. He was hemmed in by Thrace, Greece, and the northern tribes, and was, worst of all, the subject of frequent visits by hostile Roman embassies.

A long list of Roman maneuvers against Macedon testify to a continuance of the same basic policy. Philip resisted as long as he could, but in 183 after a report from Roman legates that the king could not be trusted and that, when an opportune moment came, he would openly oppose Rome, (88) the Senate warned Philip not to give even the appearance of disobedience. (89) There was little he could do short of war. Moreover, his final years were shattered by conspiracy and treachery. (90) Rome's attempt to seduce Philip's son Demetrius to its side and then install him on Macedon's throne where he would be little more than a puppet, indicates to what lengths the Senate went to achieve its ends. (91) The effort, however, was fruitless, and ended in disaster for all concerned. (92) Philip, who had executed his own son as a traitor to family and country, was especially crushed. And, if it is true that up to his dying day Philip read his treaty with Rome twice a day, it did him little good. (93) Rome knew nothing but obedience to its will. Arguments from a position of legal obligations or treaties were of no substance when compared to the necessity of keeping Roman friends secure and Macedon contained.

In like fashion, the Achaean League suffered under a similar policy during the 180s. Achaean policies toward

Another Look

Rome had long been dominated by Philopoemen and had taken the general stance that, while Achaea would support (or at least not oppose) Rome on major issues, it reserved the absolute and legal right of independence in internal League affairs. (94) Such a policy was not realistic in the world of the 180s. Philopoemen's intransigent legalism was no threat to the Romans, but it was an inconvenience, increasingly annoying as the Achaeans snubbed Rome's directives year after year. In every instance of Roman-Achaean diplomacy which transpired, the most glaring feature was Rome's desire to keep the League weak and disunited by trying to dictate Achaean relations with Sparta and Messene. In the Spartan case, Rome supported the restoration of Spartan exiles, a position which Philopoemen (and later Lycortas) opposed, since the banished men were almost uniformly hostile to Achaea. (95) To have returned the exiles to Sparta would certainly have loosed numerous troubles on the Achaean League, an objective which the Senate must have had in mind. Each year - 185, (96) 184, (97) and 183 (98) - Roman legates visited the Achaeans, and each year the case of the Spartan exiles was the major issue of debate. And despite senatorial warnings, an open threat of force, and a blatant statement that the Senate wished for the dissolution of the Achaean League, the Romans were thwarted by Philopoemen's policies. But the dispute over Messene displayed Roman policy in special vividness. Following the Roman embassy of 183, it was announced that they would not assist the Achaeans in their effort to suppress rebellious Messenians, and that, in any case, the Senate preferred to deal with separate states more than with an organized League. (99) Polybius' comment that the Romans were 'displeased if all matters were not submitted to them and if all was not done in accordance with their decision,' (100) illuminates senatorial aims and methods in the Messenian affair, and, indeed, in Roman-Achaean relations.

Roman policy, in its basest sense, was grounded on the time-honored practise of the powerful ignoring all morality - societal and religious - and imposing its will on the humble. Polybius' narrative, while not so eloquent, has the same meaning as Thucydides' Melian Debate. (101) Neither Philip nor the Achaean League was strong enough to warrant an overt show of Roman force; yet both could cause potential trouble, Philip by his efforts to strengthen Macedon, and the Achaeans by their insistence on internal independence. Roman interests could best be served by keeping Philip contained and their friends secure, and also by accomplishing the de facto end of the League by dealing with its component parts individually. Unfortunately for the Romans, this was easier said than done. Philip could barely be cowed by Rome; and the effort to upstage him and Perseus with Demetrius ended in the worst of failures. The Achaeans, too, blocked Rome's efforts at imposing its will on them by stubborn adhesion to the policies of Philopoemen. Thus, Roman policies of the 180s, although their methods and goals were clear, were in part ineffective, since, short of force, it was extremely difficult to get the Greeks to submit. What was needed was an internal force which was loyal only to Rome - this seems to have been how the Romans perceived the solution. Their efforts in Macedon failed, but in Greece itself they were to be much more successful.

The beginning of the year 180 saw no end to the problems of Sparta (102) and Messene. (103) In response to the still raging debate over whether or not to obey Roman orders concerning the Spartan exiles, the Achaeans sent an embassy to Rome to explain the Achaean position. (104) To be found among the Achaean envoys was a certain Callicrates, an opponent of Lycortas' policies but one who appears to have given in to Lycortas in order to become a commissioner to Rome. But upon arriving at the Senate, Callicrates cast off all pretension of backing Lycortas and delivered a speech, saying that if the Romans wished their commands to be followed they should support those groups in the Greek cities which were eager to follow Rome. (105) If this were done, the combination of the power of the Greek politicians and the authority of Rome would be so strong that nothing which was ordered would go unheeded. The Senate was pleased with the advice, and from this point on began a policy of actively weakening those who opposed them and strengthening those who did their bidding. (106) Anyone who dared to appeal to legality or treaties had no chance against such pressure. Thus, the Senate praised Callicrates over all other Achaeans, and also wrote to the Aetolians, Epirotes, Athenians, Boeotians, and Acarnanians in order to strengthen friendly factions in those areas. Here were the beginnings of a policy through which Rome could control the destiny of Greece by using native Greek politicans, while at the same time remaining at a discreet distance, not becoming directly involved in petty

Another Look

factionalism.

The importance of Callicrates' speech and the Roman action that followed must not be underemphasized. One need not follow the statements of Badian and Errington that Callicrates was a farseeing statesman whose course was the only logical one. (107) Nor are the vituperative remarks of those who see Callicrates as a vile traitor to be believed. (108) Especially suspect are Gruen's recent views that seek to reject Polybius' account, and the entire significance of Callicrates. (109) Gruen finds it difficult 'to imagine any politician (i.e. Callicrates) taking so extreme a stand before a gathering of the Achaeans (where he opposed Lycortas), especially at a time when Roman interference in the internal affairs of Greece had been minimal.' (110) Yet, Gruen has not cast his nets wide enough. Instead of relying on imagination, one should note that five years earlier Diophanes of Megalopolis had also opposed Philopoemen over the same questions at a meeting of Achaeans, and in front of Metellus, the Roman legate. (111) The same arguments were employed in 185, although Diophanes' declarations carried less weight since they were heard by only one legate and not by the Senate. Serious disagreements between Achaean politicans over relations with Rome were in evidence long before 180; Callicrates was simply more successful than his predecessors. As for Roman interference in Greek affairs up to 180, the evidence, as has been presented, leaves no room for doubt - Rome's interest in dividing the Achaean League is obvious. One must, then, accept the reality of Callicrates' speech before the Senate and the new direction it gave to Roman policy. (112) Rome could now affect Achaean decisions by directing Callicrates; equally important is Polybius' note that Rome also cultivated supportive factions in other major areas of Greece. Roman policy had embarked on a course which eventually led to declaration of war against Macedon.

The history of the years following 180 is exceedingly obscure and confused; the Polybian narrative is nearly entirely lost, and Livy has large gaps in his text. (113) Nevertheless, most of the light which penetrates the darkness focuses on the activities of Philip's son and successor, Perseus, and it is this avenue which must be followed - only in this way can Roman aid to its toadies and the consequences of that policy be understood. The ascension of Perseus to the throne cannot have sat well at Rome, since the senatorial scheme to use Demetrius ended with the young prince's death. Perseus, moreover, immediately showed that he was not a passive or lax king; when, only months after Philip died in 179, Abrupolis, a Thracian prince, invaded parts of Macedon, Perseus countered by decisively defeating him and expelling him from his kingdom. (114) Later Roman tradition claimed that Perseus' act was a gross deed of aggression since Abrupolis was a 'friend and ally of Rome.' (115) Yet, the 'friendship and alliance' between Rome and Abrupolis was, at most, an invention dreamed up at a later date, since, when Perseus' ambassadors appeared before the Senate a short while afterwards to renew their treaty of friendship and to ask that Rome recognize Perseus as king, there was not the slightest hint that the senators were upset over the Abrupolis matter. (116) This is not to say that cordial relations between the two powers existed; so far Rome's allies had not been threatened, and the Senate had nothing to lose by acknowledging Perseus.

Perseus' first few years were marked by intensive efforts to re-unify Macedon internally. Harmless by themselves, the king's policies, from the Roman viewpoint, were potentially dangerous. Perseus pardoned all Macedonian exiles, debtors, and political prisoners, and invited them to return home. (117) Lists of the exiles appeared in Delos, Delphi, and the sanctuary of Itonian Athena (located in Thessaly) informing them of the royal amnesty, and, so far as one is able to tell, the new policies were successful. (118) Of greater consequence was the fact that Perseus' announcement to the Macedonian exiles was greeted with enthusiasm by a large portion of the Greek population which obviously took the king's action as a prelude to a move on their behalf. (119) It is also possible that the lists, posted in such well-known areas, had deleterious effects on locals who supported Rome; they would be hard-pressed to compete against even the dream of debt abolition. Add to this the implications of Perseus' marriage to the Seleucid princess Laodice and the marriage of his own sister to Prusias II of Bithynia, and one has the <u>intimation</u> that Macedon was courting political alliances with powers unfriendly to Rome and Eumenes. (120) The evidence does not suggest an alliance, but the totality of the picture of the young king's opening years could easily lend itself to the view that Macedon was again on the move.

By 176 embassies and complaints against Perseus began to converge on Rome. The Dardanians told of savage

Another Look

warfare with the Bastarnae, a people under the control of Perseus. (121) So desperate were the Dardanians that they also enlisted the Thessalians to speak of the dangers of the invaders. (122) And, there was even the sinister notion (clearly propagandistic and fantastic) that the Bastarnae might attack Italy. (123) Roman commissioners were sent to the area, but their report made no mention of any alleged Macedonian involvement and merely confirmed the fact that there was indeed a war between the Dardanians and Bastarnae; nonetheless, the Senate kept a wary eye on Perseus' activities and cautioned him to take especial care to observe his treaty with Rome. (124)

In 174 the situation worsened considerably, with Perseus giving every indication that his independent spirit was overextending itself. From Roman envoys in Carthage came a report that Perseus was exchanging ambassadors with that city; (125) at the same time, Perseus himself struck deep into Greece proper, crushing a revolt of the Dolopians, people whom he thought were under Macedonian rule. (126) It is hard to know whether or not the invasion of Dolopia was technically illegal; yet to the Senate (which had ordered Philip to stay within Macedon's borders), both this act and the relations with Carthage (though not in the least illegal) must have caused misgivings. And from Dolopia, Perseus and his entire army crossed over to Delphi, from there returning to Macedon through Phthiotic Achaea and Thessaly. (127) Far from wishing to conquer Greece or unite it against Rome, Perseus sought to establish a reconciliation between Macedon and the Greek states, and, in particular, the Achaean League. (128) But Perseus' dabbling in Greece caused more than he imagined; messages inspired by fear criss-crossed Greece and were sent to none other than Eumenes. (129) And since Perseus was well received by the majority of people, (130) the messages can have come from only the factions which depended on Rome for their strength - they were clearly uncertain as to whether they could hold their positions in the face of a popular Macedonian king.

They had ample reason for worry. Perseus' trek through Greece was followed by a groundswell of popular feeling for him. Moreover, one can be reasonably sure that the king attracted people from various classes. To Achaea, for example, Perseus sent word that he would restore run-away slaves in return for a re-establishment of good relations; he received considerable support from the strategos Xenarchus, his brother Archon, and, one is entitled to assume, from many others who could afford to own slaves. (131) On the other hand, much more serious problems over huge debts erupted between all classes in Aetolia, Thessaly and Perrhaebia, areas which Perseus had passed near or through. (132) In Aetolia, two factions contested in what amounted to a debt war, and although both were largely comprised of members of the upper classes, (133) there is every indication that the hopes of the oppressed, which had been ignited by Perseus, were exploited in the strife. (134) The king's appeal was also felt in Thessaly and Perrhaebia where the slightest inference of debt abolition was enough to launch stasis. (135)

Gruen, however, in a recent article, has argued that evidence for support of Perseus, especially by the lower classes, is shaky at best. (136) He seeks, furthermore, to analyze every instance where the possibility exists that Perseus received popular backing, and every case is dismissed. Gruen rightly points out that the notion that the poor of Greece supported Perseus while the wealthy looked to Rome as a benefactor during 174 and, indeed, for the entire Third Macedonian War, is a gross oversimplification of the picture; (137) Xenarchus and Archon cannot be counted among the ochlos. Yet, by dismissing every piece of evidence relating to debt problems and war between the rich and poor (such as that which tore apart Aetolia, Thessaly, and Perrhaebia), Gruen has missed the forest for the trees. (138) Even if evidence can be qualified on individual bases, one would be hard pressed to deny the totality of that same evidence. It is curious and highly suggestive that debt problems and civil strife broke out only after Perseus' tour through (or very close to) Aetolia, Thessaly, and Perrhaebia. And it is equally interesting that in both 174 and 173 Rome found it necessary, because of the unrelenting bloodshed, to send a number of embassies to those very areas to try and quiet the problems; (139) it was in their own interests to do so in order that friendly groups would not be deprived of power. Perseus, for his part, clearly did not journey to Greece for the express purpose of uniting the oppressed to his cause; that presupposes that he expected an imminent war with Rome, a notion that cannot be given serious consideration. But, given Perseus' reputation for having cancelled the debts of Macedonians, and his present eagerness to win friends and normalize relations with Greece, it is probable that the oppressed eagerly grasped at the smallest hint of relief, thereby bringing on strife and creating the impression that Perseus' machinations were behind it. Anti-Persean propaganda stood ready to exploit that belief.

Apprehension born of fear for their positions and power linked the pro-Roman factions in Greece and Asia together. From dispatches which swept between Greek cities and Pergamum during and after Perseus' tour in 174, Eumenes was bonded to these groups and was constantly aware of the situation in Greece. (140) And the nature of the messages and the position which they took against Perseus reveals the heated propaganda of the day; fortunately, an important speech by Callicrates survives which illuminates this very point. (141) The speech, delivered in opposition to the proposed reconciliation between the Achaean League and Macedon, is, as one might expect, completely anti-Persean. Its main accusations, namely that war had been planned by Philip and was inherited by Perseus, that Perseus and Philip had conspired to murder Demetrius, that the Bastarnae attack on Dardania was an example of undisguised warmongering, that the recent attack on Dolopia marked the beginning of war, and that Perseus' journey to Delphi and through Greece was calculated to pull the Greeks into the war on Macedon's side, indicate the extremes to which the pro-Roman Callicrates went to discredit Perseus. And the pre-occupation with Perseus' recent activities - i.e., the attack on Dolopia and his passage through Greece - suggests that Callicrates feared them the most. Thus, it was to his advantage to hold that they were the start of a preordained war in which Perseus, the aggressor, would employ the most underhanded means possible to use the Greeks for his own ends. (142)

The Romans themselves were equally distrustful of Perseus during 174 and 173. A series of embassies visited Macedon and Greece, the purpose of each being to judge the state of affairs from the point of view of Roman interests. Those who went to Macedon reported that Perseus was indeed preparing for war, (143) while those sent to Greece did their best to suppress the civil strife in Aetolia and other areas. (144) Roman motivations snap into crystal clarity in spite of Livy's strained effort to portray their deeds as altruistic when it is noted that Marcellus, a legate in 173, went far out of bounds by calling a meeting of the Achaeans, and then taking the occasion to deliver a strong warning to his 'captive' audience that any move whatsoever toward Macedon would be met by the strongest Roman displeasure. (145) In a not-so-subtle manner Marcellus had reproved men like Xenarchus who were friendly to Perseus, thereby further strengthening Callicrates and the pro-Romans. The connections between Rome and its supportive Greek factions were firmer than ever, and in the frantic rush of events during 174/3 Rome and its legates were careful to keep a watchful eye on Perseus and a protective attitude toward allies.

Macedon's independent course still did not pause. Sometime during 173 (or perhaps late 174) a treaty was made with the Boeotian League, yet another indication that Perseus was overly bold in his interest with Greece. (146) In addition, the king sent aid to Byzantium against invading Thracians, and this last move seems to have been the final 'provocation', (147) for almost immediately afterwards Eumenes journeyed to Rome to accuse Perseus before the Senate. (148)

Eumenes was well experienced at hurling imprecations at Macedonian kings, but this time he had help. His assistance came not in the form of others appearing at his side; rather, he made use of exactly the same propaganda as Callicrates had employed in his speech before the Achaeans two years previously. The resemblance between the main points of the two speeches, taking into account Eumenes' rhetorical enhancements, is amazing and suggests a high degree of contact between the various pro-Roman groups - indeed, Eumenes was quite familiar with Callicrates and with what had transpired in the Achaean council two years before. (149) Both stressed the inevitability of a war which had been passed from Philip to Perseus, and both took particular notice of the events of 174, implying that the troubles in Greece marked the onset of hostilities. (150) Nor were the senators themselves ignorant of the situation and its possible implications; various Roman embassies and legates were in Greece and Macedon from 175 on, and their reports tended to confirm Eumenes' dire warnings. (151) The sum total of all the reports, Roman and Eumenes', finally pushed the Senate into war against Macedon; and it was Eumenes' catalog of Perseus' misdeeds which became the standard Roman justification for war. (152)

Roman motivations behind the decision for war were twofold: first, to crush a king who had shown himself too independent and too eager to disobey directives meant to keep him from expanding Macedon; and second, to protect those Greeks loyal to Rome and compliant to her will.

Another Look

Perseus' attack on Dolopia, the struggles which arose in Greece following his passage through certain areas, his treaty with Boeotia, and, finally, the aid sent to Byzantium demonstrated the king's desire for autonomy, and the disturbing fact that he could not be cowed by Roman displeasure alone. Fear of Perseus had little to do with the reason for war; (153) Roman security was never threatened by Macedon of the 170s. What had been threatened by Perseus' audacity was the continuation of the general Roman policy, begun in the 180s, of restricting the growth of Macedon and controlling the affairs of Greece. The potential for serious difficulties could no longer be ignored, and if Rome wished to maintain its dominance, then a policy of toleration was not expedient. Action had to be taken to humble an interfering Macedon, while simultaneously securing the positions of useful lackies.

Nevertheless, various prosopographers have chosen to view the advent of war, not as a logical step taken to secure Roman foreign policy and interests, but rather as the result of political infighting between factions at Rome. (154) In the prosopographers' scheme, new political groups which came into power at the end of the 170s were more war-like and unprincipled than the older Scipionic faction, an alliance of higher repute both morally and politically. At this time, however, the Scipionic group, comprised of patricians and those who were culturally 'philhellenic', was largely out of power, and had correspondingly little influence over major policy decisions. Thus it was that the newer, glory-seeking plebeian magistrates conspired to declare war on Perseus, neglecting time-honored virtues and pursuing the struggle with unprecedented ferocity. Not until Aemilius Paullus, a patrician and leader of the Scipionic faction, was elected consul for 168 did the newer groups lose their control over policy, and only then was the war fought and brought to an end in a manner befitting antique discipline and Scipionic, philhellenic nobility. Yet for all these claims, there remain serious, if not insurmountable, problems caused by the prominence of principle in foreign policy. First of all, there is the quagmire of evidential unreliability; Livy and his annalistic sources (from whom the prosopographers draw the lion's share of their material) must be openly and vigorously questioned before anything from them is to be accepted. Add to this the gross deficiency of information with which elaborate theories of factional aims, methods, goals, and even beliefs are constructed. Secondly, and just as ominous, are the preconceptions which prosopographers have inflicted on the era of the Third Macedonian War, the premier example being Scullard's treatment which blames the entire war on the crafty and cruel plebeian magistrates, and exonerates the deeds of the patrician (i.e., good) Paullus. Third, in the prosopographerical view entire groups of people are thrown together under one convenient and seemingly unchanging label - this label classifies them, types them, and restricts their freedom of individual action or thought. T.F. Carney, in a probing reconsideration of the techniques and value of proposography, has pointed out the problems of a prosopographical approach to a faction, individual, or period of time. By using a disarmingly simple example of the difficulties encountered in the average scheme of the prosopographer, Carney has shown the pitfalls of such an approach:

> Take the simplest case, that of two persons, A and B, involved in contention. Six personae are involved, as each participant is: (i) the person he appears to be; (ii) the person he thinks he is; and (iii) the person he actually is. Moreover, the person's own interests and those of the group he represents may not be identical ... Besides, A's perception of the issue may not be at all like B's perception of A's perception of the issue. B's perception of A's perception of his - B's - perception of the issue will also be in there, further confusing things. (155)

Of course, when one seeks to understand the complexities of whole groups of individuals the problems are magnified beyond any positivistic hope of solution. And given the perplexity inherent in the Third Macedonian War period, one has every right to be wary of a technique so dependent on rigidity and on the weight of principles over national interests.

Nor should one go too far in the opposite direction. The vision of a monolithic Senate (accepted by Polybius) directing its policy and commanders with an unanimous and harmonious spirit is equally misleading. Differences, such as those previously discussed between the Popilii and the Senate on whether the Ligurian wars should receive continued attention or whether Rome's forces should be committed against Perseus, were quite real, but were hardly based on humanity or principle - it was a question of which arena held the greatest opportunity. In any case, the declaration of war against Macedon cannot properly be understood as the work of perfidious men bent on their personal aggrandizement. It was a step entirely in keeping with established foreign policy.

In the months preceding the actual start of hostilities that same policy turned to propaganda and a myriad of embassies, all of which were designed to strengthen the Roman position in Greece. Stories of an attempted murder of Eumenes by Macedonian agents at Delphi complemented Rome's justification of war and were spread throughout Greece where it was hoped that such 'impiety' would work against Perseus' popularity. (156) At the same time even wilder tales, all aimed at Perseus, surfaced; the king was actually accused by a mysterious informer of planning to poison a large portion of the Roman government! (157) And on the diplomatic scene, Roman envoys travelled to every corner of the East seeking new support, firming up existing alliances, and intimidating potential opposition. (158) Most pertinent to the present discussion was the Roman achievement of replacing the current leadership in several states with men whose loyalty to Rome was unquestioned. Aetolia, constantly a source of unrest, came under the control of Lyciscus, whose election opportunely took place while Roman envoys were in the city. (159) In the Boeotian League, where the alliance with Perseus could not be allowed to stand, the Roman legates (chief of whom was Q. Marcius Philippus) not only managed the dismemberment of the League, but also replaced its officials with reliable collaborators. (160) As for the other states, most of them already had strong factions devoted to Rome and, therefore, received no more than encouragement from the legates. (161) The specter of Roman might and a possible war permitted few Greeks to exercise the luxury of choice as to which side they would support in the coming war. (162)

Perseus was not unaware of these goings-on, but it seems clear that he did not expect them and did not know exactly how to react. On two occasions messengers were sent to the Roman legates who were seeking support among the Greek cities asking why such actions were occurring and why Roman troops were now on Greek soil. (163) The second meeting with the Romans brought results; a conference was arranged between Philippus and Perseus. (164) The outcome was less than happy for Perseus; Philippus denounced the king with the same charges which Eumenes had outlined before the Senate, while Perseus, besides denying any wrongdoing, naively based his defense on formalities and legal points. (165) He was, moreover, willing to accept a temporary truce from Philippus in the hope that an alternative to war might be found. (166) This was not to be the case; Philippus' offer of peace was nothing more than a ruse so that Rome could gain time to fortify Greece. (167) Perseus' confidence that the Senate would listen to his pleas came to nothing, for, by the time he awakened to the reality of his predicament, Roman forces were in Greece and a full scale war awaited Macedon. Despite the propaganda of Callicrates, Eumenes, Polybius, and the Romans themselves, this episode gives unmistakable proof that Perseus did not inherit and further the war plans of his father. The driving force toward war was Roman self-interest - pity was for the weak and humble, but against the strong, Rome reserved the right to wield an iron fist.

Still, expectations of victory were not easily realized. The combination of Roman incompetence in the field and Perseus' boldness and daring made a travesty, from Rome's standpoint, of the opening years of the war. Both the consuls of 171 and 170 suffered reverses at the hands of Perseus, and made little, if any, progress at containing the king or his influence. (168) Indeed, following his victories Perseus found his popularity greatly heightened among many in the Greek cities. Whether they believed the Macedonian propaganda that, if Rome won the war, authority and power over the entire world would pass into the hands of one people, (169) or whether, as Polybius holds, the passion for Macedon was an irrational desire of the crowd to cheer for the underdog, (170) the fact remained that the Roman defeats only helped the image of Perseus and caused corresponding harm to Greeks loyal to Rome. Rome's problems did not end here either; other Roman commanders during 171 and 170 carried on the war with little restraint, enslaving whole cities and cruelly destroying others. (171) The Greek reaction was outrage. Embassies from many of the affected states went so far as to take their cases to the Senate itself in the hope of redress. (172) Worse still, defections to the Macedonian side were not unknown, and in one particularly disturbing case, much of Epirus deserted Rome after coming to the realization that Perseus was the lesser of two evils. (173) Faced with losses to Perseus, shifting alliances, and wavering cities the Senate adopted a policy of placating those Greeks whose loyalty (or neutrality) had been

Another Look

undermined. (174) Although Livy and his annalistic sources have tried to portray the Senate as genuinely interested in bettering the condition of the afflicted Greeks, there is no reason to believe that the men in Rome were any more humane than those in the field; the senators simply showed themselves to be more realistic.

Concessions offered to the Greeks were, in most cases, highly effective in pacifying disgruntled states; and the Senate did, in fact, restrict the power of Roman commanders who conducted the war as they saw fit and had no regard for the rising hostility in Greek public opinion. A decree was passed forbidding Roman officers to extort supplies from Greek cities. (175) Moreover, the complaints which the Greeks presented before the Senate were all heard with a sympathetic ear, and in the cases of several cities, the Senate ordered that property taken as loot be returned along with anyone who had been sold into slavery. (176) The conciliatory moves did the job for which they were intended - one hears of no major defection of Greek states (other than part of Epirus) to Macedon. But to the Greeks' misfortune this slight modification in Roman policy was, at best, momentary; senatorial humanity, principles, and humility fell by the way with the outcome of the battle of Pydna.

Nor did the indulgence of Greek complaints overshadow Rome's policy of using whatever means possible to back supportive groups. In fact, the war brought out and intensified the bitter factionalism which raged between the different parties; and Rome was hardly a disinterested observer. Collaboration with Roman commanders guaranteed the elimination of one's political enemies. The Realpolitik of the Third Macedonian War dictated that anything less than open and enthusiastic support of Rome was the equivalent of aiding and abetting the Macedonian cause. The defeat of a consular army in 171 in which a number of Aetolians had fought was all the excuse needed by the pro-Roman Lyciscus to accuse those same Aetolians of political crimes; their fate was deportation to Rome. (177) In Epirus, the pro-Roman Charops followed a similar course by representing everything which went contrary to Roman wishes as the result of his opponents' deliberate malice. (178) Here too, the Romans had absolute faith in the word of their Quisling, and a slur from Charops could bring ruin down upon a man. Often, however, Roman ventures at building local operations were more direct. After the capture of Thisbe and Coronea, cities allied to Perseus, both the commander in the field and the Senate in Rome took steps to secure the ascendancy of friendly leaders; pro-Romans in both cities were allowed to keep their property, and in Thisbe they were given an exclusive hold on all magistracies for a ten year period. (179) And where pro-Roman factions already existed but needed aid to help maintain themselves, Rome was only too anxious to assist. G. Popillius and Gn. Octavius headed an embassy to Greece in 169, the chief purpose of which was to preserve and strengthen friends during a dark period of the war. (180) The legates did take care to avoid angering anyone to the point of switching sides to Macedon, but their aims were obvious and in Achaea, Aetolia, and Acarnania contrived rumors of prosecution or banishment quieted potential opposition. (181) Thus, despite a few examples of the Senate calming ruffled Greeks, Rome never lost sight of, nor did it abandon, its long-time plan of gaining control through the use of native operatives. From the very beginning of the war in 171 down to 169, every manner of succor was accorded compliant groups.

Yet, the war was still not going well for Rome. The consul of 169, Q. Marcius Philippus, had invaded Macedon in a daring maneuver which caught Perseus totally off guard; (182) however, Philippus was himself in an awkward situation and was forced to withdraw without facing the Macedonians. With the conduct of the war an ever-increasing source of humiliation, the Romans wisely elected two experienced generals to the consulship of 168, Lucius Aemilus Paullus and C. Licinius Crassus. (183) To the lot of Aemilius Paullus fell Macedon, (184) and, if Livy's treatment is to be given any credit, the new consul prepared for his command in a most thorough fashion, carefully considering the present state of all forces and allies so that he might know what to expect and how to pursue the war. (185) Indeed, if one may judge from the speed with which Paullus crushed Perseus, the consul's planning must have been precise and painstaking. Before most of the world knew it, Genthius (Perseus' ally) had been defeated by the praetor Anicius, and the plain of Pydna was littered with the remains of Macedonian phalanxes, cut to pieces by Paullus' conquering legions; (186) it is no wonder that Polybius viewed the scene with awe and amazement.

Militarily, the lightning victory over Macedon had restored credibility to Rome's war machine, and had added still more glory to Paullus' name. Diplomatically, that same victory signalled an end to the Senate's temporary expedient of listening to Greek complaints and promising reparation or relief. Now there was no further need for such a policy; Roman might had asserted itself and was in no mood to brook further obstruction. (187) Freed from incumbencies, Roman policy toward Macedon moved to its logical conclusion; since it had proved impossible to suppress or contain the successors of Alexander by conventional avenues, there remained one alternative, the dissolution of the monarchy and kingdom of Macedon. Rome's attitude toward the Greeks was equally harsh. Whosoever had practiced anything less than total obedience to Rome during the war found himself caught up in a purge which spread from Greece, to the islands, to Asia. Neutrality was no excuse; thousands were deported, without trial, to an uncertain captivity in Rome. And it is within this framework of a policy bent on final supremacy that one must view, and judge, the actions of Paullus.

The inevitable mopping up operations following Pydna occupied Paullus for a few days, (188) during which time he received the surrender of all Macedon and the last die-hard Macedonian allies. (189) Pursuit of Perseus, who had long since fled, came swiftly, and Paullus soon took the royal treasury at Pella, then moved to Amphipolis and struck eastward after the fallen king. (190) Perseus himself begged, through envoys, that he be treated according to his rank, but Paullus refused to acknowledge any entreaty utilizing the appellation of 'king'. (191) The situation stalled for the moment; the consul urged Perseus to entrust himself to the good-will and clemency of the Roman people, while the monarch (still calling himself 'king') had no intention of simply giving up on a pledge of faith. (192) His caution was well advised; unlike his father Philip who was allowed to retain his title and kingdom after defeat, it was now clear that Rome saw Perseus as a prize of victory. In any case, time was on the Roman side, and following several futile attempts at escape, Perseus yielded to the inevitable and was taken to the consul's tent where, if one is inclined to believe Polybius' dramatic account, he was subjected to further humiliation by furnishing Paullus with a prime example with which to instruct his junior officers on how <u>not</u> to conduct one's life. (193) With the capture of the fugitive king, the war, for all intents and purposes, was over, there being no one left to defy the consul.

The settlement imposed on the cities and men of Greece after Perseus' capture is interesting for what it reveals of Roman policy and Paullus' character. Some two months after Pydna, Paullus launched attacks on three cities, Aeginium, Agassae, and Aenea. (194) The hapless cities were charged with a number of crimes, from a failure to surrender, to the cruel treatment of Roman soldiers sent to garrison the area. (195) Yet, the very timing of the assaults, weeks after the fall of Macedon, makes any excuse feeble, since Livy's earlier narrative gives every indication that all resistance had collapsed and surrendered; (196) there is no hint that these cities were still blind to the state of affairs. Thus, one may well consider the possibility that the 'crimes' were pretexts invented to justify the acquisition of plunder by the army; (197) had the offenses actually been great enough to deserve punishment, then the matter would have been dealt with immediately after Pydna when a number of other enemy cities were reduced.

This being accomplished, Paullus now embarked on a course which was to bring to fruition Rome's desire to install its own puppets in every area of Greece and to oust those men still clinging to the antiquated ideal of independence. Taking with him a small retinue, Paullus journeyed through central Greece, into the areas of Euboea and Attica, thence into the Peloponnesus, finally returning north and ending in Aetolia. (198) The trip, although described by Livy as being purely sightseeing in nature with no political overtones, (199) was hardly innocuous. Plutarch's note that Paullus restored popular governments and laid down their constitutions is enough to demonstrate the real purpose of the consul's 'holiday' and to convict Livy of his usual distortions. (200) The newly created governments can only have been those sanctioned by and servile to Rome. Furthermore, Paullus seems to have taken the occasion to become familiar with and to support Rome's long-standing Greek allies. By Livy's own admission, pro-Romans from Achaea, Boeotia, Acarnania, and Epirus were sought out by Paullus and invited to attend the consul's festive victory celebration. (201) Nor is this all. The pro-Romans in Aetolia, Lyciscus and Tisippus, had merely to assert that the victims of their recent internal purges, hundreds of murdered and exiled men, were pro-Macedonian in order to receive the consul's benedictions. (202) This last act in particular was to usher in a veritable reign of terror against all those even remotely suspected of favoring Macedon.

Roman collaborators seized the day and obliterated opposing groups by furnishing lists of enemies to Paullus himself. Men from Aetolia, Acarnania, Epirus, and Boeotia, branded as Macedonian sympathizers, were ordered by Paullus to proceed to Rome, there to stand trial. (203) Direct Roman involvement was itself striking and blatant; officials assigned to Paullus travelled to Achaea in order to assure that their commands would not be disobeyed and to see that Callicrates and his followers would not be endangered. On the most insignificant pretext, one thousand unlucky Achaeans, including Polybius, were shipped off to exile in Rome. (204) Indeed, the witch-hunt for 'promonarchical' types was not contained within Greece; inquiries and their resulting accusations made their way through the islands and into Asia. (205) The entire city of Antissa on the island of Lesbos was razed for the crime of having lent Perseus' fleet shelter and provisions. (206) Throughout the East Rome's slightest wish was obeyed and Paullus' word was law. A letter from the Roman concerning a pro-Persean Rhodian was all that was required to bring about the man's instant extradition from sanctuary. (207) And, despite Polybius' protest that Paullus did not really approve of the orders he issued or of the actions he took, (208) the evidence clearly points to Aemilius' punctilious participation in every facet of Rome's move to heighten the positions of its friends by deporting or crushing their foes. The seemingly pointless execution, on Paullus' direction, of two important men who had sinned by allying themselves with the losing side, (209) affords still further proof, if it were needed, that Polybius' patron was a man dedicated to the ruthless Roman policy which manifested itself after Pydna. (210)

An equally harsh judgement was placed on Macedon. Simply put, neither the existence of the king nor the nation as an entity was tolerated. Senatorial tactics called for the formulation of a plan under which Macedon would never again go counter to Rome - and to carry this out, a special commission of ten was assigned to take the basic outlines of a settlement of Paullus, where they would consult with him and present Macedon with their decision. (211) Livy comments, with obvious approval, that the Senate wished only that the Macedonians gain their freedom (212) (and, indeed, Cato seems to have argued thusly), (213) but this is the same self-serving propaganda that Rome had previously used, and need not be accepted. If the Senate did not actually annex or garrison territory, it was not out of a belief in freedom; rather it was out of the sure knowledge that Macedonian unity of action was all but destroyed. (214) The actual settlement, announced by Paullus in Latin and then translated into Greek, called for the division of Macedon into four separate regions, each of which was to have self-sufficiency and self-government thrust upon it. (215) Each area would have its own separate government, money, and magistrates over which Paullus laid a new law code which replaced all but minor, local regulations. (216) More interesting still was the social and economic isolation forced on the four new 'states': Paullus decreed that the right of marriage was illegal outside of one's region; that trade in land and buildings was forbidden; that the gold and silver mines which had given Macedon its wealth were to be closed; that the importation of salt was to end; that the cutting or importation of ship-timber was forbidden; and that only those areas having troubles with barbarians were permitted armed guards. (217) Rome also assumed the collection of one-half the taxes which Macedon had paid to its king. (218) The coup de grace administered to the dismembered nation approximated the same fate suffered by thousands of Greeks; that is, all Macedonians of any consequence, whether they had been personal friends of the king or lowly military commanders, were, on penalty of death, ordered into exile in Italy. (219) Although Livy justifies the act by calling the Macedonians 'haughty tyrants' who were unfit for life under the rule of law, the Roman desire to paralyze Macedon does not escape the wary eye. Indeed, one would be hard pressed to name a more brutal piece of Roman policy up to that time; the monarchy had been destroyed, the land divided, social and trading relations ended, and a large portion of the governmental/military leaders lost to their country. Had a prophet at this time foretold of a fourth Macedonian war, he would have been laughingly dubbed insane.

A hugh celebration, to which Rome's friends from Asia and Greece had been invited, capped Paullus' victory and settlement. It was, in fact, a festival of unending pomp and pageantry the likes of which the Greco-Roman world had not seen before; entertainment was constant, as were the banquets, and a saying is supposed to have made the rounds, complimenting Paullus on being equally adept in directing a thanksgiving and in waging a war. (220) Magnificent gifts were freely handed out to those who attended; but for Rome was reserved the wealth of Macedon, a treasure of booty so great that Romans were free from taxes for over one hundred years. (221) This was loaded on the fleet for transport to Rome. Paullus preferred to cross Greece and Epirus and to embark for Italy from there. Thus, after bidding his Greek friends farewell, he and the army moved west across Greece on a journey which was to bring destruction to cities which had surrendered long before and thought themselves to be perfectly safe.

Cities in Illyria soon came under the sword of a contingent of the army commanded by Paullus' son, Quintus Maximus. (222). Officially, the attack was a punitive measure against towns which had aided Perseus in the war, but the excuse is altogether lame; almost a year had passed since Pydna during which time the praetor Anicius had both captured the Illyrian king and garrisoned several important cities in the area. (233) Unofficially, the sorties are better seen as a sop offered to the legions in place of the Macedonian gold which was kept from them. However this may be, Paullus' next move was hard even for the ancients to justify. The army was encamped at the city of Passaron, and from there Paullus sent messages to Anicius, whose camp was very near, telling him not to interfere with what was about to take place, for the Senate had decreed that the Molossian cities in Epirus which deserted to Perseus should serve as plunder for the army; Anicius, who had subdued Epirus and Molossia months before, made no move. (224) Paullus then sent envoys to the cities, promising to remove all Roman garrisons so that freedom might be had, but on the condition that each town's gold and silver be collected and piled in the square. Troops were dispatched to oversee the operation, and when all were in position, and on a specific day and hour, a systematic attack was launched against seventy cities. One hundred and fifty thousand people were sold into slavery in a maneuver so devastatingly complete that over one hundred years later Strabo could comment that the once-populated land was now a desert. (225) Those few of rank who escaped the slaver were either put to death on the spot or were shipped to Rome. (226) The feat of sacking an entire country, a stroke so ruthlessly precise and efficient, shocked even Plutarch, who exclaimed that it was contrary to Paullus' humane and generous spirit. (227) And many moderns have, in their turn, tried to exonerate Paullus from any responsibility, laying all blame and liability on the shoulders of the Senate whose orders

Paullus obeyed. (228) Yet, excuses tend to hide more than they reveal; time and energy is better spent trying to determine whether the sack of Epirus was an aberration or whether it can be understood by appealing to the outlines of Roman policy for a guide.

That at least one reason for the attack was to obtain booty for the legions is beyond question. (229) One may further suggest that Epirus was sacked as an object lesson, showing what happens to those who desert the Roman fold. (230) Similar practices were not unusual in the post-Third Macedonian War period: for a long time after the war, when the Senate believed that Rhodes' abortive efforts to bring about a peace between Rome and Perseus had been totally pro-Macedonian in nature, serious consideration was given to, as Polybius puts it, making an example of the island-state by utterly destroying it. (231) When, finally, the Senate decided not to crush Rhodes but merely to extinguish the economic and political vitality of the state, it was not out of a change of heart; as Badian has pointed out, 'war was totally unnecessary at a time when the prospective enemy was begging for his own humiliation.' (232) The 'example' in the eyes of the rest of the world could not be mistaken. But the supreme lesson, especially to the kings who remained, was the miserable Perseus who graced Paullus' triumph. In this light alone one can understand the reasons for the barbarity employed in Epirus: no one would dare turn on Rome in the future. There remains, nevertheless, a third factor influencing Roman actions, and this may be discovered in the figure of Charops, the chief pro-Roman of Epirus.

Charops is, perhaps, the most enigmatic part in the complex puzzle. (233) His family had supported Rome for years, and he himself was educated in Rome where he is said to have cultivated many useful friendships. A young man at the beginning of the war, Charops soon proved his political astuteness by traducing his opponents, on charges of being pro-Macedonian, to the Romans. Interestingly enough, the men against whom he made his accusations were Molossians; (234) and, though at first the Molossians shrugged off Charops as a harmless irritation, it soon became apparent that the Romans were quite capable of believing malicious slurs (as in the Aetolian case where Lyciscus' word condemned five men to exile) and using them as pretexts for deportation. And, not wishing to end their days in a Roman internment camp, the Molossians - Antinous, Cephalus, and

Theodotus - switched their allegiance to Perseus, carrying with them all the cities of the area. It is not pure speculation to suggest that the sack of Molossia was undertaken to benefit the political position of Charops; for, although he was powerful before this, Polybius clearly implies that after the thorn of his Molossian foes had been removed by Paullus, Charops was at liberty to do whatever he wished. (235) Political assistance of this kind (without, of course, the same wholesale destruction) was in keeping with the common policy of strengthening the pro-Roman factions. To go a step further, one must combine all three factors of Roman motivation - the need for booty, the desire to use the incident as an object lesson, and the aid to Charops - in order to explain the brutality in Epirus. Otherwise, the attack takes on the appearance of a spasm of irrational bloodletting and greed. But viewed from the standpoint of how it complements Roman policy (and remembering the senatorial decree giving the territory up to Paullus), the fate of Molossia is in keeping with the harshness shown to both friends and enemies after the war.

Responsibility for the sacking of Molossia must fall equally on the Senate and on Paullus. No weight need be given to Scullard's claim that Charops conspired with new, unprincipled plebeian senators to achieve the destruction of his remaining Molossian opponents; Scullard's leaps of unwarranted assumption show the weakness of his thesis: 'If there is any truth in the supposition that birds of a feather flock together, (Charops) would be more likely to find friends among those cruel unprincipled newcomers than among the older aristocracy with its more honourable tradition of public service.' (236) Nor is there any reason to think that the senatorial decree opening Epirus to plunder was forced on Paullus who was then compelled to follow his orders and was taken aback at the deed. (237) There is, on the contrary, every indication that the Senate was following the basic outline of Roman policy when it passed judgement on Molossia, and that no one group or faction in Rome was worse than the others. And Paullus himself never hesitated in performing the execution; his warning to Anicius to stay away, the clever ploy of promising freedom in return for gold and silver, his dispatch of troops, and the precision with which the attack was made all point to a man who knew exactly what he was doing and who agreed with it. (238) Paullus, as he had done throughout the war, continued to back senatorial policy. Moreover, amidst the ruins of seventy cities and one hundred and fifty thousand lives, there is no room for the image of Aemilius as a man of benevolence and humanity.

Paullus' homecoming from Greece, though welcomed by the populace and by the Senate, which voted him a triumph, was, however, marred by a disaffection among the troops over their share of the booty. (239) According to Livy (relying on annalistic sources), vicious, petty men opposed Paullus' triumph, and it was only the intervention of the Senate's noblest personage that turned the tide for Paullus. (240) Whatever the reality of the situation, the triumph was the most splendid ever witnessed in Rome, lasting three full days and exhibiting the wealth of Macedon and, most of all, the pathetic last king of that country. (241) Were it not for the loss of his youngest sons, one before and one just after the triumph, Paullus' victory would indeed have been complete. (242)

There remains but one note, almost an epilogue, on the war - the fate of Perseus. Paullus, it will be remembered, had refused to recognize Perseus' title of 'king' and had kept the fallen monarch under tight guard after his capture. Indeed, it appears that Aemilius failed to give Perseus any consideration as befitted his former rank; when, before the triumph, Perseus appealed to the triumphator not to be led as a spectacle in the procession, Paullus mocked the request and suggested instead that suicide would be the only way to escape the dishonor. (243) Livy states that, following the triumph, Perseus was sent to prison at Alba Fuceus, but was permitted to retain his staff and riches. (244) Yet, the Augustan historian fails to note, as Diodorus does, that the cell at Alba into which Perseus was cast was an underground room of the most loathsome nature, filled to overflowing with other prisoners, all of whom were in wretched condition. (245) A sword was thrown down to Perseus so that he might commit suicide, and, when this failed, his jailors lowered a hangman's noose into the dungeon. There he remained until, by the grace of Aemilius Paullus, he was removed and placed in better conditions. (246) This did Perseus little good; for, although Plutarch mentions that he may have starved himself to death (an unlikely act given Perseus' aversion to suicide), both the moralist and Diodorus assert that Perseus' guards took a disliking to him and kept him constantly awake through sundry vexations until he finally died from lack of sleep. (247) A truly ignoble end for a successor of Alexander the Great.

Yet this is what Paullus' achievement had wrought. His actions during 168/167 had both amazed and cowed the known world, and the disgrace and death of Perseus served notice as to how Rome would handle future troublemakers. Polybius was quite correct in his estimation of the state of affairs after Pydna, for now, Roman power - absolute and unavoidable - held dominion over every king and nation. (248) Throughout the 160s, matters in Greece remained as they had been after Paullus' settlement; that is, Rome's supportive factions continued in power, constantly receiving encouragement and backing from the Senate. (249) On the other hand, Asia now became the chief focus of attention, with Rome aiming 'at establishing a balance of power ... and making the kings and people (of that area) directly dependent upon herself.' (250) Eumenes, because of charges that he had negotiated with Perseus a plan under which, for a fee, he would withdraw from the war, or, if the price were right, actually try to arrange a peace with Rome, (251) lost favor with the Senate and suffered mightily. (252) As the power of Rome's former watchdog in Asia waned, the strength of his enemy Prusias was raised correspondingly. (253) Similarly, in Egypt the Ptolemies seemed incapable of accomplishing anything without Roman supervision or intervention. (254) Even the powerful king of Syria, Antiochus IV, was humbled and embarrassed when he was forced to leave Egypt on the threat of Roman displeasure. (255) The manipulation of eastern politics allowed the Senate a discreet distance from the inconvenience of direct rule, while at the same time seeing to it that no one had the audacity, independence, or power to defy Roman will.

Of particular interest for the present study are the affairs of Syria, for here, if anywhere, one is able to see the hand of Paullus operating in Roman policy. The death of Antiochus IV in 163 markedly changed the political scene in Syria and in Rome. At Rome the Senate was faced with two choices: should Demetrius, the son of Antiochus' brother and a hostage, be proclaimed king and allowed to return to Syria as he had requested, or should the Senate recognize Antiochus' young son as heir to the throne? (256) The second choice was opted for, chiefly because of the nine year old king's apparent weakness. (257) Taking immediate advantage of the new monarch, and on spurious pretexts, an embassy was sent to the area, the sole purpose of which was to weaken Syria's military machine; the fleet was set ablaze, the war elephants hamstrung, and, as Polybius notes, every effort was made to cripple royal power. (258) Circumstances were not, however, as under control as the Senate imagined. Anti-Roman sentiment pervaded much of Syria, and men of learning and influence felt free to criticize and mock the Romans openly. (259) Furthermore, the advisers of the young king were themselves anti-Roman; it appears certain that Lysias, one of these counselors, went so far as to mastermind the murder of a Roman legate who was involved in the destruction of Syria's fleet and elephants. (260) Indeed, Syria's unsettled condition had already become infamous among the other kings in the East, and dire warnings were made concerning the future of that country. (261) Now, in light of the escalating troubles in Syria, and especially of the murder of the Roman envoy, Demetrius again appealed to the Senate to let him return home and assume the kingship. (262) Again he failed to convince the senators. Few options remained for the young hostage. Thus, he contacted Polybius, who was his good friend, and together they plotted a daring escape from Rome. (263) The part of Polybius in the escape, a part which the historian freely admits and relishes, is a puzzling one for a political exile/prisoner to engage in; it can, in fact, only be explained by the assumption that the historian was acting on the orders of important men of power who wished to see Demetrius return to Syria and the throne. And one is obliged to suspect that Polybius' patrons (most probably Paullus himself) were those Romans who directed the escape. (264)

It has been conjectured that the escape of Demetrius set into highlight deep differences between senatorial groups over Roman policy toward the East. (265) Those who wished that Demetrius stay a hostage are seen as favoring an aggressive policy, while Paullus and the others who helped Demetrius flee are supposed to have adopted a more lenient attitude. (266) Yet, such arbitrary and definite distinctions tend only to obfuscate the positions of Demetrius and Rome. There is no denying the fact that Demetrius turned to flight only after having been rebuffed by the Senate. This does not necessarily mean, however, that factions in Rome had different goals in mind concerning the fate of Syria. Had there been major disagreements over Demetrius and Syria, the 'belligerent' senators would have pursued Demetrius' escape ship; instead, chase was not given, and the Senate calmly accepted what had taken place. (267) Rather than envisioning a dichotomy within the Senate over Roman

Another Look

foreign policy, it is, perhaps, more realistic to see this situation as little more than dissension over which government would be most compliant to Roman directives; the body of the Senate wanted to keep the child-king on the throne, while Paullus, who was quite familiar with eastern politics, saw the problems there as potentially explosive and decided that the young Antiochus and his advisers had to be ousted. As for the bold method of escape, replete with secret messages, meetings after dark, etc., this may be attributed to Polybius' taste for drama and adventure. (268) Nothing gives any hint that the goal of Roman policy had changed from its original plan designed to shatter Syrian might.

Demetrius himself suffered as much as his predecessors. The disposition of young Antiochus V, his advisers, and the anti-Romans who had been involved in the murder of the legate and in criticizing Rome was calculated to win backing from the Senate. (269) And while these acts certainly calmed the turbulance which Syria had been undergoing, the senate was scrupulously careful not to bestow favorable recognition for this on Demetrius. Rome noted that Demetrius, in fact, ruled Syria, but refused to go beyond this cursory acknowledgment; it appears that the Senate never honored him with the formal title of 'king'. (270) The official attitude held that, only when Demetrius' conduct pleased the Senate, would there be kindnesses shown in return. (271) Unfortunately for Demetrius, his conduct never entranced the senators. In the years that followed, Rome was to establish a treaty with Syria's enemy, the Jews, and to lend its approval to those who opposed Demetrius. (272) The king's usefulness, it seems, was in the suppression of Syrian elements which were hostile to Rome; after that, he was just another monarch whose power had to be curbed.

Demetrius' ultimate fate, however, hardly concerned Paullus. The conqueror of Perseus died in 160, less than two years after Demetrius had taken the Seleucid throne. (273) Paullus' last years were graced with as much honor as any Roman could hope to achieve. In 164 he was censor with Q. Marcius Philippus, and together they were remembered by Plutarch for their moderation and excellence. (274) And when, in 162, there occurred irregularities with the consular elections, Paullus was appointed to the respected position of interrex. (275) He was also, it seems, an augur throughout his adult years, right up to his death. (276) His death and funeral, if one believes the sources, brought forth an overwhelming flood of emotion from all people of all classes, and Plutarch is even willing to state that Paullus' former enemies whom he had conquered carried his bier to its resting place. (277) Indeed, the funeral games organized by his sons were extraordinarily magnificent, costing at least thirty talents (and probably more), and including two plays by Terence, a gladiatorial show, and a splendid procession. (278) It was, in all respects, a fitting send-off for a man who had made Roman dominion over the world a reality.

NOTES

1. The exact date is unknown, but Paullus was approximately sixty years old during his second consulship in 168. See Plutarch Aem. 10.2; Livy 44.41.1 (P); Diod. 30.65.
2. Plutarch Aem. 2.6.
3. Plutarch Aem. 2.5; Polyb. 31.26-1-3.
4. This information is found in his elogium, but there are no details. See the Corpus Inscriptionum Latinarum 12.1, p.194.
5. Broughton, M.R.R. I.340. 195 is the latest possible date since he was aedile in 193.
6. Livy 34.35.3-5 (A).
7. References in Broughton, M.R.R. I.347.
8. Plutarch Aem. 3.2-5. Broughton, M.R.R I.352 accepts 192 as the date of the augurate.
9. Election: Livy 35.24.6 (A). Spain: Livy 36.2.6 (A). Also Plutarch Aem. 4.1.
10. On Rome and Spain before 197, see conveniently, C.H.V. Sutherland, The Romans in Spain 217 B.C. - A.D. 117 (New York: Barnes and Noble, 1971 reprint of 1939 ed.), pp.45-63; and Badian, F.C., pp.116-20.
11. For the division into provinces, see Livy 32.27.6-7 (A); and 32.28.2 and 11 (A). The beginnings of the revolt, see Livy 33.21.7-9 (A). Tiberius Gracchus finally ended the revolt in 179/8; cf. Badian, F.C., p.119 n.5.
12. Exploitation: Livy 32.7.4 (A); 33.27.1 (A). New praetors: Livy 32.27.6 (A); 32.28.11 (A). Also see Broughton, M.R.R. I.333.
13. Broughton, M.R.R. I.339.
14. Broughton, M.R.R. I.353; Plutarch Aem. 4.1. Plutarch claims that Paullus was never defeated in Spain,

and that he won two great victories. Yet, Livy 37.46.7-8 (A) admits Paullus' defeat. Suspicion must fall on Plutarch's idealized version.

15. On the victory, see Livy 37.57.5-6 (A). Paullus is sometimes thought to have celebrated a triumph for this, but the notices are quite late and just as false - see Broughton, M.R.R. I.362.

16. Corpus Inscriptionum Latinarum II.5041. Also E.H. Warmington, Remains of Old Latin, Vol. IV ('The Loeb Classical Library'; Cambridge, Mass.: Harvard University Press, 1959), 254.

17. Theodor Mommsen, 'Bemerkungen zum Decret des L. Aemilius Paulus,' Gesammalte Schriften IV, pp.52-62, esp. p.57.

18. Livy 32.21.7-9 (A); cf. 28.13.3 (A).

19. Badian, F.C., p.122.

20. Polyb. 21.11.7.

21. Cf. Badian, F.C., p.122; and Sutherland, Romans in Spain, p.74.

22. Sutherland, Romans in Spain, p.74.

23. In 186 Hasta was finally taken - Livy 39.21.1-4 (A).

24. For an overview of the entire situation, see Maurice Holleaux, 'Rome and Antiochus,' in The Cambridge Ancient History, Vol. 8 (Cambridge: The University Press, 1954), pp.199-240. And, E. Badian, 'Rome and Antiochus the Great. A Study in Cold War' Classical Philology 54 (1959), 81-99.

25. Such is the view of, J.W. Swain, 'The Theory of the Four Monarchies. Opposition History Under the Roman Empire,' Classical Philology 35 (1940), 1-21, esp.2-3, and 3, n.5. Swain's argument depends heavily on Velleius' citation (1.6.6) of Aemilius Sura's comments on the progression of empires. This is accepted by Oost, Roman Policy, pp.66-7, and pp.128-29, n.175.

26. On the political divisiveness and struggles, based not on any regard for the conduct of foreign policy, but on a simple desire for power, see Scullard, Roman Politics, pp.133-45.

27. References in, Broughton, M.R.R. I.362-64, and n.5.

28. Ibid., I.364, n.5.

29. Scullard, Roman Politics, p.137, and n.1.

30. The evidence comes from Livy's coverage of the Scipionic trials and is therefore somewhat suspect - Livy

38.58.11-12 (A).
31. For the charges and the speech, see Livy 38.45-46 (A).
32. See Nissen, Untersuchungen, p.212, for a statement on Livy's source and its value. Valerius was also the source for Manlius' defense, Livy 38.47-50 (A).
33. The Senate had foreseen the probability of war with the Gauls. See Livy 37.8.4; 37.18.7; 37.38.3; 37.40.10; 37.40.13; 37.51.10; and Manlius' own defense, 38.48.9. All references from annalistic sources.
34. Nissen, Untersuchungen, p.212, severely questions the validity of the charges against Manlius.
35. See Walbank, J.R.S. 31, 87-89. Also, 88-89, n.50, where Walbank accepts the accusations against Manlius.
36. The only indictment of which Manlius was afraid was a possible one based on a charge of introducing eastern luxury and vice into Rome; on this and his triumph, see Livy 39.6.3-7.5 (A).
37. Livy 38.45.5 (A).
38. See Cicero, In Pisonem 50.
39. Nissen, Untersuchungen, p.212.
40. On the situation, see F.W. Walbank, Philip V of Macedon (Hamden, Conn.: Archon Books, 1967 reprint of 1940 ed.), pp.217-17.
41. Livy 38.40-41 (P); and Appian, Syr. 43.
42. Livy 39.32.6 (A).
43. Livy 39.32.6 (A).
44. Scullard, Roman Politics, Appendix IV, pp.290-303, for the trials.
45. Ibid., p.170.
46. Livy 40.16.4 (A); 40.17.6-7 (A). Plutarch Aem. 6.1-3.
47. Broughton, M.R.R I.384.
48. Nissen, Untersuchungen, p.235, chiefly on Livy 40.25-28.
49. Plutarch Aem. 6.4-7.
50. Plutarch Aem. 6.5.
51. Plutarch Aem. 6.8.
52. Plutarch Aem. 6.9-10.
53. Pliny Natural History 35.135.
54. Livy 45.29.3 (P); cf. 45.8.6 (P).
55. Plutarch Aem. 28.11. But see Niese, Geschichte, III.186.
56. Livy 45.27.7 (P); Polyb. 30.10.2.
57. Pliny Natural History 35.135.

58. Cicero Orat. 232.
59. Colin, Rome et la Grece, p.444, n.3.
60. Polyb. 18.35.6.
61. Polyb. 18.35.4-5; 31.22.3-4.
62. Polyb. 18.35.6; 31.22.3.
63. Polyb. 31.28.3.
64. As Plutarch Aem. 28.11 intimates. Niese's comments, Geschichte, III.186, are well worth quoting: 'nur aus der Bibliothek des Perseus liess er seine Söhne auswählen.'
65. Polyb. 31.29.3-5.
66. Livy 45.32.8-33.7. (P).
67. There exists, so far as I know, no other direct reference to another contemporary Roman's fortune with which one could compare Paullus' wealth. The richest Greek of the time, Alexander the Isian, was worth over 200 talents - Polyb. 21.26.9 and 14. Within Rome, however, money seems to have been more abundant; Scipio Africanus Maior allowed each of his daughters a dowery of 50 talents (Polyb. 31.27.1-2); Scipio Aemilianus had enough of a fortune to give the entire inheritance from Paullus (all 60 talents) to his poorer brother Fabius (Polyb. 31.28.3); the funeral games for Paullus (probably) came to around 30 talents (Polyb. 31.28.6).
68. Plutarch Aem. 5.1-2.
69. Plutarch Aem. 5.3-4.
70. Polyb. 31.26.6-7.
71. Polyb. 31.26.6.
72. Polyb. 31.26.1-5.
73. For the short notice of Paullus' life, see de Viris Illustribus 56; esp. 56.6. In the Teubner text, the editor reads continentiam et paupertatem, and the Teubner reading sheds a completely different light on the meaning, thus conforming to what most writers say about Paullus. But, as a recent editor, W.K. Sherwin, De Viris Illustribus (Norman: University of Oklahoma Press, 1973), pp.ix-xvi, has shown, the manuscripts followed by the Teubner - Mss o and p - are highly emended products of the fifteenth century. On the other hand, a majority of the older Mss give the reading as licentiam.
74. Livy 43.2.1-12 (A).
75. Livy 43.2.2 (A).
76. Livy 43.2.4 and 7 (A).
77. Scullard, Roman Politics, p.201.
78. Livy 43.2.11 (A).

79. Livy 43.2.12 (A).
80. For these years in general, see Walbank, Philip V, pp.224-57; and Badian, F.C., pp.92-3.
81. See the earlier discussion of the attack on Manlius. The cities in Thrace were Aenus and Maronea: Polyb. 22.6.7; Livy 39.27.7-10 (P).
82. Economy: Livy 39.24.1-4 (P). Thessaly: Walbank, Philip V, pp.225-6.
83. Livy 39.24.6-12 (P).
84. Aenus and Maronea: Polyb. 22.6; Livy 39.24.7 (P). Consent of Roman generals: Livy 39.24.10 (P). Commission: Polyb. 22.6.5-6; Livy 39.24.13-14 (P).
85. Livy 39.25-26 (P); esp. 39.26.14 (P). Walbank, Philip V, p.233f.
86. Livy 39.33.3-4 (A); Polyb. 22.11.1-4. Also Broughton, M.R.R I.376-77.
87. Polyb. 22.14.7-8. See Walbank, J.H.S. 58, 65.
88. Polyb. 23.9.4-6. Broughton, M.R.R. I.379.
89. Polyb. 23.9.7.
90. For an overview of Philip's last years, see Walbank, Philip V, pp.242-57.
91. Polyb. 23.3.4-10, and 23.7. See Polyb. 23.1-2 on the embassies against Philip and on Demetrius' visit to Rome. Also, Walbank, J.H.S. 58; and Edson, H.S.C.P. 46.
92. For Livy's grand drama, see 40.5-16.3 (P), and 40.20.5-24.8 (P).
93. Livy 44.16.5 (A).
94. In general, see R.M. Errington, Philopoemen (Oxford: The Clarendon Press, 1969), pp.221-26. Also Polyb. 24.11-13 on Philopoemen's policies and the opposition to them by Aristaenus.
95. There were four groups of exiles: Polyb.23.4; Livy 39.35.5-8 (P). Also Livy 39.48.2-4 (P).
96. Q. Caecilius Metellus visited Achaea in 185 and severely chided League officials about their treatment of the Spartans. He was joined in his criticism by Diophanes of Megalopolis, an oppoent of Philopoemen. Diophanes disapproved of current Achaean policy and also suggested that Metellus look into the problems at Messene. But, blocked by Philopoemen, Metellus called for an assembly of the people - an illegal move - and when this too was denied on legal grounds, Metellus left in a fury. See Polyb. 22.10; Broughton, M.R.R. I.373; Errington, Philopoemen, pp.166-69. The Senate later backed Metellus' actions and cautioned the Achaeans to pay more respect to Roman envoys: Polyb.

22.12.5-10; Broughton, M.R.R. I.377.

97. Appius Claudius Pulcher was the legate in 184. Claudius stated his position that the Senate was unhappy over the treatment of the Spartans, and was answered by Lycortas who followed Philopoemen's legalistic policies. Appius replied from a position of strength - if the Achaeans did not come to terms of their own free will, they would soon be forced to do so. The meaning was obvious, as the Achaeans recognized. Livy 39.35.5-37.21 (P); J.A.O. Larsen, 'Was Greece Free Between 196 and 146 B.C.?' Classical Philology 30 (1935), 193-213; Errington, Philopoemen, pp.177-79; Pausanius 7.9.3-5.

98. Q. Marcius Philippus was the legate in 183. Again the Spartan problem was the major issue, but now Messene gained prominence as a trouble spot. Philippus' report to the Senate (Polyb. 23.9.8-14) demonstrates that Rome desired the dismemberment of the Achaean League. On the expendiency of Roman policy, see Polyb. 23.17.3-4. Also, Errington, Philopoemen, pp.185-7; Briscoe, J.R.S 54, 66-7; Livy 40.2.6-3.7 (P).

99. Polyb. 23.9.12-14; 23.17.2-4.

100. Polyb. 23.17.3-4.

101. Thucydides 5.85-111.

102. Sparta was taken into the Achaean League in 182, but the exiles were not restored. Thus, the main problem remained active. Polyb. 23.17.5-18.5.

103. Messene was recaptured in 182 by Lycortas who, by his generosity (so Polyb. 23.17.1), brought it back into the League - Polyb. 23.16.1-17.1.

104. Polyb. 24.8.1-8.

105. Polyb. 24.8.9-9.15. Callicrates specifically cites the Spartan and Messenian problems as examples.

106. Polyb. 24.10.4.

107. Badian, F.C., pp.89-90; Errington, Philopoemen, pp.202-5.

108. E.g., Niese, Geschichte, III.59-61; Stier, Roms Aufstieg, pp.179-84; Oost, Roman Policy, pp.68-69.

109. Gruen, A.J.A.H. 1, 32-33, and notes.

110. Ibid., 32.

111. Polyb. 22.10.4-7.

112. Such is the basic conclusion of A. Passerini, 'Studi di storia ellenistica-romana, VI, I moti politico-sociali della Grecia e i Romani,' Athenaeum 11 (1933), chiefly 324-35.

113. For the most complete account of these years, see Meloni, Perseo, pp.61-161; also E. Bickerman, 'Notes sur

Polybe, III: Initia belli Macedonici,' Revue des Études Grecques 61 (1953), 479-506; and, A. Giovannini, 'Les Origines de la troisième guerre de Macédoine,' Bulletin de Correspondence Hellénique 93 (1969), 853-61. The standard works usually provide as good an outline as the evidence permits. Also note the discussion by Pedech, Methode de Polybe, pp.134-37, where the evidence and especially Polybius' treatment of it is considered.

114. Polyb. 22.18.2-3; see note 115.
115. Eumenes, in Livy 42.13.5. (P), and Philippus, in Livy 42.40.5 (P) both call Abrupolis a 'socius et amicus' of the Roman people. See Livy 42.41.10-12 (P) for Perseus' defense.
116. See Livy 40.58.8 (P); and esp. Appian Mac. 11.6 where the Senate accepts Perseus' explanation.
117. Polyb. 25.3.1-4.
118. Polyb. 25.3.2-4.
119. Polyb. 25.3.3-4.
120. Perseus' marriage: Polyb. 25.4.8; Livy 42.12.3-4 (P). Marriage of Perseus' sister: Livy 42.12.3-4 (P). See Meloni, Perseo, pp.119-24, on the marriages, and Perseus' relations with the East in general.
121. Polyb. 25.6.2-6; Livy 41.19.4 (P).
122. The Thessalians were certainly trying to remove Perseus' influence from their lands - Polyb. 25.6.4.
123. Livy 40.57.6-7 (P). The original plan was said to be Philip's.
124. Livy 41.19.4-6 (P). See also Broughton, M.R.R. I.403.
125. Livy 41.22.2-4 (P). Meloni, Perseo, pp.127-29.
126. Livy 41.22.4 (P); Polyb. 22.18.2.
127. Livy 41.22.5-6 (P).
128. Livy 41.22.7-8 (P).
129. Livy 41.22.5 (P).
130. Livy 42.5.2 (P).
131. Livy 41.23.4, and 24.1 (P).
132. Livy 42.5.7. (P).
133. Livy 41.25.1-7 (P).
134. Livy 42.12.7; 42.40.7 (P).
135. Livy 42.5.7-10 (P); 42.13.9 (P); Diod. 29.33.
136. The entire article is concerned with this question; Gruen, A.J.A.H. 1.
137. See, e.g., Ibid., 46-48.
138. Ibid., 35-39 for Aetolia, and 39-40 for Thessaly.
139. References in Broughton, M.R.R. I.405 for 174;

and M.R.R. I.409 for 173.

140. Dispatches: Livy 41.22.5 (P). Eumenes knew Callicrates: Livy 42.12.6 (P).

141. Livy 41.23.6-18 (P). Cf. Errington, Philopoemen, pp.207-8; and Walbank, J.H.S. 58, 65-66, n.51. One has to wonder, especially noting Callicrates' point that Philip conceived of the war which was carried out by Perseus, how much Polybius himself was affected by the propaganda espoused by his hated enemy.

142. In opposition to Callicrates, Archon spoke on behalf of re-establishing friendly relations. He based his argument (Livy 41.24.1-18 (P)) on a desire for neutrality while also saying that careful consideration should be given to Perseus' request. Archon backed this last point by appealing to the authority of the vetusta coniunctio between the Achaeans and Macedon. It appears to be a rather unrealistic attitude given the situation in 174; yet the Achaeans were habitual in their resurrection of ancient arguments to defend present-day policies; see Walbank, Ancient Macedonia, pp.296-99.

143. See Broughton, M.R.R. I.405, and 409.

144. Ibid.

145. Livy 42.6.1-3 (P).

146. Livy 42.12.5-6 (P); 42.38.5 (P); 42.40.6 (P); 42.42.4 (P). Polyb. 27.1.8 and 11. Also Gruen, A.J.A.H. 1, 43-44; and Will, Histoire, II.221-22.

147. Livy 42.13.8 (P). Meloni, Perseo, pp.145-49, including the treaty with the Boeotian League; Pedech, Methode de Polybe, p.135.

148. For his speech and the charges against Perseus, see Livy 42.11.4-13.12 (P). Also Nissen, Untersuchungen, p.245; and Appian Mac. 11.1-2, for a shortened version of the speech.

149. Livy 42.12.6 (P).

150. Livy 42.11.4-9 (P): Idea of inherited war. Livy 42.12.7 (P); 42.13.4 (P); 42.13.8-10 (P); 174. Cf. Giovannini, B.C.H. 93, 859-61.

151. Broughton, M.R.R. I.403; 405; 409; 412-13, provides a convenient list of the embassies and legates. Cf. Appian Mac. 11.1.

152. Compare the Roman declaration of war, Livy 42.30. 10-11 (A), with Eumenes' charges, Livy 42.11.4-13.12 (P), and the speech of Philippus to Perseus, Livy 42.40 (P). But see especially the inscription detailing Perseus' 'crimes' which was set up at Delphi - W. Dittenberger, Sylloge

Inscriptionem Graecarum 3rd. (Leipzig, 1915-1924), n.643. This duplicates the standard charges found in other sources.

153. Fear of Perseus is considered a primary cause of the war by Bickerman, R.E.G. 66, 479-506. Cf. Will, Histoire, II.227; and Leo Raditsa, 'Bella Macedonica,' Aufsteig und Niedergang der Römischen Welt, Vol. I (Berlin: Walter de Gruyter, 1972), p.578.

154. I feel it unnecessary to provide a detailed treatment of the various prosopographical arguments and the subtle differences between them. In general, Münzer, Römische Adelsparteien, pp.199-223, views the 170s as beginning with a dominant Fulvian group; toward the end of the decade the Postumii gained considerable strength. Against them stood the Scipionic faction which included Paullus and other men of distinguished background. Scullard, Roman Politics, pp.177-206, accepts the same basic pattern regarding the different groups. But he makes much more of a point that the chief magistrates of the late 170s were violent, glory-seeking plebeians who stood against the noble, moral, lenient, and patrician (i.e., good) Scipionic faction. Briscoe, J.R.S. 54, 73-77, modifies the picture slightly; he sees no plebeian-patrician conflict, and also views the Fulvians as the major power group of the late 170s. Against them he still places the Scipionic coalition. For a discussion of the evidence, see my earlier chapter on Livy's treatment of these years.

155. T.F. Carney, 'Prosopography: Payoffs and Pitfalls,' Phoenix 27 (1973), 171. One should read the entire article to appreciate the impact of Carney's criticism.

156. On the attempted murder, which, in reality, was most probably merely an accident, see Livy 42.15.3-16.9 (P). One wonders if it was not Attalus who was behind the accident; cf. Livy 42.16.8-9 (P). For the use of this event as propaganda, see Livy 44.1.10 (P), and 45.5.5 (P).

157. Livy 42.17.1-9 (P).

158. References in Broughton, M.R.R. I.412-13.

159. Livy 42.38.2 (P). Gruen, A.J.A.H. 1, 37, denies that the Romans had a hand in the election, but the opposite seems clear to me. Cf. Meloni, Perseo, p.184.

160. Polyb. 27.1.1-2.10. Livy 42.43.4-44.6. (P); esp. 42.44.6.

161. Cities of the Peloponnese: Livy 42.37.7-9 (P). Epirus: Livy 42.38.1 (P). Acarnania: Livy 42.38.3-4 (P). Thessaly: Livy 42.38.6-7 (P). Achaea: Livy 42.44.7-8 (P). Rhodes: Livy 42.45.1-7 (P); Polyb. 27.3.1-5.

162. Cf. Appian Mac. 11.4.
163. Livy 42.37.5 (P); 42.38.8 (P).
164. Livy 42.39-42 (P).
165. See Meloni, Perseo, pp.445-46; Will, Histoire, II.227. Cf. Appian Mac. 11.5-8, for another version of Perseus' defense, this one taking place before the Senate at Rome. Perseus was so diligent in his observance of the treaty that when envoys from allied cities (Coronea, Thisbe, and Haliartus) begged that he send aid to them, the king refused on account of the truce; Polyb. 27.5.8.
166. Livy 42.43.1-2 (P). On the reaction of some senators to the truce and the 'new wisdom' it represented, see Livy 42.47.1-9 (P).
167. Livy 42.43.3 (P); 42.52.8 (P). Walbank, J.R.S. 31, 91-93.
168. References in Broughton, M.R.R. I.416; 419-20.
169. Livy 42.46.4 (P); Polyb. 27.4.7.
170. Polyb. 27.9-10; Livy 42.63.1-2 (P).
171. References in Broughton, M.R.R. I.416; 420.
172. On embassies and complaints from Greece, see Livy 43.4.8-13 (A) for Abdera; 43.5 (A) for envoys of Cincibilus, king of the Gauls; 43.6.1-3 (A) for Athens; and 43.7.5-11 for Micythion, the envoy from Chalcis.
173. The case is that of Cephalus who, on account of fear of the pro-Roman Charops and because of the Roman treatment of other Greeks, led Molottis (during or after 170) into Perseus' camp; see Polyb. 27.15; 30.7.2.
174. The senatorial reaction to the embassies listed in note 172 was uniform in its desire to calm ruffled feelings. For an interesting comment on this policy, see Diod. 30.8.
175. Polyb. 28.13; Livy 43.17.2-3 (P). The amount of supplies demanded from the Athenians, Livy 43.6.2-3 (A), was probably not unusual.
176. Cf. the cases of Abdera (Livy 43.4.5-13 (A)), and Chalcis (Livy 43.7.5-11 (A)). But see note 179.
177. Polyb. 27.15.4; Livy 42.60.8-10 (P) leaves out mention of Lyciscus and the political charges. See also Appian Mac. 12.
178. Polyb. 27.15.6-13.
179. Most of the evidence comes from inscriptions. See Sherk, Documents, n.2, for the decree of the Senate clearly favoring the pro-Roman faction at Thisbe. Yet, this decree seems to have been a mere confirmation of what Lucretius, the praetor (171) who took Thisbe, had already done; Livy 42.63.12 (P), but note that Livy has 'Thebes'

instead of 'Thisbe'. The fate of the pro-Macedonians was extinction. At Coronea (Documents, n.3) there appears the same basic decree, but no mention is made of a monopoly on offices; however, the inscription is quite fragmentary. There is a curious passage relating to Coronea in Livy 43.4.11 (A); Q. Maenius, the praetor who issued the decree on Thisbe (Broughton, M.R.R. I.420), is said to have also issued the one for Coronea. But the interesting part is that the city of Abdera is said to have received the same decree that Coronea did. If true, Roman efforts at building new, friendly factions were even more widespread, and we need not believe that the Senate was being noble in helping Abdera - still another example of annalistic/Livian distortion.

180. References in Broughton, M.R.R. I.426.

181. Polyb. 28.3-5. Livy's version, 43.17.2-9 (P), is heavily censored.

182. Livy 44.5 (P); confused and dramatic.

183. Broughton, M.R.R I.427. On Crassus' military record, see Livy 45.58.12 (P).

184. Plutarch Aem. 10.3, and Paullus' elogium both hold that he was elected to the position of general for the Macedonian War; but such an action would have been highly irregular, if not illegal, and is probably a later invention. See Livy 44.17.10 (A).

185. In general, Livy 44, 18-21 (A). One must beware of the stock dramatic devices in these sections, e.g. the drama of a delay, 44.19.1-5 (A). Concerning Paullus' speech to the people before leaving for Greece (Livy 44.22 (P) with moralistic touches; Polyb. 29.1; Plutarch Aem. 10) censuring those who openly criticized the conduct of the war, Meloni, Perseo, p.320 doubts its authenticity. But, if it did occur, I suggest that it was not directed at the mass of people, but at those senators who preferred a less aggressive course because of Greek protests - Paullus thus declared that he would carry the war to its most immediate conclusion by any means he saw fit.

186. References in Broughton, M.R.R. I.427-28. Cf. Will, Histoire, II.234-35; Meloni, Perseo, pp.319-26, 349-54, 359-409. Also E. Meyer, 'Die Schlacht bei Pydna,' Kleine Schriften, Vol. 2 (Halle, 1924), pp.463-94. On the chronology of 168, see S. Oost, 'The Roman Calendar in the Year of Pydna (168 B.C.),' Classical Philology 48 (1953), 217-30; and Meloni, Perseo, pp.466-68. Pydna took place on June 22, 168 (Julian calendar).

187. For a general overview of the policy, see Badian,

F.C., pp.96-115; Errington, Dawn of Empire, p.221; and the various standard works.

188. Livy 44.45.1-7 (P); 44.46. (P).
189. Livy 44.45.5 (P); 44.46.1-3 (P).
190. Livy 44.46.4-11 (P); cf. 45.4.2 (P).
191. Livy 45.4.2-7 (P).
192. Livy 45.4.6-7 (P).
193. Livy 45.5-9.1 (P); Polyb. 29.20; Diod. 30.23; Plutarch Aem. 26-27.
194. Livy 45.27.1 (P).
195. Livy 45.27.1-4 (P). For the earlier alliances and activities of these cities, see Livy 44.46.4 (P) on Aeginium; 44.7.5 (P) on Agassae; 44.10.7 (P) and 44.32.8 (P) on Aenia.
196. Livy gives no indication that any cities or areas did not surrender: Livy 44.45.5-8 (P); Beroea, Thessalonica, Pella, Macedon, Pydna; Livy 44.46.9 (P): Thessaly; Livy 44.46.1-3 (P): Aeginium, Amphipolis, Sintica; Livy 45.4.2 (P): Sirae in the Odomantian territory.
197. A point also made by A.C. Schlesinger, the Loeb editor of Livy, vol. 13, pp.338-39, n.1, but his chronology is inaccurate.
198. Chiefly Livy 45.27.5-28.6 (P); also Polyb. 30.10.
199. Livy 45.28.6 (P).
200. Plutarch Aem. 28.2.
201. Livy 45.32.8 (P); Polyb. 30.13.3-4 names the Roman puppets: Achaea: Callicrates, Aristodamus, Agesias, Philippus. Boeotia: Mnasippus. Acarnania: Chremas (and perhaps Aeschrion and Glaucus), Polyb. 28.5.1. Epirus: Charops, Nicias. Aetolia: Lyciscus, Tisippus.
202. Livy 45.28.6-8 (P) reports the massacre, etc., but disassociates Paullus from the deeds. The consul, it seems, was angry that Roman troops had taken part in the killings. It appears that where there existed a strong pro-Roman faction in a particular city, Rome acted as an overseer, preferring to have all dirty work done by the Greeks themselves. Concerning the Aetolian massacre, Paullus, at a later date, clearly supported the acts of the pro-Romans - Livy 45.31.1-2 (P).
203. Livy 45.31.9 (P). Also cf. Polyb. 32.5.6, but the text here is difficult. The passage concerns the deportation of notables to Rome, and by whose orders this was done. The MSS reading is anikion kai. Hultsch brackets the kai and leaves the name anikion. But Büttner-Wobst retains the kai and inserts the name, Leukion Aimilion. B-W cites Livy 45.34 (P); Polyb. 30.15; and Plutarch Aem. 29 as support for

his collation. Thus, the text now reads that both Anicius the praetor <u>and</u> Paullus put notables to death and shipped others to Rome. The collation is entirely warranted, especially given Paullus' ruthless acts in other areas of Greece, and should stand. One may also note that, apparently under Paullus' guidance, the Acarnanian League was deprived of the city of Leucas, an important coastal town - Livy 45.31.12 (P).

204. Livy 45.31.9-11 (P); Polyb. 30.13.6-11; Pausanias 7.10.

205. Livy 45.31.13-15 (P).

206. Livy 45.31.14 (P). On the Fabius (Labeo ?) who carried out the attack, see Broughton, <u>M.R.R.</u> I.435, and 436, n.3.

207. Polyb. 30.9.18, and the entire episode of the capture of Polyaratus. One may note with interest that, at least, in this case, the aims of G. Popilius, the plebeian consul of 172, and Paullus, the patrician general, were identical - both carried out senatorial policies.

208. Polyb. 30.13.11.

209. Livy 45.31.15 (P). From Polybius' point of view anyone foolish enough to choose the losing side should pay for the error with his life; see Polybius' extended defense of himself, and the condemnation of the pro-Macedonians, 30.6-9; also the inevitable Polybian moralizing, 30.9.20-21.

210. Hints that such a policy was in the making during the war can be seen in the deportation of five Aetolians to Rome after Lyciscus' accusation, the actions of Charops which drove Cephalus to Perseus, and the embassy of Popilius and Octavius to Greece in 169. The policy was not, therefore, suddenly conceived at the war's end, but was already in practice - to a limited extent - by 171.

211. Livy 45.17-18 (A); 45.29.3 (P).

212. Livy 45.18.1-2 (A); 45.29.4 (P).

213. Cato argued that Macedon must be set free since Rome could not guard her; see H. Malcovati, <u>Oratorum Romanorum Fragmenta</u> 2nd. ed. (Italy, 1955), Cato, frg. 161.

214. Rome did not count on the 'false Philip' who fell from the skies; Polyb. 36.10.1-2.

215. Livy 45.29.1-9 (P); Diod. 31.8.4-9. Significantly, and unmentioned by Livy, Diod. 31.8.6 notes that the Romans also destroyed the walls of Demetrias, one of the 'fetters of Greece'. Also, see A. Aymard, 'L'Organisation de la Macédoine en 167,' <u>Classical Philology</u> 45 (1950), 96-107; J.A.O. Larsen, 'Consilium in Livy XLV.18.6-7 and the

Macedonian Synedria,' Classical Philology 44 (1949),73-90.
  216. Livy 45.29.10 (P); 45.31.1 (P); 45.32.1-2, and 7 (P). Also Justin-Trogus 33.2.7. But cf. Livy 45.29.4.
  217. Livy 45.29.4-14 (P).
  218. Livy 45.29.4, and 11 (P).
  219. Livy 45.32.1-6 (P).
  220. So great was Paullus' celebration that Antiochus IV felt obligated to try and out-do it; see Polyb. 30.25-26. For Paullus' festival, see Livy 45.32.8-33.7 (P); Plutarch Aem. 28.7-12; Polyb. 30.14. To delight his guests, Paullus threw a number of unfortunates to the beasts; Valerius Maximus 2.7.13; Livy Per. LI.
  221. Gifts: Livy 45.33.4 (P). Booty: Livy 45.33.5-7 (P).
  222. Livy 45.33.8 (P).
  223. See Oost, C.P. 49, 83, for the date of the attack. See Livy 45.26.1-2 (P) for Anicius.
  224. Livy 45.34. I (P). The attack is clearly described in Livy 45.34.1-6 (P); Plutarch Aem. 29; Poly. 30.15. On Amicius' conquest of Epirus, see Livy 45.26.3-11 (P).
  225. Strabo 7.327.
  226. Polyb. 32.5.6. See note 203.
  227. Plutarch Aem. 30.1.
  228. Chiefly Scullard, Roman Politics, p.213; and Scullard, J.R.S. 35, 59; also many of the works already discussed.
  229. This is clear from Livy and the senatorial order which he paraphrases; Livy 45.34.1 (P); also Plutarch Aem 29.1.
  230. See note 194 in the chapter on Polybius.
  231. Polyb. 29.19.5; Livy 45.3.3-8 (P). The standard histories give the details of the situation. See also E.S. Gruen, 'Rome and Rhodes in the Second Century B.C.: A Historiographical Inquiry,' Classical Quarterly 25 (1975) 58-81.
  232. Badian, F.C., p.101; cf. pp.100-2.
  233. The background and actions of Charops are described in a number of passages: Polyb. 27.15 (=Diod. 30.5); Polyb. 32.5-6 (=Diod. 31.31); Polyb. 30.32.12; and Polybius' extremely harsh estimation of Charops, 30.12. Livy, as one should expect, fails to mention Charops. For a modern discussion of Charops, see Scullard, J.R.S. 35, 58-64; Oost, Roman Policy, pp.83-87, and corresponding notes (the best discussion); Gruen, A.J.A.H. 1, 40-2, and corresponding notes; Passerini, Athenaeum 11, 331-33.
  234. Antinous, Cephalus, and Theodotus were

Molossians and enemies of Charops: Polyb. 27.15.7; 30.7.2. The Theodotus of Molossia is not to be confused with the Theodotus who attempted to kidnap the consul Hostilius in 170; the Molossians at that time still supported Rome: Polyb. 27.16. On the fates of Antinous and Theodotus, see Livy 45.26.5-9 (P); they died when Anicius took Epirus.

235. Polyb. 32.5.6-8.
236. Scullard, J.R.S. 35, 63.
237. Ibid., 59-60.
238. Cf. Oost, Roman Policy, pp.83-87; and esp. 133-35, nn.106 and 112.
239. Homecoming and triumph: Livy 45.35.3-4 (A). Disaffection among troops and resistance to the triumph: Livy 45.35.5-36.8 (A). Also Plutarch Aem. 30-31.2. One should keep in mind that the sources for Livy and Plutarch are annalistic; their treatment of events is highly dramatic and suspect.
240. See note 239; for the speech supporting Paullus, see Livy 45.36.9-39.20 (A); Plutarch Aem. 31.20-10.
241. Livy 45.40.1-5 (A); Plutarch Aem. 32-34; Diod. 31.8.10-12.
242. Livy 45.40.6-42.1 (P); Diod. 31.11; Plutarch Aem. 35-36; Appian Mac. 19.
243. Plutarch Aem. 34.3-4.
244. Livy 45.42.4 (P); cf. Velleius 1.11.1.
245. Diod. 31.9; cf. Plutarch Aem. 37.2.
246. Plutarch Aem. 37.2, states that Paullus got Perseus' release; but Diod. 31.9.4, states that it was Marcus Aemilius, the princeps senatus; the different names are probably due to the epitomizer's sloppy handling of Diodorus.
247. Plutarch Aem. 37.3; Diod. 31.5. See Meloni, Perseo, pp.437-38, for a discussion of Perseus' imprisonment and death.
248. Cf. Polyb 29.21.
249. Polyb. 30.32.
250. Badian, F.C., p.104. On Asia in general, see the comprehensive survey by Niese, Geschichte, III.207-311. For a short overview, see Errington, Dawn of Empire, pp.242-56.
251. Polyb. 29.5-10; 30.1. Badian, F.C., pp.102-3; Scullard, Roman Politics, pp.286-7.
252. Eumenes forbidden to land in Italy: Polyb. 30.19. Asian Gauls receive tacit Roman support in war against Eumenes: Polyb. 30.19.12; 30.29; Livy 45.34.10-14 (P). Romans try to persuade Attalus to take control of

Another Look

Pergamum: Polyb. 30.1-3; Livy 45.19 (P). Embassy sent to Asia to hear complaints against Eumenes: Polyb. 31.1; esp. 31.6. Note the similarity between Roman efforts against Philip V years earlier and these newer moves against Eumenes. See Badian, F.C., pp.102-5, and Note K, pp.294-95.

253. On Prusias' reception at Rome after the war, see Polyb. 30.18; Livy 45.44.4-21 (P and A). Polybius records many instances of Prusias attacking Eumenes before a believing Senate, e.g., Polyb. 30.30.2-6. Yet Prusias himself was not allowed to become too powerful. When he attacked Pergamum after Eumenes' death, Rome forced him to stop: Polyb. 32.15-16; 33.1 and 12.

254. See Polyb. 31.10, and esp. 31.10.7 for a statement concerning Roman motivation which could not be more blunt. Also numerous other sections, e.g., Polyb. 31.17-19; 33.11.

255. Polyb. 29.27; Livy 45.12.3-6 (P); and 45.13.1-3 (A) for wild annalistic claims.

256. Polyb. 31.2.1-6.
257. Polyb. 31.2.7-11; Appian Syr. 46.
258. Polyb. 31.2.9-11.
259. Polyb. 32.2.4-7.
260. Appian Syr. 46-47; Polyb. 31.11.1, and 12.4; Livy Per. 56; Livy Obseq. 15.
261. Thus the warning of Ariarthes to the envoys themselves before they went into Syria; Polyb. 31.8.5-8.
262. Polyb. 31.11.
263. Polyb. 31.12-15.
264. Badian, F.C., p.108; Walbank, Polybius, p.9, n.42; Briscoe, Historia 18, 61.
265. Chiefly Briscoe, Historia 18, 60-70.
266. Ibid., 67.
267. Polyb. 31.15.7-10.
268. Polyb. 31.12-15; esp. 31.13.8-14.
269. Appian Syr. 47; Polyb. 32.2-3; Livy Per. 46.
270. Polyb. 31.33, together with 32.3.13. Also Badian, F.D., p.108, n.1.
271. Polyb. 32.2-3; esp. 32.3.11-13.
272. Treaty with Jews: I. Mac. 8.17f. Support to opposition: Polyb. 33.18. Cf. Polybius' remarks on Demetrius' personal condition, 33.19.
273. Livy Per. 46; Diod. 31.25.
274. Broughton, M.R.R I.439; Plutarch Aem. 38.8.9.
275. Broughton, M.R.R. I.442.

276. Ibid., I.445.
277. Plutarch Aem. 39.6-9; Diod. 31.25.
278. The Hecyra and the Adelphoe by Terence. See Diod. 31.25; Plutarch Aem. 39.6-9; Polyb. 31.28.5-6.

BIBLIOGRAPHY

(Note: all ancient references belong to the Loeb Classical Library with the exceptions of Valerius Maximus, Justin-Trogus, and the author of de Viris Illustribus for whom the Teubner text is used.)

Africa, Thomas, W. Phylarchus and the Spartan Revolution. Berkeley: University of California Press, 1961.

Africa, Thomas W. The Immense Majesty. New York: Thomas Y. Crowell, 1974.

Aymard, A. 'L'Organisation de la Macédoine en 167.' Classical Philology, 45 (1950), 96-107.

Badian, E. 'Early Historians.' Latin Historians. Edited by T.A. Dorey. New York: Basic Books, 1966.

Badian, E. Foreign Clientelae (264-70 B.C.). Oxford: The Clarendon Press, 1972.

Badian, E. 'Rome and Antiochus the Great. A Study in Cold War.' Classical Philology, 54 (1959), 81-99.

Badian, E. Titus Quinctius Flamininus: Philhellenism and Realpolitik. Cincinnati: University of Cincinnati, 1970.

Benecke, P.V.M. "The Fall of the Macedonian Monarchy." Cambridge Ancient History, Vol. 8. Cambridge: The University Press, 1954.

Bickerman, E. "Notes sur Polybe, III: Initia belli Macedonici." Revue des Etudes Grecques, 61 (1953), 479-506.

Brink, C.O., and Walbank, F.W. "The Construction of the Sixth Book of Polybius." Classical Quarterly, 48 (1954), 97-122.

Briscoe, J. "Eastern Policy and Senatorial Politics; 168-146 B.C." Historia, 18 (1969), 49-70.

Bibliography

Briscoe, J. "Q. Marcius Philippus and Nova Sapientia." Journal of Roman Studies, 54 (1964), 66-77.

Broughton, T.R.S. The Magistrates of the Roman Republic, 2 volumes. The American Philological Association, 1951.

Carney, T.F. 'Prosopography: Payoffs and Pitfalls.' Phoenix, 27 (1973), 156-79.

Colin, G. Rome et la Grece: de 200 a 146 avant J.C. Paris, 1905.

Corpus Inscriptionum Latinarum. Berlin: G. Reimeri, 1862.

Dittenberger, W. Sylloge Inscriptionem Graecarum. 3rd edition. Leipzig, 1915-1924.

Duruy, Victor. History of Rome and of the Roman People, 8 volumes in 16. Translated by M.M. Ripley and W.J. Clarke. Edited by J.P. Mahaffy. Boston: Dana Estes and Charles E. Lauriot, 1884.

Eckstein, F.A. 'Lucius Amilius Paullus (4).' Allgemeine Encyclopädie der Wissenschaften und Kunste III, 14 (1840), 176-82.

Edson, C.F. 'Perseus and Demetrius.' Harvard Studies in Classical Philology, 46 (1935), 191-202.

Errington, R.M. Dawn of Empire: Rome's Rise to World Power. Ithaca: Cornell University Press, 1972.

Errington, R.M. Philopoemen. Oxford: The Clarendon Press, 1969.

Forde, Nels W. Cato the Censor. Boston: Twayne Publishers, 1975.

Fowler, Warde. 'Polybius' Conception of Tyche.' Classical Review, 17 (1903), 445-49.

Frank, Tenny. Roman Imperialism. New York: The MacMillan Co., 1914.

Geiger, J. 'Plutarch's Parallel Lives; the Choice of the Heros.' Hermes, CIX (1981), 85-104.

Gelzer, M. Kleine Schriften, 3 volumes. Wiesbaden: F. Steiner, 1962-64.

Giovannini, A. "Les Origines de la troisieme guerre de Macedoine." Bulletin de Correspondance Hellenique, 93 (1969), 853-61.

Gruen, E.S. "Class Conflict and the Third Macedonian War." American Journal of Ancient History, 1 (1976), 29-60.

Gruen, E.S. 'Rome and Rhodes in the Second Century B.C.: A Historiographical Inquiry." Classical Quarterly, 25 (1975), 58-81.

Gruen, E.S. The Hellenistic World and the Coming of Rome. Berkeley: University of California Press, 1984.

Gundel, H.G. "L. Ae. Paullus (Macedonicus) (22)." Der Kleine

Bibliography

Pauly, 1 (1964), 92-93.
Holleaux, Maurice. "Rome and Antiochus." Cambridge Ancient History, Vol. 8. Cambridge: The University Press, 1954.
Jacoby, Felix. Die Fragmente der griechischen Historiker. Leiden: E.J. Brill, 1954.
Jones, C.P. Plutarch and Rome. Oxford: The Clarendon Press, 1971.
Kahrstedt, U. "Zum Ausbruch des dritten römisch-makedonischen Krieges." Klio, 11 (1911), 415-30.
Klebs. "L. Aemilius Paullus (114)." Paulys Realencyclopädie der classischen Altertumswissenschaft, I, 1 (1893), 576-80.
Klotz, A. "Zu den Quellen der vierten und fünften Dekade des Livius." Hermes, 50 (1915), 481-536.
Laistner, M.L.W. The Greater Roman Historians. Berkeley: University of California Press, 1971.
Larsen, J.A.O. "Consilium in Livy XLV. 18. 6-7 and the Macedonian Synedria.' Classical Philology, 44 (1949), 73-90.
Larsen, J.A.O. 'Was Greece Free Between 196 and 146 B.C.?' Classical Philology, 30 (1935), 193-214.
Lehmann, G.A. 'Die Endphase des Perseuskriegs im Augenzeugenberichte des P. Cornelius Scipio Nasica.' Beiträge zur alten Geschichte (Festschrift Altheim). Berlin, 1969, 387-412.
Liedmeier, Christiana. Plutarchus Biographie van Aemilius Paullus: Historische Commentaar. Utrecht: Dekker & van de Vegt N.V., 1935.
Lind, L.R. 'Concept, Action, and Character: The Reasons for Rome's Greatness.' Transactions and Proceedings of the American Philological Association, 103 (1972), 235-83.
Machiavelli. Chiefworks and Others. Translated by Allan Gilbert. Durham: Duke University Press, 1965.
Malcovati, H. Oratorum Romanorum Fragmenta. 2nd edition, Italy, 1955.
McDonald, A.H. 'Paullus (2) Macedonicus.' The Oxford Classical Dictionary. 2nd ed. Oxford: The Clarendon Press, 1970.
Meissner, E. Lucius Aemilus Paullus und seine Bedeutung für das Romische Reich (229-160 v. Chr.). Bischberg: Oberfranken Selbstverl., 1974.
Meloni, Piero. Perseo e la fine della Monarchia Macedone. Rome, 1953.
Meyer, E. 'Die Schlacht bei Pydna.' Kleine Schriften, Vol. 2.

Halle, 1924, pp.463-94.
Michelet, J. History of the Roman Republic. Translated by William Hazlitt. London: David Bogue, 1847.
Mommsen, Theodor. 'Bemerkungen zum Decret des L. Aemilius Paullus.' Gesammalte Schriften, IV, pp.52-62.
Mommsen, Theodor. The History of Rome, 4 volumes. Translated by W.P. Dickson. New York: Charles Schribner's Sons, nid.
Münzer, F. Römische Adelsparteien und Adelsfamilien. Stuttgart: Metzler, 1963 reprint of 1920 ed.
Nissen, H. Kritische Untersuchungen über die Quellen der vierten und fünften Dekade des Livius. Berlin: Weidmannsche Buchandlung, 1863.
Niebuhr, B.G. The History of Rome from the First Punic War to the Death of Constantine. Edited and translated by L. Schmitz. London: Taylor and Walton, 1844.
Niebuhr, B.G. The Life and Letters of Barthold George Niebuhr. Translator unnamed. New York: Harper & Brothers, 1854.
Niese, Benedictus. Geschichte der Griechischen und Makedonischen Staaten seit der Schlacht bei Chaeronea, 3 volumes. Darmstadt: Wissenschaftliche Buchgesellschaft, 1963, reprint of 1893-1903 edition.
Oost, S.I. Roman Policy in Epirus and Acarnania in the Age of the Roman Conquest of Greece. Dallas, 1954.
Oost, S.I. 'The Roman Calendar in the Year of Pydna (168 B.S.).' Classical Philology, 48 (1953), 217-30.
Passerini, A. 'Studi di storia ellenistica-romana, VI, I moti politico-sociali della Grecia e i Romani.' Athenaeum, 11 (1933), 309-335.
Pavan, Massimiliano. 'Du Discoursi di Lucio Emilio Paolo.' Studi Romani, 9 (1961), 593-613.
Pedech, P. La Methode Historique de Polybe. Paris: Societe d'Edition 'Les Belles Lettres', 1964.
Pedech, P. 'Un Grec a la découverte de Rome: l'exil de Polybe (167-150 av. J.C.).' Orpheus, 11 (194), 123-40.
Polybius. Histoires Livre I. Edited and translated by p. Pedech. Paris: Societe d' Editions, 1969.
Raditsa, Leo. 'Bella Macedonica.' Aufsteig und Niedergang der Römischen Welt, Vol. 1. Berlin: Walter de Gruyter, 1972, pp.564-89.
Rollin, Charles. Ancient History, 2 volumes. New York: Derby and Jackson, 1857.
Scullard, H.H. 'Charops and Roman Policy in Epirus.' Journal of Roman Studies, 35 (1945), 58-64.

Bibliography

Scullard, H.H. Roman Politics: 220-150 B.C. 2nd ed. Oxford: The Clarendon Press, 1973.

Sherk, R.K. Roman Documents from the Greek East. Senatus consulta and epistulae to the Age of Augustus. Baltimore: Johns Hopkins Press, 1969.

Sherwin, W.K. De Viris Illustribus. Edited and translated by W.K. Sherwin. Norman: University of Oklahoma Press, 1973.

Shorey, P. 'Tyche in Polybius.' Classical Philology, 16 (1921), 280-83.

Smith, R.E. 'Plutarch's Biographical Sources in the Roman Lives.' Classical Quarterly, 34 (1940), 1-10.

Stanley, Alice D. 'Lucius Aemilius Paullus.' Unpublished Ph.D. dissertation, Bryn Mawr College, 1954.

Stier, H.E. Roms Aufstieg zur Weltmacht und die griechische Welt. Koln: Westdeutscher Verlag, 1957.

Strasburger, H. 'Poseidonius on Problems of the Roman Empire.' Journal of Roman Studies, 55 (1965), 40-53.

Sutherland, C.H.V. The Romans in Spain 217 B.C.-A.D. 117. New York: Barnes and Noble, 1971 reprint of 1939 ed.

Swain, J.W. 'The Theory of the Four Monarchies. Opposition History Under the Roman Empire.' Classical Philology, 35 (1940), 1-21.

Syme, Ronald. The Roman Revolution. Oxford: Oxford University Press, 1968.

Vianoli, Rosanna. 'Carattere e tendenza della tradizione su L. Emilio Paolo.' Contributi dell'Instituto di storia antica, 1 (1972), 78-90.

von Fritz, K. The Theory of the Mixed Constitution in Antiquity: A Criticial Analysis of Polybius' Political Ideas. New York: Columbia University Press, 1954.

Walbank, F.W. A Historical Commentary on Polybius, 2 volumes. Oxford: The Clarendon Press, 1957 and 1967.

Walbank, F.W. 'A Note on the Embassy of Q. Marcius Philippus, 172 B.C.' Journal of Roman Studies, 31 (1941), 82-93.

Walbank, F.W. 'Philippos Tragodoumenos: A Polybian Experiment.' Journal of Hellenic Studies, 58 (1938), 55-68.

Walbank, F.W. Philip V of Macedon. Hamden, Conn.: Archon Books, 1967 reprint of 1940 ed.

Walbank, F.W. 'Political Morality and the Friends of Scipio.' Journal of Roman Studies, 55 (1965), 1-16.

Walbank, F.W. Polybius. Berkeley: University of California Press, 1972.

Bibliography

Walbank, F.W. 'Polybius, and Macedonia.' Ancient Macedonia: Papers Read at the First International Symposium Held in Thessaloniki, 26-29 August 1968, 291-307.

Walbank, F.W. 'Polybius and the Growth of Rome.' (Summary in the) Classical Association Proceedings, 43 (1946), 11.

Walbank, F.W. 'Polybius and the Roman State.' Greek, Roman and Byzantine Studies, 5 (1964), 239-60.

Walbank, F.W. 'Polybius on the Roman Constitution.' Classical Quarterly, 37 (1943), 73-89.

Walbank, F.W. 'The Fourth and Fifth Decades.' Livy. Edited by T.A. Dorey, London: Routledge and Kegan Paul, 1971.

Walbank, F.W. 'The Scipionic Legend.' Cambridge Philological Society Proceedings, 93 (1967), 54-69.

Walbank, F.W. A Historical Commentary on Polybius, Oxford, Clarendon Press, 1957.

Walbank, F.W. Review of "Filino-Polibio-Sileno-Diodoro" by Vincenzo LaBua, The Classical Review, 1968.

Walbank, F.W. 'The Historians of Greek Sicily', Kokalos XIV-XV 1960-69.

Walsh, P.G. Livy. Cambridge: The University Press, 1961.

Wardman, Alan. Plutarch's Lives. Berkeley: University of California Press, 1974.

Will, E. Histoire Politique du Monde Hellenistique (323-20 av. J.C.), 2 volumes. Nancy, 1957.

Will, E. Studies on the History of Roman Sea-Power in Republican Times, Amsterdam, 1946.

INDEX

Abrupolis 124
Acarnania 84
Achaeans 82
Achaean League 121
Aemilius Paullus 36, 71, 98, 113-14, 134, 53f
    augur 100
    conduct 37-8
    consulship of 168, 182
    death 37, 105
    early career 109-10
    financial matters 33
    Livy's image 80
    military discipline 101
    statesman/conqueror 56
    tour of Greece 78, 136
    triumph 104, 142
    virtues 21, 77
    wisdom 38-9
Aetotia 82
Alexander the Great 30, 43-4
Anicius 78
Antiochus V 145
Antigonus Doson 40, 44
Antias 112
Antias, Valeruis 72
Antiochus IV 143
Apelles 45
Aristeides 35

Athens, constitution 24
Augustus 70

Badian, Ernst 12
Boeotian League 82, 128

Callicrates 38, 82, 122, 127
Carthage 34
    constitution 26
Charops 38, 133, 140
Cleomenes of Sparta 44
Colin, C. 9
Crassus, Licinius 83
Crete, constitution 24
Culchas 111

Demetrius 120
Demetrius of Phalerum 29, 40
Demetrius of Pharos 45
Demonsthenes 43
Diophanes of Megapolis 123
Duruy, Victor 7

Eckstein, F.A. 5
Epaminondas 35
Epirus 85, 103, 139
Eumenes 52, 127, 128, 143

Fabius, Quintus 20

Index

Forde, Nels 14
Frank, Tenny 10

Genthuis 78
Greek, factions 76, 81, 84, 136-7
  social unrest 126
Gundel, H.G. 12f

Illyria 139

Klebs (Raelencyclopadie) 8

Liguria 74
Livy 69, 81
  methods 71
Lyciscus 83
Lycortas 122

Macedon, dissolution after Pydna 138
  fall of 41
Machiavelli 2
Maiestas 79
Mamercus 100
McDonald, A.H. 10
Meloni, Piero 11f
Messene 122
Michelet, J. 5
mixed constitution, Roman 25, 27
Molossia 141
Mommsen, Theodor 6f

Niebuhr, Barthold 3f
Niese, Benedictus 8f
Nasica, Scipio 99

Oost, S.I. 12

Papiria 116
Perseus 31, 39, 50, 53f, 85, 99, 131, 135
  Polybian portrayal 50f
  Plutarch's image 102

policies of unification 124, 131, 135
fate 142
Philip II 30, 40, 42
Philip V 38, 41, 45, 48, 119
  and Carthage 46
Philippus, Marcius 74
Philopoemen 121
Phylarchus 53
Plutarch 78, 97
Polybius 115
  empires and conquest 30f
  Greek cupidity 34
  Histories' purpose 22
  madness 31
  patron of Paullus 32-3
  Paullus' family 20-1
  political constitutions 22-5
  progression of empires 47f
  reason and traitors 42-3
  resistance to Rome 31
  Roman conquest 21f
  Roman decline 35
  theme of evil councellors 45
  use of the dramatic 55
Popillius Gauis 73
Popillius, Marcus 73
Poseidonius 99
Ptolemy Epiphanes 46
Pydna 53

Quadrigarius, Claudius 72

Rhodes 72, 85, 140
Rollin, Charles 2f
Rome 47
  law and mixed constitution 27
  policy against Philip V 120
  traditional virtues 70
  funeral rites 27-8

Index

virtus 26-7
Roman embassies 83

Scipio Aemilianus 20, 36, 105
Scullard, H.H. 11
Senate 74, 79, 130
   policies after Pydna 135
Spain 110, 117
Sparta 121
   constitution 26
Stanley, Alice 12
Stier, H.E. 12
Syria 144

Thearides, Polybius' grandfather 43
Thebes 43-4
   constitution 24
Theopompus 42
Thessaly 82
Third Macedonian War 75, 87, 129f
   propaganda 131
   Roman policies 133
Treaty of Apamea 119
Tyche 29, 40, 41, 42, 104
   and Antigonus Doson 44
   and Philip V 45
   Philip V and war with Rome 48-9
   Roman favor 31
   virtus and Tyche 29

Vianoli, Rosanna 13

Will, E. 13